THE STRUCTURAL APPROACH
TO DIRECT PRACTICE IN SOCIAL WORK

GALE GOLDBERG WOOD AND RUTH R. MIDDLEMAN

The Structural Approach to Direct Practice in Social Work

COLUMBIA UNIVERSITY PRESS

NEW YORK

Parts of this book were taken from the previous edition of this book, which was published by Columbia University Press in 1974 as *Social Service Delivery: A Structural Approach to Social Work Practice*.

Columbia University Press
New York   Chichester, West Sussex
Copyright © 1989 Columbia University Press
All rights reserved

Library of Congress Cataloging-in-Publication Data

Wood, Gale Goldberg.
The structural approach to direct practice in social work.

Rev. ed. of: Social service delivery / by Ruth R. Middleman and Gale Goldberg.
Bibliography: p.
Includes index.
1. Social service.   2. Social service—United States.
3. Social workers.   4. Social workers—United States.
I. Middleman, Ruth R.   Social service delivery.
II. Title
HV40.W66   1989   361.3   88-35217
ISBN 0-231-5506-4

c 10 9 8 7 6 5

Printed in the United States of America

Casebound editions of Columbia University Press books are printed on permanent and durable acid-free paper.

To the memory of our mothers
Matilda Rubin Meyers
Corinne Lorch Rosenbloom

Contents

PART V: SURROUNDINGS

12. The Organizational Context   239
13. Conclusion: It Matters   254

    Notes   261
    Index   275

THE STRUCTURAL APPROACH
TO DIRECT PRACTICE IN SOCIAL WORK

The man who wears the shoe knows best that it pinches and where it pinches, even if the expert shoemaker is the best judge of how the trouble is to be remedied.

John Dewey

Introduction

Much has occurred since our ideas on social work practice first appeared in *Social Service Delivery: A Structural Approach to Social Work Practice*. The thrust of that volume has remained robust and valuable to some portions of the social work profession, despite the turnabout we all have experienced in the cultural context that now surrounds, infuses our daily lives. We think our orientation is, if anything, even more appropriate today and more necessary. It is not surprising to us that the newish emphasis, case management, seems to be informed by the structural approach.

Several other textbooks appearing since the *Structural Approach* have used its Quadrant typology as orienting and sorting the work of social work, and have used its boundaries and divisions centrally in their compositions.[1] The structural approach has been described in a historical review of social work's technology as coming closest to providing a framework for a social work science and "loci for knowledge-building activities and the means for sorting out social work objectives, processes, and technologies."[2] In these few years the Department of Health and "Human" (sic!) Services appeared (1979). No more Health, Education, and Welfare! The "new" spirit of the times emphasized self-sufficiency values, assurances and insurance for the employed, and little for the others, e.g., for the unemployed, for students, women working in the home, welfare recipients, the elderly. The social welfare policy priorities have been disability, cyclical unemployment, retirement, and preservation of the family wage. They have not been for better income distribution, long-term unemployment, involuntary part-time employment, or retraining redundant workers.[3]

Our book's previous title, *Social Service Delivery . . .* , reflected a

central preoccupation in American life—economics. Production, promotion, distribution, exchange, and consumption occupy most of the
energy of those in the mainstream, while concern with the pressures
that result from noninvolvement or limited involvement in the economy occupies much of the attention of those who are out of the
mainstream. A *consumer* orientation has dominated American life,
and thus social work.

The Age of the Consumer

Many were relieved that 1984 came and went without the realization
of Orwell's dire predictions—without Big Brother, or thought control,
or truth concealed from them. Yet what of this nation's addiction to
TV? It is watched, on average, $7\frac{1}{2}$ hours a day. According to one
twenty-year study of the medium, "the lessons of television involve a
mean world of violence and power dominated by white males in the
prime of life. . . . The consumer-oriented populism of the medium is
reflected in the fact that the more viewers watch, the less they want
government to cut back on spending for health, the environment,
education, the cities. And yet (they say) taxes are too high."[4] While
Orwell thought we would be marched singlefile and manacled into
oblivion, our TV situation is more like Huxley's *Brave New World:* we
shall dance ourselves into oblivion—smiling, buying, and con-
suming.[5]

Those in the Age of the Consumer have learned that the world does
not beat a path to the door of the person who builds a better mouse-
trap. They know that the key elements determining a product's usage
include what it looks like, how many people know it exists, who else
has one, and how widely it is publicized. Hence, they invest heavily in
package design, commercials, and distributive mechanisms. And as
consumers become more aware of the power that inheres in their role
—the power to use or avoid a given item—as they become more
sophisticated about the products offered for their consumption, they
have gained more control over what goods are to be produced and
sold.

For a time, when social justice was an ideal, social programs were
popular, community control flourished, and human services came to

be viewed in the same way. In the 1960s and early 1970s, client's rights were emphasized and strategies favoring the consumer appeared. There was client participation on agency boards and review boards, occupational opportunities for paraprofessionals, and even promise of long-term careers in the human services Establishment. Not only might employing paraprofessionals diffuse angry criticism by the poor, might cool some of the critics out, but it was hoped the paraprofessionals might navigate the communication barriers that stymied many middle-class would-be helpers.

With respect to the consumption of human services, quality was only one measure of a service—necessary, but not sufficient. The nature of the service, its goal, its distribution, and its delivery were seen as equal, if not more significant determinants of consumption. Consumers made the point with increased stridency in the '60s and '70s that "human" services were not human, that they were ill-conceived, that they were palliative fragments designed by those with biased frames of reference who lacked sufficient knowledge about the users.

The consumers questioned the nature and form of services; they questioned the arrogance of the providers; and they questioned the professionals' competence. These "Who says so?" questions attacked physicians' control over health systems, teachers' control over parents in educational systems, and social workers' control over clients in social service systems.

Questions of professionals' knowledge and practice competence were raised in the intellectual arena too. Harvard president Bok assailed graduating students with speeches about their too narrow education as preparation for future challenges. One year he spoke of medical education, the next about law and the legal system.[6] Additionally, as a result of a study of various professions (architects, psychotherapists, engineers, planners, and managers), Schön spoke of their "babble of voices," of their internal diversity, and, thus, the competing views about practice, professional role, central values, and necessary, relevant knowledge and skills. "In sum (there is a) mismatch of traditional patterns of practice and knowledge to features of the practice situation—complexity, uncertainty, instability, uniqueness, and value conflict . . ."[7]

Specialized Knowledge

Year by year, the professions have become increasingly specialized, a development that causes concern. Fuller commented on this issue as follows:

> Advancing science has now discovered that all known cases of biological extinction have been caused by overspecialization, whose concentration of only selected genes sacrifices general adaptability. . . . Specialization has bred feelings of isolation, futility, and confusion in individuals. It has also resulted in the individual's leaving responsibility for thinking and social action to others. . . . Specialization tends to shut off the wide-band tuning searches and thus to preclude further discovery of the all-powerful generalized principles.[8]

This book is about the wide-band tuning which remains a hallmark, an imperative for the social work profession. It is about the individual worker's responsibility for imaginative thinking and *social* action.

This seems important especially in our increasingly complex world that seeks and rewards specialists. But specialized knowledge should grow out of broad, basic appreciation of the fullness of social work practice rather than its intracacies—breadth before depth. It is important for the social work profession that has searched so long for its unifying bonds, for its central purpose, mission, domain, and voice as a collectivity of practitioners with a shared affinity—one for another. And it is important, as Fuller warns, so that the individual practitioner (and the profession itself) will be able to adapt to the ever changing realities of the world. The structural approach is a focused, specialized orientation toward life-problems.

Economic-Political Influences on Social Conditions

The economic-political exigencies of the times pit whole segments of the population against each other. The person in the street, the politician, and the provider of services blame each other and/or the populations in need, for it is simply incomprehensible to find and attack the more abstract common enemy—a system of economic arrangements that has produced an industrial technology far out of line with the social arrangements needed to live with it. Like the broom of the sorcerer's apprentice, the economic system takes on a life of its own and sweeps furiously with ever-increasing momentum, while the system of social services, which was never actually meant to provide a comfortable life, desperately hangs on, ill-attended, underfinanced, and viewed at the moment as a wasteful, burdensome investment.

The political system is more responsive to the vested interests of the economically powerful than to the interests of the poor, the aged, the unemployed black teenager, the homeless street person, the chronically mentally ill, the physically disabled, the AIDS victim, or the displaced workers of all varieties. If interests were to be represented equally, Gans claimed in the early 1970s, the poor would have about fifty congressmen and thirteen senators to represent them.[9] The numbers of representative congresspersons would need to be far greater now.

The massive influence of poverty on human suffering, on social and health needs, can be appreciated by considering these figures from a report to the Joint Economic Committee of Congress: "for a 1% increase in unemployment over a period of one year: there are attributed 1,540 suicides, 5,320 state hospital admissions, 7,660 state prison admissions, 1,740 homicides, 870 deaths traced to cirrhosis of the liver, 26,440 deaths caused by cardiovascular and renal disease."[10]

In the early '70s, we wrote of the increased general recognition that existing social arrangements were inadequate, that differentials in access to means systematically kept the poor and other powerless groups from attaining their goals, and that these "voiceless" segments of the population would no longer settle for palliatives and promises. We wrote that the posture of social workers had begun to shift toward greater participation in politics, toward using their clout where it counts in matters affecting social legislation, and hence social conditions. The social work literature directed social workers to become advocates for clients' entitlements and to support clients movement into the political arena. We aimed to add some specifics in the "how-to-do-it" area, the gap between injunction and action at the direct practice level.

The Rise of Conservatism

How quickly the national temperament has turned around with the advent of the Reagan Administration and the institution of a Conservative ideology! This philosophy is built upon entrepreneurial, "American" spirit and free enterprise, assumedly aimed to spark economic growth. It was hoped that social problems would be solved by the church, family, and neighborhood. National freedom (supremacy) and military prowess ("defense"!) were top priorities.[11]

Nonprofit charitable organizations, especially those in social services, housing and community development, legal services, employment and training which were focused on services to the poor, were hit especially hard by the federal cutbacks. Unlike agencies in health-related fields, the arts, and culture that were able to maintain or even increase their spending by replacing lost government funds with increased private donations and fees, agencies focused chiefly on the poor could not fill the gap of lost federal income (estimated at 35 percent between 1980 and 1984). Some agencies survived through fees, service charges, and insurance reimbursements and the adoption of a mercantile mentality.

The Reagan administration emphasized private solutions to public problems, e.g., through volunteerism, nonprofit and voluntary organizations, and businesses. Domestic policies and practices were reversed: e.g., restrictions on business were lifted, and government's role as protector of workers, consumers, minorities, the environment, and occupational health and safety vanished. Social security and health programs took the lead over poverty. Gradually, domestic services have succumbed to the entrepreneurial drift, in programs for the elderly, day care, employee assistance programs, home health care, case management, self-help groups, group therapy and so forth.

Deregulation, weapons escalation, the dismantling of monopolies in public schools, telephone, postal, and airline services, and the privatization of such services as hospitals and nursing homes, fire and police protection, garbage collection, and even correctional facilities are commonplace features in the present day. For social work, fear has been expressed that "a growing implicit assumption that the fee-for-service private practitioner is the ideal form for truly professional practice."[12] Whether to escape the constrictions of bureaucracies and their voluminous red tape, to assert professional status, focus on specialized services, or earn more money, increasing numbers of practitioners have drifted into private full-time or part-time practice.[13]

The Influence on Social Work

Indeed, the economic and ideological context of the times must affect social workers, embedded as they are within the fabric of the social programs and services. Their own economic and job security depend on their certainty in self-definition as professionals, depend ultimately on the economic conditions which affect the dominant class. One's sense of personal autonomy and security in bureaucratized systems resonates with the threat or reality of layoffs, size of caseloads, salary scale and opportunities for advancement, ambiance and dignity at the office, and more.

Gummer discussed the politicization of the environment of social agencies: the intense competition for the declining resources and scramble over turf; the diffuse control system involving professional bureaucrats, state and local politicians, community élites, and numerous interest groups; and the concentration upon apolitical and technical matters. Social work administrators, to compete with the MBAs and others, have adopted whole new management technologies, particularly those derived from "the command and control school of industrial and business management."[14]

For some social workers, becoming a licensed independent practitioner has been a way out of the grip of the formal service systems. Yet, all social workers are affected by the New Federalism: the move away from the Great Society, from civil rights and affirmative action, from promoting social welfare, from federal involvement in regulating the behavior of organizations, and from the move to return decision-making and responsibility to lower levels of government.

The entreprenuerial spirit flourished and invaded what once was only a nonprofit array of services. Since agencies and independent practitioners depend upon third-party payments and definitions determined by insurance coverage, the economic survival of organizations (and private practitioners) depends upon the adoption of more businesslike values and procedures. The for-profit "service" organizations and chains now proliferate in the social, health, and education arenas.

The Age of the Customer

Rather than think of these times as *The Age of the Consumer,* a more fitting designation would be *The Age of the Customer!* Professional services are now being "sold;" commercialism surrounds us. TV, radio, and newspapers tout the services of lawyers, dentists, physicians, optometrists, and others who can afford the ads. Hospitals compete with full page spreads, credit card offers, seminars, "free" lectures, and discounts for healthcare and cultural events. This is the heyday of the marketing specialist. We shall not be surprised by special sales (Moonlight Madness, Door Openers), Opportunity-Discounts, or dated coupons as the commercial mentality and competitive spirit continue to invade professional realms.

The editor of the new *Journal of Independent Social Work* argues for a fixed fee scale for practitioners in private practice as follows:

> a fixed fee system is consistent with the goal of consumerism as opposed to paternalism . . . one's dollar is worth the same as anyone else's . . . any retail store (would) have dubious ethics if they charged different prices for the same product, depending on how much money the customer claimed to have.[15]

Following this commercialized analogy, we assume that poor, vulnerable, stigmatized clients—already at great risk—will have to shop in the bargain basement since they have fewer dollars to begin with no matter their worth, and suffer from the lack of available, comparable services since chances are they are dealing with some service provider monopoly. Many persons wonder whether we now have a two-tiered system of social services—the poor served by persons with the occupational title of "social worker" and the more affluent paying for the services of the professionals.

Direct Social Work Practice

Direct social work practice (sometimes called microlevel practice, or direct front line practice, or face to face practice) refers to a practice in which the unit of attention is the plight of particular individuals (as will be elaborated in chapter 1). This contrasts with indirect (or macrolevel) practice, which views society from the perspective of general problems, such as poverty or delinquency. This book describes a practice derived from a social welfare-through-social-change philosophy. We have touched on the economic-political currents of the times since these comprise a formidable backdrop to all practice activities. We do not operate in a vacuum; we work in a context.

The book was written for the social worker who must question the systematic inequities surrounding the distribution of society's resources, who must stand for the powerless client because of an ethical commitment to how life ought to be. It was also written for the supervisor and administrator, the planner of social programs, the developer of social policy, and the researcher who devises the measuring instruments that assess the effectiveness of a practice or a program. Persons in roles that support and make room for the basic services will do so more effectively to the extent that the various approaches to direct practice are described and opened to public scrutiny. And it was written for the social workers who want to be therapists, for they will never be able to do so in quite the same way again.

Let us take, for example, the instance of twelve-year-old Tommy whose distraught mother brought him for therapy after he was expelled from three separate schools. Tommy was small for his age and already two grade levels beyond his peers. When asked what led to his expulsion, he "didn't know, except that his teachers thought he lied about his homework." Exploring a bit further, the social worker learned that he did his homework, but never turned it in because he couldn't find it in his backpack. Further discussion revealed that the backpack, in Tommy's unlocked locker, was easily accessible to other children who had discovered his good homework material. The worker also learned that Tommy enjoyed knowing more than other students and would get back at classmates who picked on him in the playground by showing them up in class.

At this point the social worker could have pursued Tommy's apparent interpersonal problems with other children; but, having been taught to look first to environmental structures as the possible locus of problems, she chose to consider the organizational arrangements for intellectually gifted children before assuming Tommy's plight to be intrapsychic and of his own making. In other words, if Tommy could be with other children like himself, he might not have "interpersonal problems."

So instead of engaging Tommy and his parents in a therapeutic enterprise, the social worker connected his parents with a private school which was designed for special children like Tommy. After Tommy and his parents visited the school, felt welcome there and pleased with its potential, the social worker helped the family to get financial assistance with tuition and Tommy was immediately enrolled. At a follow-up meeting three months later, there were no signs of interpersonal problems at all. In fact, for the first time since he started school, Tommy had friends. Even if Tommy's plight were psychological in origin, a clinician using this text would provide treatment in a somewhat different, less traditional way, for the perspective offered here encourages the social worker to return the situation to the client as soon as he can cope with it on his own. This obligation that the worker not assume a central position in the helping process, that the worker in effect try to work herself out of a job, demands inordinate respect for client strength.

The book furthers the continued interest of social workers in matters of social justice, particularly their interest in how unjust social conditions are experienced by individuals in their everyday lives, and how a difference can be made. It describes, and illustrates with examples of workers in action, the ways in which the social worker can respond to clients and their social distress, as these clients come with their needs to the social agency, or as they are encountered in present day urban industrial life, in the public schools, mental health centers, by parole boards, in housing projects and boarding homes, mental hospitals, nursing and retirement homes.

This book is for the front line practitioner, whether BSW, MSW, ACSW, or licensed clinician, who wants to assume a social worker orientation rather than a method-based orientation, who wants to deliver services through a social work methodology equally applicable in a one-to-one, group, family, or community context. That is, the book is directed to the social worker who wants to work and will work with clients wherever they are met, and be free to pursue what needs to be done according to the tasks worked out together.

Partnership

Social worker and client are joined to each other as fellow strugglers through the vast bureaucratic mechanisms that control their everyday lives. The specialized know-how for negotiating and surviving the morass is sometimes possessed by social worker, sometimes by client, sometimes by neither. This partnership is a different perspective on their work together.[16]

Some social workers might wish to fight and try to explain away the client's anger, frustration and disappointment with the services. Some social workers might suffer pangs of exasperation (and self-doubt) with client "ingratitude" for their well-intended ethical and moral commitment to serving others as a helping person. But these reactions help no one. It behooves the social worker to "get with" clients in a new way, to be for them even in their anger—to be their partner every step of the way.

This will be a different, possibly uncomfortable, position for social workers. For their expertise may be identified by the client as having been used to maintain the social arrangements planned by some "élite" in behalf of others. And the client is right. All too often the social worker has served as society's gatekeeper of the *status quo* rather than as an informed strategist who offers a special know-how to help clients change their social situations. In many instances the social worker is seen by the client as "the system". And, in fact, this is true. The system has been good to many social workers; they are of the system. Social workers used to be "the conscience of society."[17] They no longer have a monopoly on this role; other advocates have been even more successful. But social workers can, if they work hard enough, lend their special knowledge where it counts. They can bring to bear their specialized knowledge and skills to help others in their quest for the material and personal resources that make for social well-being.

The general awakening of the public to social conditions, the alarm at the accelerating pace of economic forces that threaten to engulf all —the discontent is shared by those who have "made it," by those who now see that they are outside it and demand full-fledged membership in society, and by those struggling at some midpoint within the system. Just as some persons protest the devastation of the physical environment by the business-industrial-military complex and force some perhaps costly response, so should they protest the neglect of the social environment that spawns even greater social problems for tomorrow's world and forces the costly investments that must be made for human survival. For the increased public dissatisfaction with the precariousness of today's life is now part of the consciousness, regardless of attempts to redefine who should bear the financial cost of meeting human needs. More people know that the promises of the Constitution have been more rhetoric than reality: domestic tranquility has not been insured; the general welfare has not been promoted, and the other basic rights enumerated for individuals have not been assured for all.

It is now all too apparent that the myth of America as a nation of equals, a classless society, is an ideal that has never been energetically pursued. And now more segments of the population are aware of their powerlessness and are objecting to the political, economic, and social inequalities of the times. The poor, the blue-collar workers, and the white-collar workers alike—each from their own vantage point—feel the crush of the ever increasing pressures of an economic system which consigns them to increasingly insignificant slots as the bureaucracies and corporations compete and grow bigger. And with a level of affluence visibly increased for some and a greater awareness that there is economic and technological potential that could be deployed more frequently to social and human needs, the expectations for a better life and the impatience with present conditions make the mission of social work, as a part of the struggle, ever more urgent.

A Structural Approach

In contrast to other orientations to practice that may aim to help individuals adjust to their situations, to understand their motivations, to gain insight, or to change their ways of thinking and acting, the structural approach aims to modify the environment to the needs of the individuals. Social work, theories and practice, has long claimed concern for both persons and environments. But the predominant attention has been focused on the persons, not their situations (perhaps because it seems harder to change situations/environments or because agencies and workers are not paid to do this!).

Certain conceptual tools for understanding and dealing with situations have been described by Siporin. He elaborated situation theory from a historical and current perspective.[18] Further attention to dealing with environmental issues and practicing with an ecological orientation has been heightened and clarified through the work of Germain.[19] The ecological approach has exerted great influence in social work.

The structural approach asks the practitioner to consider *first* the structural surround before placing the problem(s) within the person of the individual(s). If there is no pressure stemming from outside the person, then the focus can shift to a more internal realm. There is a logic here: if you start with the environment, make changes there, and the problem still remains, you have demonstrated that the pressures are not external to the person. But if you start with the situation internal to the person, you can not demonstrate that there were pressures outside the person at work.

The basic assumptions underlying this orientation are elaborated in chapter 1. Because the orientation differs, the practice principles, the guidelines for practice, also differ from those presented in other texts. These principles are explained and illustrated in chapter 3. Chapter 4 describes the dynamics of the Structural Approach, i.e., its process over time from beginning to end with a given client.

Ideological Antecedents

The reader will find connections between some of the ideas presented here and those of earlier social critics and social workers who held similar interests and concerns about their world. We are not the first to suggest, for example, that:

social and economic conditions and the intellectual and political spirit
of the times exert profound influences upon the particular . . . problems
which concern us and upon the forms of help which develop and
flourish.[20]

Others have pointed this out with respect to social services[21] as well
as education.[22] Neither were we the first to note that two modes of
social service helping have derived from the *Zeitgeist* of the times,
popular according to the particular values and view of the person that
flourished with the times. For it is well documented that

situational modes of help, demanding as they do the questioning of the
social environment and change in the social environment, will flourish
during periods of political or social reform . . . periods of "acute social
change" . . . Intra-psychic modes of help will be prominent during
periods of political or social conservatism.[23]

In the early 1920s Mary Richmond saw the need for a social work
practice that emphasized more than casework and wrote:

Social casework would be only a fragment if separated from the much
larger field occupied by social work in general . . . family case workers
(should) study and develop their work at its point of intersection with
social research, with group activities and with social reform or mass
betterment.[24]

We cannot claim first discovery for the notion that the social worker
should aim to "work herself out of a job." This has its counterpart in
Wooton's contention that social work should be "self-liquidating."[25]
And emphasis upon more than the intrapsychic phenomena was pointed
to by Charlotte Towle, in declaring:

that families live in streets amongst neighbors, not in a vacuum, that
much of most lives is spent in factories or other workplaces, and that
people are affected by what happens outside their homes as well as by
their domestic relationships.[26]

Towle also proclaimed loud and clear to the workers in the 1940s:
"The social caseworker has labored all too long in futile attempts at
helping the individual feel better on an empty stomach."[27] Bertha
Reynolds' concerns about the inadequacies of the social environment
and its effect upon persons' distress runs through all her writings.
Here is one of her pointed comments to school social workers:

The contribution of social casework is to supplement the best public administration, not to struggle to make up for the mistakes of a poor one. If a faulty school curriculum is causing every year thousands of school failures, it would be stupid to engage visiting teachers to work individually with the unsuccessful children. Why not change the curriculum and do away with that particular problem at one stroke? [28]

Why is Reynolds' directive so reminiscent of this old Cornish tale?

As a test of insanity the person to be tested is placed in a small room facing a sink in which there is a spigot, a pail underneath the spigot and a ladle in the pail. The spigot is turned on and the testee is told to keep the water from overflowing from the pail. The person who continues to ladle, however energetically and successfully, without attending to the flow from the spigot, is judged insane.

Harry Lurie summed matters up this way:

We have assumed the existence of freedom of opportunity for adjustment of the individual and have blinked the gross obstacles to adjustment which exist in the social order . . . have given little attention to such demoralizing factors in social life as the venality of business and of politics, and the prevalence of unethical practices. . . . Casework . . . is usually a poor substitute for inadequate income and is not a genuine solution for the problems of poverty . . . it is not likely to be better than the social work program in which it functions. [29]

The structural approach seems to fit congenially with John Rawles' concept—distributive justice—as its underlying value. This view holds as primary each person's need of a fair share of the benefits and burdens of society. This includes the need for a fair distribution of economic goods and services, but also a fair allocation of nonmaterial goods like opportunity, power, rights, liberties, and the self-respect that accompanies these social benefits. The social worker is concerned for the deprived that they gain a just level of these basic goods and gain access to them when blockages create their deprivation. [30]

Conclusion

The major focus will be on present practice rather than on history. Throughout social work's brief history, practice has been conceptualized differently from time to time. Perhaps this stems from social work's view of itself as essentially a *responding* profession. Social workers have responded throughout history to what the times seemed to demand according to the knowledge and tools they had available. Unlike the scientists and engineers of the space industry who hold a public sanction to create the times, social workers hold a societal mandate mainly to deal with the times. Social workers have been trouble-shooters for an imperfect set of social arrangements, often equipped with blank cartridges that make more noise than impact.

Now, more than ever, many social workers need to have a hand in designing and creating the times—to initiate, not merely to respond. They do not wish to remain agents of social control, no matter how humane. They do not want to perpetuate an inadequate *status quo*. This book aims to translate these social change imperatives into specific principles that can guide the practitioner's work with clients.

Basic Assumptions

Two central assumptions are inherent in the approach: 1) Individuals' problems are not viewed as individual pathology, but as a manifestation of inadequate social arrangements.[31] Thus, clients of social services are not categorically seen as impaired or deficient individuals, a different breed from the rest of society. Rather, their life circumstances may be more precarious, more restrictive, more crushing than those of other populations. 2) The response of the social work profession to the need for social change is the obligation of all social workers wherever they are in the bureaucratic hierarchy. In fact, it *begins* with how the direct service practitioners conceptualize their response to a specific client. Social change is not separated from social work, not relegated to specialists within the social work profession (community organizers, planners, social policy-makers). Rather, it is pursued at every level of assignment, every working day by all social workers, and especially by those who must face the clients directly.

PART ONE

Roots

1. A Frame of Reference for Social Work Practice

The history of social work has been characterized more by diversity than unity. Practice has differed in accord with different fields of practice (medical social work, psychiatric social work, child welfare work, gerontological social work, occupational social work), different methods (casework, family social work, group work, community organization), different schools of thought (psychosocial, behavioral, problem solving, ecological, task-centered, interactional), and different purposes (rehabilitation, socialization, resocialization, education, social action).

So what, if anything, is there about social work's diverse practice that makes it one profession? Subscription to a single set of ethics? Standing for oppressed peoples? The stigma we bear due to being frequently identified with our clients because, like them, we *cost* money in this commercial world where market mentality is king? While these similarities are significant, they are by no means sufficient to provide a clear and stable professional identity.

A profession *is* what it *does;* therefore it should be defined by its actions. Thus we must look to the activities of social work practitioners for the data from which to define our boundaries.

Since this book's first edition, there is increasing recognition that the following model connects accurately and usefully the diverse activities of social work. It has been seen as valuable for helping workers identify where they are in any given instance of practice. It helps workers keep their primary goal in mind despite "happy accidents", as when teenagers have good experiences providing recreation for disabled children. The social worker remains clear about the fact that the children are her intended beneficiaries, and the teens are an "action system"[1] engaged by her in behalf of the disabled children. The worker, therefore, cannot inadvertantly focus on the teenagers having a good experience, nor does she even divide her attention between the children and the teens.

Moreover, as Germain[2] notes, the model comes out of social work itself. It does not rely upon theory or practice in psychology, biology, sociology, or theology. It derives from what the worker is doing, with what interested parties, toward what end. That is to say, the model consists of four categories of activity (what the worker is doing), formed, as per figure 1.1, by juxtaposition of two bi-polar dimensions —persons engaged, and intended beneficiary.

FIGURE 1.1. A Frame of Reference

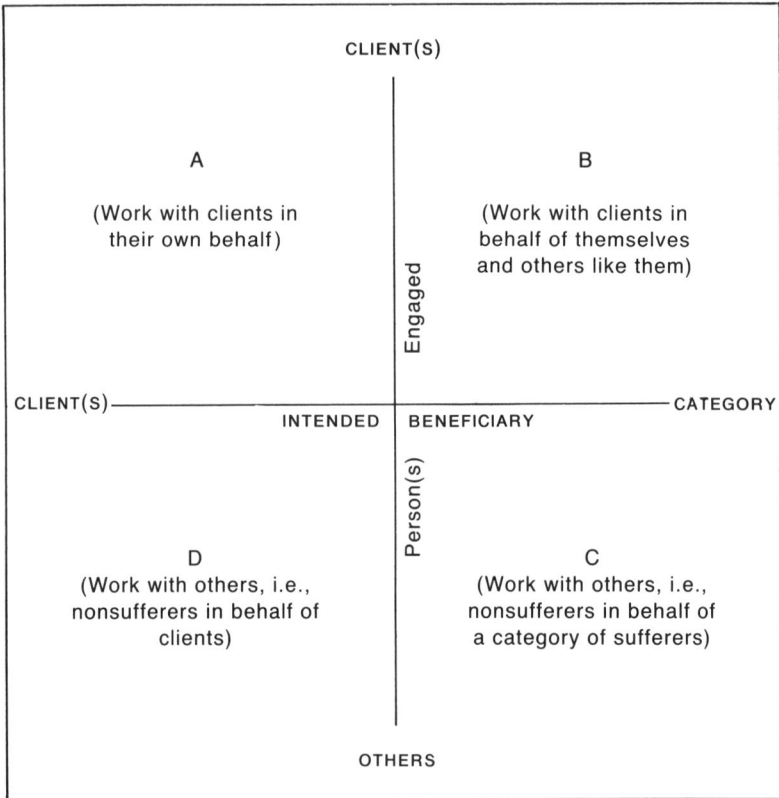

Two Dimensions

"Intended beneficiary" is the worker's locus of concern, which constitutes the rationale for social work intervention. The poles on this dimension are 1) client(s), specific people suffering in relation to particular facets of various problems (for example, a man who cannot get a job because he is chicano and cannot get decent housing because he is poor, or a poor white who is consistently turned down for jobs due to body odors he cannot eliminate because one is not permitted to purchase soap, deodorant, and/or toothpaste with food stamps); and 2) categories of persons at risk, sub-populations of persons identified as sufferers by definition of a social problem (the poor, for example, or peoples of color).

"Person(s) engaged" refers to those people with whom the social worker works at various times in accord with his rationale for intervention. The poles on this dimension are 1) client(s), and 2) other(s). On the one hand, the social worker may engage individuals and/or families and/or community groups in helping themselves and each other to change the particular situations that limit their functioning and exacerbate their suffering. Or the social worker may engage others (neighbors, congressmen, local merchants, other professionals such as teachers, lawyers and/or nurses) to help an individual, or a family, or a group or a category of persons. Congressmen, for example, may be approached by the social worker to amend archaic housing laws that protect landlords, not tenants. Local civic leaders may be mobilized to demand additional day-care centers, more accessible and affordable health services, an improved system of monitoring employment practices in local branches of large business organizations. Or neighbors may be enlisted to provide specific supports during a particularly trying time in the life of an individual or a family.

Four Categories of Social Work Activity

The four categories of social work activity bounded by these two coordinates (intended beneficiary and person(s) engaged) are labeled A, B, C, and D. Quadrant A (figure 1.2A) designates all activity in which the social worker directly engages clients out of concern with their particular plight. To illustrate, one worker at a community mental health center found isolation and loneliness to be the major recurrent themes expressed by her clients. To help alleviate this problem, she directly engaged the clients in forming a telephone network through which they communicated with each other every day. That is, Client 1 called Client 2 who then called Client 3. Client 3 called Client 4 who then called Client 1. (See chapter 3 for a description of the process.) The creation of such a self-help network comprised of and for the sole benefit of the few, specific people engaged is typical of activity in Quadrant A. A-type activity also includes work with families concerning problems various members are having with each other, and work with individuals who are having problems with themselves.

Quadrant B (figure 1.2B) designates all activity in which the social worker directly engages specific clients out of concern with an entire category of people suffering from the situation which the plight of these clients typify. B-type activities also include working with some tenants (clients) to press for home improvements for all tenants (a category of persons at risk), and working with a committee of senior citizens to plan programs for a larger senior citizen population. In other words, the typical Quadrant B activity involves direct engagement of one or a few specific people for the benefit of themselves and other persons in situations similar to theirs.

FIGURE 1.2A   FIGURE 1.2B

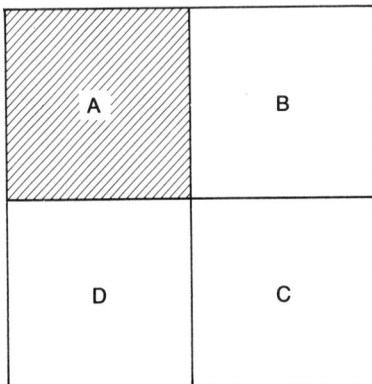

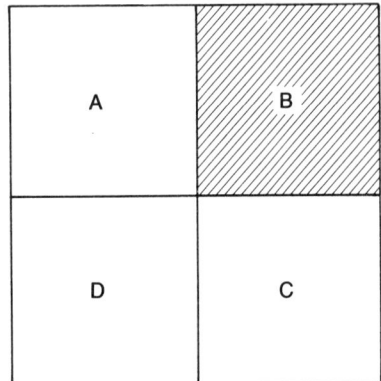

Quadrant C (figure 1.2C) designates all activity in which the social worker directly engages others, e.g., nonsufferers, out of concern with a category of sufferers. Examples include research, social policy development and analysis, social planning, fund raising, lobbying, and organizing scattered programmatic efforts to manage or alleviate a particular social problem into coordinated units for comprehensive social service delivery.

Quadrant D (figure 1.2D) designates all activity in which the social worker directly engages others (nonsufferers) out of concern with the plight of particular clients. To illustrate, another worker at a community mental health center learned that some of her clients were spending a whole day in line awaiting their prescriptions for tranquilizers, while other sufferers were on a long waiting list, unable to get needed prescriptions at all. The situation was largely a function of the limited number of staff psychiatrists. In an effort to deal with the problem, the social worker sought to organize general practitioners and family physicians in the community to take on the prescription-writing function for persons in their neighborhoods whose well-being required psychotropic medicines.

Had the social worker organized some of the people who had to stand in line (the sufferers) for purposes of pressuring the mental health center to hire more psychiatrists or pressuring the local physicians to extend their general practices to include supervision of people

FIGURE 1.2C   FIGURE 1.2D

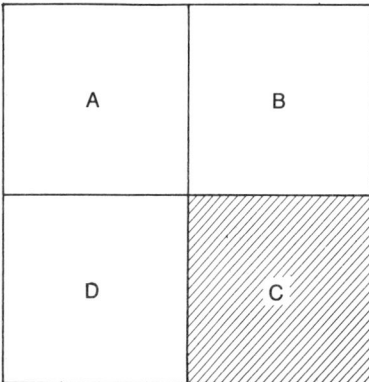 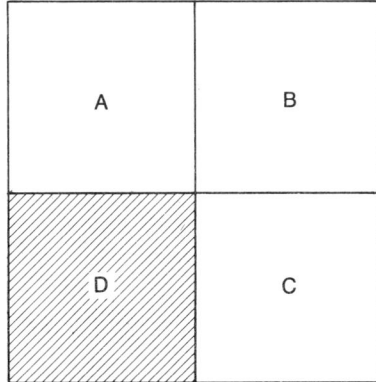

on psychotropic drugs, the worker's activity would have been classified as type B. That is to say, organizing some sufferers to do something that will benefit both themselves and others (direct work with clients to benefit their category of persons at risk) is a B-type activity, while organizing nonsufferers (others) to do something that will benefit clients who are suffering is a D-type activity. Other D-type activities include supervision of line workers, consultation, and staff training.

RESEARCH VALUE

In addition to providing a classificatory scheme for ordering thoughts about social work practice, the four-quadrant model has some potential for guiding research. For example, it can be used to track the activities of a given social worker at work in a particular instance, or to compare his activities across instances, thus providing a mechanism for determining the typical activity of a particular worker in different problematic situations. Holding the type of situation constant, it is possible to track the activities of different workers in order to determine typical social worker activity in that kind of situation. So too, holding the type of situation constant, differential social worker activity as a function of 1) school of thought, 2) field of practice, and 3) methodology can be examined. In such ways as this, we can collect data that will tell us what social workers do irrespective of differences in orientation and setting for practice (basic activities), and what social workers do as a function of their different orientations and practice contexts (specialized activities).

BEYOND RESEARCH

What social workers do may be quite different from what social workers ought to do. Research can contribute to knowledge of the former, and it can provide evidence to substantiate or disclaim the existence-in-action of a single, unified social work profession. But research cannot tell us what social workers *ought* to do.[3] When the data are in, we will have to decide whether we like all of it, part of it, or none of it —and that decision will be made quite independent of the data itself.

Nevertheless, the frame of reference and the information collected and organized can focus our attention on possible gaps in the range of approaches to social service delivery. And recognition of gaps can serve as a springboard for redetermining specializations and for developing new approaches to serving the heretofore unserved and underserved segments of the population frequently labeled "unreachable" as if, somehow, our own limited repertoire of intervention strategies were their fault.

2. The Philosophical Base for Structural Social Work Practice

Definition of a problem is a potent force in determining action to alleviate it, for the way in which the problem is formulated places constraints on the range of alternatives from which solutions can be chosen. For example, if a problem such as unemployment is defined as lack of motivation, then efforts to alleviate the problem will be directed toward motivating the unemployed. On the other hand, if the problem of unemployment is defined as a lack of jobs and/or systematic biases in the structure of opportunity, then efforts to resolve the problem will take a very different direction.

While it is obviously ridiculous to define a psychological problem such as fear of heights in social terms (e.g., buildings are too tall?), the tendency to define social problems in psychological terms is a more subtle version of the same fallacy. And it is just such a fallacy of the latter type that has made some social workers with good intentions unwitting parties to the mounting conspiracy against the poor and peoples of color.

The tendency to define social problems in psychological terms has its roots in a remedial paradigm, a set of assumptions foisted upon us as children and reinforced throughout our further "education". We were taught to believe that an individual's economic limitations stem from his own personal deficits, that he is an exception in an otherwise functional set of social arrangements, and that he needs to be changed in some way—made more adequate via counseling, education, socialization, acculturation, rehabilitation, and so forth—in order to "hold his own" in society. From this perspective, the social worker is an agent of social control, maintaining the inequitable *status quo* by placating an otherwise dangerous population of have-nots.

At this point, it seems important to note that the term "inadequate", which, when applied to people, leads to such goals as increased ego strength, can be insidiously tyrannical, for it is not merely a descriptive term. It refers to a disparity between the skills and resources of a given person and the demands of a given situation. If one believes that the person ought to be more skillful and/or resourceful, better able to meet the demands of the situation, then the person will be labeled "inadequate". If, on the other hand, it is believed that the situation ought to place fewer demands on the person, then the situation will be labeled "inadequate." Thus, to say that a given person is inadequate is both a description of disparity between that person and a particular situation, and a value judgment attributing blame for that disparity at one and the same time.[1]

An alternative perspective considers most social problems to be predictable, deliberately built into the system for the benefit of some at the expense of a systematic population of others. This line of thinking suggests that opportunities and resources are unequally distributed and that members of deprived populations are social victims. Thus it appears that social workers ought to be changing oppressive situations instead of the people trapped in them. That is to say, social workers should bring to bear, modify, and/or create resources to meet human needs; social workers should be agents of social change, not status quoticians. And this perspective considers public social services to be the right of every man, woman and child who, for whatever reason, cannot provide for themselves.

Unfortunately, neither perspective is unequivocally correct. The issue of problem definition is always a choice. Knowing how to define problems from both perspectives, however, provides the social worker with a choice, not just a habit. Structural social work is based on the choice of defining problems in the environment, not in the client.

The practice model presented in this text presupposes that sufferers are not necessarily the cause of their problems and therefore are not always the appropriate targets for change efforts. The point is that inadequate social arrangements may be responsible for many of the problematic situations that are frequently defined as products of those who suffer from them. Poverty, for example, was not created by the poor. Nor was racism invented by blacks.

Structural social work procedes from the assumption that in any given instance of suffering, environmental pressures should be considered *first,* 1) to see if environmental change would alleviate the suffering, and 2) to see if it is possible to change the environment in the necessary manner. If it is not possible to change the environment, or if it is possible and the change still does not alleviate the person's suffering, then psychological help for the individual may be indicated. The rationale for considering the situation first is to avoid getting locked into a tautological and self-confirming system. To presume that the problem is psychological is to preclude proof that it is not. To presume that the problem is rooted in the social structure, however, allows for observable evidence to indicate that the assumption is fallacious if, in fact, it is.

Given this philosophy, we propose the following four-part professional assignment for the structural social worker in direct practice:

1. To help people connect with needed resources;

2. To change social structures where existing ones limit human functioning and it is feasible to change them;

3. To help people negotiate problematic situations, whether real or as they have construed them to be, and

4. To help oneself and one's colleagues toward on-going professional development and delivery of high quality service.

This professional assignment can and should hold across agency settings. The service delivered by a social worker is conceptualized as a professional social work service rather than the service of a particular agency. Much as an obstetrician delivers babies, and delivers them in the same way irrespective of what hospital employs her, the social worker should perform the same professional assignment irrespective of the employing agency. In both instances, the service that the professional renders is the service of the profession.

Agencies define client populations, e.g., residents in a particular catchment area, and provide resources, e.g., emergency financial assistance. They do not determine the professional practice of the professionals they employ. This is not to deny that the way in which a worker implements the professional assignment must be modified in accord with the organizational restrictions of different agencies. The point is that the basic thrust does not change, although the specific movements of the worker may need to change.

Fulfillment of the professional assignment specified here demands performance of all four types of work defined by the Quadrant Model in Chapter 1. And this is a tall order for any one social worker to carry out. Moreover, while the worker is involved in C-type activities (research, social policy development), what happens to the persons he left behind in Quadrant A? For example, who will help Robert Hernandez to get a job while the social worker is engaged with congressmen, local businessmen, and government agencies about putting into operation policies that guarantee equal employment opportunity for all? Conversely, who will work toward alleviating the common plight of minority groups through changing discriminatory employment practices while the social worker is busy helping Robert Hernandez to get a job? For pragmatic reasons at least, some division of labor is necessary.

Specialization

Social work practice has always been divided in some way. But the specializations were not designated *a priori* in accord with definitive knowledge or a hypothetical construct of the whole. Rather, specializations evolved in the course of actual work, and partial theories to justify them appeared later.

One problem posed by evolutionary development, as opposed to a priori designation of specializations, is that of determining the amount and kind of additional specializations that are required. In other words, how will we know when we have arrived at the whole? Perhaps this partially accounts for social work's reluctance either to completely embrace or completely reject any innovation in practice. With no overall, orienting scheme, with no image of what the whole should look like, there is no basis for separating the relevant from the irrelevant.

Related to this is the problem of recognizing gaps in social work practice. The absence of a scheme that organizes and gives meaning to the various specializations suggests that each is a whole unto itself, and that the profession is a loose federation of functionally autonomous units. How can there be gaps when social work is so conceived? If there is a whole of social work practice with an assigned or an assumed social function to perform, then specializations must be seen as parts in relation to other parts, each deriving its special responsibilities from, and having meaning only in relation to, the whole.

It should be noted that social work practice does not fall "naturally" into any particular set of subunits as opposed to any other particular set of subunits. Practice specializations must be arbitrarily defined, and in this sense, any scheme for partitioning the whole is as logical as any other scheme. The important issue is that there be some scheme, some theoretical construct (albeit tentative) that represents the whole and specifies the relationship among parts, irrespective of the particular way in which that whole is partitioned.

The four-quadrant model is one way to conceptualize the whole of social work practice. It guides our discussion of practice here, and serves as a point of origin for dividing social work practice into the two complementary areas of specialization diagramed in figure 2.1. Since specialization was necessary for pragmatic reasons, so too the overlap in Quadrants B and D is necessary for pragmatic reasons. The overlap is intended to prevent built-in gaps that hound theorists, confound practitioners, and frustrate clients.

Quadrants A, B, and D can be used to describe the *micro* practice of social work, while Quadrants C, B, and D can be used to describe

FIGURE 2.1

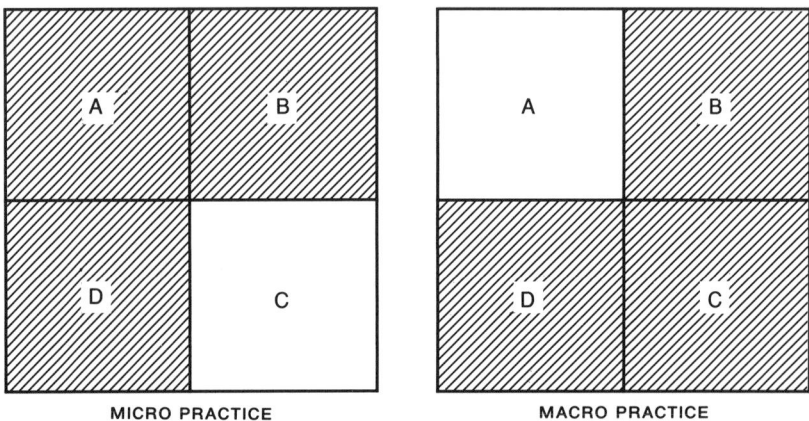

MICRO PRACTICE   MACRO PRACTICE

the *macro* practice of social work. Since Quadrant A is presumably specific to micro practice, and Quadrant C is presumably specific to macro practice, Quadrants A and C could be considered the exclusive categories of activity that provide the needed division of labor. With respect to the example cited earlier, the social worker in micro practice could help Robert Hernandez to get a job while the social worker in macro practice could work on policies to assure equal employment opportunity for all.

Since both practice specializations would operate in Quadrants B and D, these could be considered the mutual categories of activity that provide the overlap to control for gaps between areas of specialization.

Given the above, it seems reasonable to assume that every instance of micro social work would begin in Quadrant A, with the expressed needs of particular persons, and extend to Quadrants B and/or D in accord with the demands of the client task. "Client task" is defined as the deleterious aspect of a problem impinging on the client, translated into a change goal. On the other hand, every instance of social work in macro practice would begin in Quadrant C and extend to Quadrants B and/or D in accord with the demands of the social task. The "social task" is defined as a social problem translated into a change goal.[2] In other words, the objectives of macro-level social work practice would grow out of the social problem itself, while the objectives of micro-level social work practice would grow out of the expressed needs of a particular client system.

Since both specializations would operate in Quadrants B and D, their respective activities might, at times, look alike. In terms of Quadrant B, for example, either specialist may organize a group of tenants to press for improved maintainance and repairs for themselves and others living in the same housing project. As the specialists proceed from different loci of concern, however, their work manifests certain important differences.

The social workers in macro practice may organize tenant councils in various housing projects in an effort to bring about broader social change with respect to tenants' rights. Their concern is with a category of sufferers (the residents in public housing projects) rather than with any single instance within that category (the plight of client 1, client 2, client 3 and others in the Glenrock Housing Project). Thus their organizing job is not finished when any one tenants' council is organized, but their work with those particular tenants is finished. These social workers move on to organize other councils in other housing projects.

The social workers in micro practice, on the other hand, organize a group of tenants in response to their expressed need for improved maintenance. The worker's concern is with the plight of these particular tenants. When this group of tenants, with the worker, has accomplished the task (the manager has arranged for necessary repairs and improved maintenance), the worker is out of the tenant-organizing business. The worker may still be involved with these particular tenants in any number of other problematic situations, however (prejudicial attitudes of teachers in the local school toward the children of these tenants, inadequate public welfare grants).[3]

To specify a professional assignment and designate areas of specialization in terms of activity provides an orientation to practice, but it does not describe practice itself. In other words, such a formulation, while essential to a coherent, systematic practice, is too abstract to guide intervention. Elaboration of a practice requires specification of a set of principles, operational definitions of the principles, the functional roles that derive from those operationally defined principles, and the explicit acts which the worker should perform in order to implement the professional assignment in accord with the operational definitions of those principles.

PART TWO

Principles and Process

3. Basic Principles of the Structural Approach

Every instance of social work involves an intervention into the relationship between people and their social environment in order to improve the quality of that relationship. The ultimate target of change may be the people, the social environment, or the relationship itself. The accumulated body of recorded experience in social work includes a variety of conceptual models to guide people-changing and relationship changing. In the structural model described here, the social environment is the primary target of change. The social worker intervenes to improve the quality of the relationship between people and their social environment by bringing to bear, changing, or creating social structures.

The structural model rests on six basic principles:

1. The worker should be accountable to the client(s).

2. The worker should follow the demands of the client task.

3. The worker should maximize the potential supports in the client's environment.

4. The worker should proceed from an assumption of least contest.

5. The worker should identify, reinforce and/or increase the client's repertoire of strategic behavior for minimizing pain and maximizing positive outcomes and satisfaction.

6. Workers should apply principles one through five to themselves.

The Principle of Accountability to the Client

This principle translates the basic assumption of "adequate person vs. inadequate social arrangements" into action. People suffering in relation to their social situations are presumed competent to describe the pressures upon them and to explain their need. Therefore, social work practice takes, as its starting point, the task confronting a particular client or set of clients as it is expressed in terms of their felt need. In other words, the pressures on the client(s) define the task, and the task is always to lessen those pressures. This task, explicitly understood by worker and client alike, constitutes one of two essential parts of the service contract.

The service contract operationalizes the principle of worker accountability to the client. The service contract may be said to exist when both worker and client explicitly understand and agree upon the task to be accomplished and what the worker and client will do to help accomplish it. This contract is not a written document, as a literal interpretation of the word would suggest. Rather, the term is used metaphorically to indicate that worker and client have verbally agreed upon what will be done and how it will be done. The service contract is a working agreement.

The client, with the help of the worker, describes the pressures on him (job discrimination, poor housing), and these pressures, in turn, define the task to be accomplished, what must be done to alleviate the pressures which the client describes. In the instance of poor housing conditions, for example, the task may be that of obtaining necessary repairs or obtaining a different house, depending upon the preference of the client. In the event that all possible efforts of worker and client do not accomplish the client's preferred task, they may jointly agree to work on an alternative task. Or, if there is no alternative acceptable to the client, the contract may be terminated.

When a task acceptable to both client and worker has been determined, the worker defines the way in which she will help the client to accomplish it. Should the worker's definition of her part be unacceptable to the client, either the worker or the client may suggest an alternative way for the worker to help. If the worker and client cannot agree on what the worker's part should be, then no contract can be made. Should worker and client agree, then the contract is established.

As changes in the definition of the task may occur as the work proceeds, so the definition of what the worker will do may also change. This change may be necessitated by changes in the task, or by the implications of additional information obtained in the course of working on the original contract. In any event, changes in the contract must be discussed and agreed upon before action continues.

The extent to which the terms of the service contract are specified in detail is less important than the social worker's intent to be completely open. That is, the worker should not have goals or methods kept secret from the clients. The mandate to establish a contract with each client or set of clients requires that worker's state their intentions explicitly. This not only insures the client's right to decide whether or not the worker's intended behavior is acceptable, but it also insures workers' awareness of what they are about.

Because the contract openly specifies what worker and client have agreed upon as the task to be accomplished and the worker's part in helping to accomplish it, at least theoretically, the client is able to hold the worker to that task and the part they both agreed that the worker would play. That is, the client can hold the worker accountable for actions specified in the contract. While it is recognized that clients who feel (because they frequently are) powerless are unlikely to confront a worker who may be subverting the terms of the service contract, recognition of their right to do so sets a different tone for the worker-client relationship.

Social work by contractual agreement has advantages such as reducing the relative powerlessness of the client in a helping relationship. Rather than being a dependant recipient of worker behavior beyond one's control, the client is a partner in determining, every step of the way, what will be done and how it will be done. And the client is not called upon to trust blindly a person hardly known in order to get help.

SALIENT SKILLS

To serve as an accountability device, the contract must be developed at the beginning of the worker-client relationship. While necessary, this is unfortunate, for in the beginning it is very hard for many clients to talk openly about their private thoughts and feelings, to describe in detail, to a stranger, the nature of the situations that are causing them pain. Yet this is exactly what is necessary for the contract to reflect the client's needs and problems. Thus it is very important for the social worker to do everything possible to ease the way for clients to provide well-detailed, minimally distorted pictures of their plight. Six key skills can facilitate the interaction at this early and vulnerable point in the helping process: positioning, attending, reaching for feelings, getting with feelings, reaching for information, and giving feedback.

Positioning is intended to provide a social-emotional environment congenial to connection or rapport. It involves placing one's self physically at a right angle to the client,[1] approximately 29 to 36 inches away.[2] It also involves avoiding the desk, a potentially separating middle-class and businesslike accoutrement that can be both a physical and cultural barrier to communication. *Attending* refers to occasional head nods and unobtrusive "uh-huhs" that tell clients "I am following you" and encourage them to say more.

Reaching for feelings and getting with feelings are significant throughout the work and critical at the outset. If the feelings that surround a description of pressures or an expression of need are not promptly and openly engaged, they become obstacles to the work, skewing perceptions and subtly distorting information that is sent and received. The social worker can *reach for feelings* that may be present but are not verbally expressed by verbalizing the client's nonverbal behavior in a statement such as "You're frowning," or by suggesting feelings that the client's situation is likely to evoke, such as "That can be frightening." When the client does express affect in words, the worker can *get with feelings* by making a congruent statement, such as "That *is* exhausting," or a congruent noise, such as "Wow." Getting with feelings indicates to clients that the essence of their inner experience has been communicated, that what they feel is understandable and has been understood.

To *reach for information* is to ask the client for facts, opinions, values, and/or judgments that increase knowledge of a situation or event. The worker can reach for information using two different forms: open-ended questions, such as "What happened?" to explore, and close-ended questions, such as "Who went with you?" in order to clarify details.

Giving feedback, another skill essential to the development of authentic contracts with clients, involves repeating the essence of what the client has said in a way that asks if the meaning received by the worker was, in fact, the meaning intended by the client. The worker's version of the client's statement can then be confirmed, if accurate, or if inaccurate, can be corrected by the client.

In sum, the principle of accountability to the client translates the basic assumption of "adequate person" into action through the structural mechanism of the service contract, comprised by the task which is defined by the pressures on the client and the part the worker will play in helping to accomplish that task.

The following episode illustrates the accountability principle and the way in which use of the six skills described above facilitate the interaction process. Examples of skills are underscored in the practice excerpts.

> One of the fifth-grade teachers stopped me in the hall to tell me that a girl in his class was having problems with some of the other children. He asked me if I would talk to her, and I said I would. A short while later Debby came into my office and sat down without saying anything. I moved to a nearby chair and angled it so we were knee-to-knee. I waited several moments and then said, "I was talking with Mr. Taylor a little while ago and he seemed concerned that you were having some problems with some of the other kids in class." I paused and waited to see if Debby would say anything. When she didn't, I asked her if she thought that there was any problem.

The social worker presumes that Debby is competent to describe the pressures on her. She does not act according to the teacher's perception that Debby has a problem, for it is quite possible that what may seem like a problem to the teacher may not be felt as a problem to Debby. And even if Debby does consider it a problem, she has a right to refuse the social worker's offer. But Debby does feel some pressure, and with the help of the worker positioning herself to maximize the child's comfort and reaching for information, she begins to describe her situation.

Debby then replied that the other kids have been teasing her, and that she has been upset. I said that teasing could make you feel pretty bad. She nodded and began describing some examples of it. I listened, nodding at points. When she finished, I asked her if she'd like me to help her talk to the kids that tease her. She said that it seemed like a good idea, but from the look on her face I could tell that something was bothering her. I said, "You don't look as if you think it's a good idea."

The worker gets with Debby's feelings, then attends as the child tells more of her painful story. Note that when the worker picks up a non-verbal clue that Debby is not really in agreement with her suggestion, she does not violate the intent of the contract by accepting Debby's verbal "yes" when her expression seems to indicate "no." Rather, the worker reaches for her feelings and invites her to voice her doubts. In response to the worker's use of empathic skill, Debby begins to describe a feared consequence.

Debby hesitated and then said that she was afraid the other kids might start a fight with her afterward. I told Debby that I had not thought of that and agreed that it could be a problem. I said that I guessed that could really be upsetting and pointed out that if she really wanted to get together with the kids who tease her, this could be one of the risks she would have to take. I asked Debby if she understood what I was saying and she said that she did.

The social worker does not try to convince Debby to take action. Rather, she gets with the child's feelings, confirming that such a consequence is possible and encourages Debby to consider whether talking with the children who tease her is worth the risk. The choice belongs to Debby, for the consequences of the choice are hers to bear.

Debby decides to wait until the children tease her again, and a service contract is established.

Debby was silent for a few moments and then said that she didn't want to do anything until the children started to tease her again. She said that when they did, she would tell me. I asked her if she wanted me to wait until I heard from her again and at that time she would tell me if she wanted me to help her talk to the kids. She said yes, and I agreed to her plan.

The terms of the contract between Debby and the social worker were openly specified and agreed upon by both parties. The worker checked to be certain of this by giving feedback to Debby. When Debby acknowledged that the worker's formulation was accurate, it was clear that a contract had been established. No action would be taken unless another incident arose and Debby indicated to the social worker that she wanted help. Hence, Debby possessed the power to determine the direction of the worker-client relationship, if in fact she wanted to continue it at all.

The Principle of Following the Demands of the Client Task

This principle requires the social worker to move from quadrant to quadrant. For example, the worker may help a Puerto Rican child suffering from racism at school to talk with the teacher about it (Quadrant A). In addition, the worker may engage the faculty and administration in creating an atmosphere more congenial to the needs of Puerto Rican children (Quadrant D). Or, if necessary, the worker may organize the parents of Puerto Rican children at that school to confront teachers and administrators (Quadrant B).

Prerequisite to B-type activity is the identification of others suffering in the same situation. If the workers are to include B-type activities among their alternatives, they must consistently and systematically look beyond the client to see if there are others facing the same tasks.. For example, B-type activity is not a viable alternative when only one Puerto Rican family is suffering the effects of racism at the local school. When other Puerto Rican families are also victims of racism at that school, however, the need for structural change rather than an individualized plan which results from a case-by-case approach is more evident, and B-type activity, by the social worker, becomes an alternative for accomplishing the desired change. The demand that the worker consistently look beyond the client to see if others are suffering in relation to the same phenomenon translates the essence of a structural approach to social work—meeting social needs through social change—into actual practice behavior.

As workers move from quadrant to quadrant in pursuit of the client task, they engage both the client and others, in different configurations, at different times. A-type activity may be carried out with an individual, with a family, or with a group. Similarly in Quadrant D, the worker may engage one community person or a group of community people in behalf of client interest. And in Quadrant B, the worker may engage an individual, a family, or a group in behalf of themselves and others suffering from the same pressures. In other words, the worker not only moves from quadrant to quadrant in accord with the demands of the client task, but also engages different configurations of people as the work demands.

For example, when the worker agrees to help three residents of a public housing project to get needed home repairs, the client is this three-person group with the common task of obtaining the repairs. In the course of working on this task the worker may engage the local representatives of the city housing authority (D-type activity with an individual), or engage the housing authority representative along with representatives from related agencies (D-type activity with a group) in an effort to obtain the repairs.

Following the demands of the client task also implies the need for role flexibility. That is, the worker needs to use different sets of behaviors at different times, depending upon the nature of the task and the situation at any given point.

Four recognizable sets of behaviors can be subsumed under the role names: 1) broker, 2) mediator, 3) advocate, and 4) conferee. The role of broker is perhaps the most familiar one. The broker stands at the interface between client need and community resources, helping the former to connect with the latter. But brokerage is not enough; for clients and agencies do not always recognize their complementarity of interest, that each needs the other in order to survive. As a result, needed service may not be rendered. In the role of mediator, the social worker tries to help client and agency to recognize their complementarity of interest and to act accordingly.

But complementarity of interest between client and agency is more often apparent than real. Many agencies have a more than sufficient number of clients to validate their raison d'être, and are well able to survive without the patronage of any one individual—especially no-choice monopolies and involuntary clients. Hence, the client needs the agency more than the agency needs the client. In such a situation, agencies are not necessarily responsive to all who need service, particularly when responsiveness to a given client requires great effort. Rather, there is a tendency for agencies with large consumer populations to serve the "good client" and, perhaps unwittingly, to ignore the "hard to reach." The phenomenon, when noted in poverty programs, was termed "creaming the poor,"[3] but it is hardly problem-specific. It extends to the powerless in general, whether poor, black, aged, gay, or defined as mentally ill.

When the presumed complementarity of interest between client and agency breaks down (or never existed) and mediation fails, the client needs an advocate. As advocate of client interest, the social worker demands that the agency provide the clients with the benefits to which they are entitled.

A fourth set of expectations for behavior can be organized under the role name "conferee." The social worker takes the role of conferee for the purpose of determining, with clients, the task to be accomplished and the course of action to be pursued. The social worker confers with clients, providing information on alternative actions and the possible consequences of each, and encourages clients to decide which alternatives, if any, are congenial to their needs and life styles.

The four social work roles are elaborated in part 3. To recapitulate, the principle of following the demands of the client task requires the worker consistently and systematically to look beyond the client to see if others are facing the same task, and to assume different roles at different times while performing different types of activities (A-type, B-type, and D-type) with various configurations of people.

The following episode illustrates the principle of following the demands of the client task.

Mrs. Fuller had asked the County Board of Assistance to help her sixteen-year-old son, Joe, who was experiencing difficulty at school. In response to her request, Mr. Rand, a social worker at the agency, visits Joe. He begins his activity in Quadrant A, and takes the role of conferee.

I met with Joe in his home one morning before he went to school. We sat across from each other at the kitchen table. I began by asking him if he had some idea about why I was there, and he said

that he guessed so, that he had trouble with school work. I told him
that his mother had said as much, and asked him if the difficulty in
school was worrying him. He shook his head slightly in an affirmative way and, not looking directly at me, asked if I was going to get
him into welding school. I said I didn't know and asked him if that's
what he would like. He said he guessed so, but that he didn't know.
He said he wasn't doing well in school. His speech was hesitant at
this point. I said, "You seem as if you're not too sure of yourself."
There was a long silence.

Joe broke the silence, saying that he knew some guys who were
going to college and that's what he'd like to do but that it's impossible. I asked him if he meant his grades would get in the way, and
he said that was partly it but it was mainly because he can't read.
He spoke slowly and hesitantly, but articulately. I remained silent,
nodding my head in acknowledgement. There was another silence.

Again Joe broke the silence. "I really can't read," he said. "I can't
even understand some of the instructions in shop 'cause I can't
read." He said that in school they don't care if you don't learn as
long as you stay out of trouble. "You stay out of trouble, you pass."

We do not know what led Mr. Rand to sit across from Joe instead
of using the preferable corner-to-corner arrangement. Perhaps in the
Fuller kitchen there was no way to maneuver himself into a better
position. Nevertheless, from Joe's allowing himself to be vulnerable by
volunteering the information that he is not able to read, we can
suppose that in this instance, the worker's position did not adversely
affect the interaction process.

The statement "You seem as if you're not too sure of yourself," in
the excerpt above, demonstrates *checking out an inference,* a skill
useful across the board, but especially important when the worker is
trying to integrate seemingly separate bits of information that have
been generated while following the demands of the client task. It is at
this time that the worker is most likely to draw consequential inferences. Therefore, it is at this time that the worker must be most
careful to state all inferences aloud and ask the client if they are valid.
When workers do not do this, there is danger that unfounded assumptions and interpretations could be acted upon—resulting in actual or
felt harm to the client.

In addition to increasing accuracy, checking out an inference often results in both worker and client becoming clearer about sometimes elusive elements of thought and feeling. This, too, is illustrated in the above excerpt. In response to Mr. Rand's statement of the first inference he drew, Joe clarified what he would like, and when Mr. Rand checked out a second inference, Joe revealed the far more basic nature of the problem he was facing.

Having something solid to go on, Mr. Rand reaches for information in order to look beyond the client to see if others are in a similar predicament.

> We talked about needing to know how to read, whether for welding or for college, and I asked Joe if he knew of other guys in a similar predicament. He said that he did, and I wondered whether he could talk to them about getting a group together for reading or whatever. He said he would try, and we ended with the understanding that we would get together again.

While Joe contacted some of the others who shared his plight, Mr. Rand moved from Quadrant A to Quadrant D, and shifted his role from that of conferee to that of broker.

> I talked without success to the Educational Unit of the County Board of Assistance. This unit is set up to service the educational needs of all Public Assistance, or food stamp recipients in the county, a 50,000-plus population. The unit is supposed to deal with tutoring, liaison between schools and parents, and whatever other needs may develop in the area of education. The unit consists of one social worker with obviously not enough time even to consider the problem until maybe several months from now.
>
> Later, I spoke with Joe's counselor at school. The counselor was not aware of the exact nature of Joe's difficulties but seemed interested in helping out. There was a class for improving reading, but it was, as a rule, not available to students as old as Joe and his friends. The counselor said he would look into making an exception, however. I said that I would talk further with Joe about it.

The term "exception" poses a dilemma, for it suggests that the service is a gift as opposed to an entitlement. In this instance it implies that, due to the good will of this particular counselor at this particular

time, Joe and his friends will be taught to read. But others, who have
a different counselor, or who have the same counselor but do not find
reading a problem until next month or next year, may have no place
to turn. In addition to the obvious need to redesign the school program
so that students will learn to read before reaching the tenth grade, a
high school reading program should be consistently and systematically available to all students who wish to use it. A structure is needed,
and this leads directly to a discussion of the third practice principle.

The Principle of Maximizing Potential Supports in the Client's Environment

Maximizing potential supports in the client's environment suggests
modification of existing structures and/or creation of new structures
to meet human needs, and this embodies the essential thrust of the
structural approach to social work practice. With respect to the preceding example, the worker may engage teachers and administrators
in setting up a reading program in the high school. In a social agency
where clients wait several weeks between their application for help
and the beginning of service, and this lapse in time can be traced to
cumbersome intake procedures, the worker may engage agency personnel in changing the procedures or creating a program to serve
clients during those weeks of processing. As a third example, in order
to counteract the debilitating effects of a teacher's frequent disparagement of one or several black children, the worker may enlist the local
butcher, grocer, and newspaperman to tell these children regularly
that they are all right. In all of these examples, the worker attempts to
maximize potential environmental supports by either modifying an
existing structure or creating a new structure. And in all these examples the structures involve others (non-clients) in behalf of clients,
and can therefore be considered D-type structures. The telephone
network described in chapter 1, on the other hand, was comprised of
the persons who directly benefited from it, and is therefore considered
an A-type structure.

It should be noted that the creation of all A-type structures, and
such D-type structures as the corps of community people enlisted to

counteract the teacher's disparagement of some children, shifts the helping relationship from client-worker to neighbor-neighbor, and a neighbor-neighbor relationship has the potential advantage of endurance over time. This is not true of a client-worker relationship, which by its very nature must end.

The professional helping relationship is a temporary one, and an emphasis on changing existing structures and creating new structures to meet human needs recognizes this. The workers do not occupy the central position in the helping process. Instead, they change structures and create structures that can operate without them. In other words, the social workers work themselves out of a job.

In sum, the principle of maximizing potential supports in the client's environment tells the worker not to occupy the central position in the helping process. Rather, the worker is directed to change and create structures to reduce the pressures on clients—to meet social need through social change.

The following episode describes the process through which Operation Switchboard was created and illustrates the principle of maximizing potential environmental supports.

The first step in forming the self-help network to lessen somewhat the isolation and loneliness expressed by several clients of the Mental Health Center involved phone calls to potential candidates.

> I called Mrs. M and introduced myself as one of the social workers at the Mental Health Center. I said I wanted her to get involved in a kind of phone network where people call each other a few times a week to see how each other is doing. This would be a way of letting people feel that they have someone to talk to when things are on their mind. Mrs. M said it sounded like a good idea. I said the first meeting would be November 9 at 1:00 p.m. She said she would come.

Not everyone responded as Mrs. M did. Approximately half of the people whom the social worker called refused to get involved, and several others said they "would see." Eight people agreed to come to the first meeting to find out more details.

> At the first meeting, three people showed up. They all looked at me with suspicion. I welcomed them and explained briefly the

thought behind the program. I invited them to share with one another what they thought of the idea. All three seemed to agree that it sounded like a pretty good idea and began to share tentatively with one another their feelings of loneliness and isolation. . . . The meeting ended with exchanging phone numbers.

After the meeting, I called all of those who said they were coming or made some tentative commitment to come, to find out what happened and to encourage them to attend the following week.

At the second meeting, two of the original three members showed up, plus Mrs. M, who could not make it to the first meeting. I asked Mrs. H and Mr. P how things worked out for them this week. Mrs. H. said that Miss T (who was not present at this meeting) did call her last week, but she never got to return her call because so many things came up. I asked Mrs. H how she thought Miss T may have felt about not being called back. She said she really did not know but that she would explain everything when she called her later today or tomorrow. I said that of course she cannot know for a fact how Miss T may have felt, but if she were in Miss T's shoes, how may she have felt? She thought about this for a moment and said that she guessed she may have felt a bit hurt. I said yes, that could well be the case.

We talked a bit more about telephoning one another, and I asked Mrs. M how she felt about the program, especially since she thought it was a good idea, but she did not care for the idea of people calling each other a set number of times a week. She thought this would mean that some weeks she would call someone just to fill a "quota," and not because she really wanted to talk to that person. I said I could see what she meant, but had she thought of it from the other person's point of view, the person expecting the call from her? Maybe the time she really does not feel like calling is the very time that person needs to get a call from her. She thought about this for a while and said, "You have a point there." She added that she would like to have the telephone numbers of all the people so that she could call not only the one person she was responsible for but the others as well. I said that was a really good idea and that I would have them for her next week.

I turned to Mr. P and said that I was glad to see him this week, especially since he did not know if he would come back, since his wife may object to his getting calls from other women. (Last week he said he may not be able to participate because of this). He smiled and said he told his wife what the program was about and she did not seem to mind the whole thing. I said I was glad about that. There was a short silence during which Mr. P looked pensive. He broke the silence by asking what was the "ultimate purpose" of this whole program and why did I start it in the first place? I reviewed the purpose as I saw it and asked Mr. P what purpose he saw in it for himself, since he is taking part in it. He thought for a while and it seemed to him that a program like this helps people to come out of their shell. He went on to say, with much feeling, that sometimes when he talks to other people for any length of time or over a period of a few days, they begin to look at him funny, or ask his family what's wrong with him. "So I just withdraw, and sit back and don't say nothing." I said to Mr. P that it must be very upsetting to be afraid to talk to other people. He said it certainly was. I said it must also hurt to hear comments questioning whether there was something about him that was not "right." He said, "You're darn right it does." I said, "No wonder you withdraw." I asked Mr. P how he felt talking right now. He said he felt okay, that he likes the idea of this group coming together and talking every week, but he is not ready yet to make phone calls. "Let me go at my own pace." I said we will do exactly that, and that I was sure all of us were more than happy to have him just come to the group meetings for a while, knowing how he feels about talking to other people. He seemed quite satisfied with this arrangement.

Mrs. H said she had called Miss T to find out why she had not come to the last meeting, but was unable to reach her. She said she also called Mrs. M and chatted with her for about an hour. She said that Mrs. M even put her two-year-old son on the phone to talk. She said they both enjoyed the conversation.

Though the contract had been developed quite a while ago and work on the task was well under way, when Mr. P spoke about his recurrent, emotion-laden experience, the worker appropriately reached for his feelings—both the fear and the hurt. And when he acknowledged that the feelings for which the worker reached were, indeed, the feelings inside of him, the worker got with his feelings with a precision that not only validated them, but connected them to his behavioral response as well (i.e., "No wonder you withdraw"). Such precision is not always possible, but where it is, the impact can be quite powerful.

As the telephone network continued to operate, members began to call each other on occasions other than those agreed upon.

> The participants in the telephone network have been connecting well with one another on the outside. While they do not call each other every day, they do call one another a couple of times a week. Two of the women have started sewing together, and the third one may join them. They do call one another when one of them does not show up for the Monday meeting. Around the Christmas holidays they exchanged cards, and one member called another on New Year's Eve to wish him and his family Happy New Year. Attendance has been excellent on the whole, with members calling me when they cannot come for any reason. It is hard to say just what it is that is making them come to the meetings in rain, snow, and bitter cold.

In an effort to extend the network to include other lonely people who might benefit from such a self-help action system, the social worker introduced the idea at a staff meeting. These meetings had tended to be largely pro forma, and real issues of consequence to staff, clients, and the process of service delivery were rarely discussed. Staff members seemed distrustful of each other, and instead of collaboration, there was a series of internecine conflicts.

> I outlined the whole program at a staff meeting and asked other staff members to keep the network and its rationale in mind, and see if they come across any people who could benefit from this program. The announcement and request were met with the usual noncommittal silence and lack of interest, with an occasional, vague Mona Lisa smile on a few people's faces. The Element Head said the program sounded interesting and worthwhile, and that he was sure staff members would keep it in mind for possible referrals. I was not so sure at all, and I am certain that neither was he.

The worker's second attempt to involve other staff members in locating isolated persons and connecting them via the telephone network took the form of individual contacts.

I began approaching individual staff members, reminding them of my concern and asking them whether they had come across any persons who could benefit from the program. The answer was invariably, "No," but they each gave me a verbal pat on the back as if to say, "That's nice, dear." Only one person showed any real interest, and has since referred one person to Operation Switchboard.

Since both efforts to involve other staff members were unsuccessful, the worker stepped back to reassess the situation in order to determine yet a third strategy. She recognized that, except for herself, the staff was primarily oriented toward and engaged in providing therapy, and that she was proposing that therapists refer "their patients" to a nontherapy service. Perhaps the unspoken message was, "I have found a better way," which could be felt as a threat to the status quo. An additional obstacle was the apparent unwillingness of staff persons to help each other. In a setting where everyone is equal, "sameness" can become confused with "equality", resulting in a lack of role differentiation. So, too, equality can produce a kind of "status anxiety"[4] which may manifest itself in fear that helping colleagues may put them a little ahead of you. In other words, the social worker seemed to be asking other staff people to help her in a project that appeared to threaten the therapy model.

The social worker did have a continuing network that was serving a useful function for its members and could be expanded to include other clients. As staff time was limited, and staff was not able to serve all persons in need, the telephone network could actually help the staff by lightening the burden of attempting to see more clients than time allowed. Thus, the worker could give something to other staff members—a resource to help remedy some of the isolation their clients were experiencing, and a service for people on the waiting list with whom they were concerned yet did not have sufficient time to engage in therapy. It was from this perspective that the social worker made her third attempt to obtain the cooperation of her colleagues in increasing service to their clients.

In the staff meeting I reviewed the history of Operation Switchboard and gave a very positive report. I said I knew how hard it was to serve the number of people each of them was trying to serve in their limited time, and that I knew how much they cared about providing service to as many people as possible. I said it was because of this that I wanted to tell them about this resource and make it available if they thought it could be helpful to any of their clients. There was much more interest this time. One staff person wanted to know the criteria for joining—neurosis, psychosis, schizophrenia, or something else. There was much amazement when I said the only criterion was the possession of a telephone, and that for people who couldn't afford a phone, the Department of Public Assistance could arrange for one to be installed since this was a mental health service. While there was surprise at the thought that clients could benefit from something other than therapy, staff seemed willing to try. Several people asked if they could refer clients they were seeing in therapy as well as those they were unable to see, and I said they could refer anyone they thought would benefit, that I respected their professional judgments.

As time went on, the members of Operation Switchboard extended their contact with each other from phone calls and weekly meetings to visits to each other's homes. The sense of isolation decreased markedly, and members attempted to come to grips with some of the social factors that fostered their isolation.

Mrs. D went on to say that she would like to invite Mrs. H to her house but she is afraid she will be harmed coming into the project where she (Mrs. D) lives, being that Mrs. H is white and whites often get knocked down or robbed. I said it must be difficult for her to want to reach out to a friend in such a nice way and to have such fears at the same time. Mrs D looked sad and said it was really a shame to have things like that get in the way of a friendship. I suggested that perhaps there was a way she could help insure Mrs. H's safety so that she could visit her. She thought for a few minutes and said that she could tell Mrs. H exactly at which entrance to be and she could meet her downstairs. Mrs. H had thought that perhaps she could meet her even at the corner or at the bus stop. Mrs. D said that was a good idea and decided to invite Mrs. H as soon as she speaks to her on the phone.

And within the network itself there were differences that had to be confronted. Obstacles to self-help had to be challenged by the worker even when the group would have preferred to deny their existence.

Shortly after the meeting began I informed the members of the group that the following week we would be joined by a new member, Mrs. K. Everybody seemed quite happy about this, and there was general agreement to the effect that it would be nice to have more members in the group. I told the group that I quite agreed and then turned to Mr. P and asked how he felt about having another woman in the group, since right now he was the only man, with three women members and a woman worker. He laughed and said he felt fine about that and it will be all right to have another lady in the group. I turned to the women and asked if they had any thoughts or feelings about this. They agreed that they have felt very comfortable with Mr. P, that he was "open-minded," a nice person, and easy to talk to, that the fact that he was a man "made no difference." Mrs. D said that "we all have common problems; that's why we are here and can help each other; it makes no difference whether you are a man or a woman." The other two women agreed with this. I said that there was much to what they were saying and that it must be good for each of them to hear that they can be accepted and cared for simply because they are people with human problems. But could they now try to put themselves in Mr. P's place and try to imagine how it would feel to be the only man in a group of five women? The women laughed and Mrs. H said she would love it since it would bring a lot of attention to her. The other two agreed, and Mr. P said laughingly that there was something to that, although he would prefer to be thought of as "just another member of the group." The women assured him that he was and that they would treat him "exactly the same."

A bit later on I inquired as to how the telephone network was working. The three women told me who had called the other during the week. They seemed quite satisfied with the arrangement. I asked at this point if anybody had called Mr. P. There was a deafening silence and obvious discomfort. After a pretty long silence, Mr. P admitted that he was more than equally responsible for this. "I really have not made an effort to call any of the ladies, except once when I called Mrs. H." Mrs. D said that the women were just as responsible, since they have not called him. Mrs. D said, "I guess we have not treated you as equally as we thought." Mr. P said he doesn't blame the women for not reaching out to him being that he has not really reached out to them. "Before I started coming here I was so withdrawn I did not want to talk to anybody. I feel different now and I think you have been very patient with me and let me go at my own speed. But I agree with the social worker that I can go a little faster now."

Mr. P did "go a little faster," as he said he would. With the support of the members of Operation Switchboard who encouraged him, and who listened to his excited reports, Mr. P volunteered his services on the men's ward of the hospital, and was accepted as an official volunteer—complete with badge, which he wore to every meeting. It may be the first palatable label that has been tacked on him in years.

The principle of Maximizing Supports in the Client's Environment is appropriately applied not only in instances where clients live in the community at large, as in the two prior examples, but also in instances where the client's environment is a total institution. In fact, in a total institution the need to maximize environmental supports for clients is often more urgent and more compelling than it is for clients whose surroundings are not as circumscribed. In the following example, the social worker at Rafferty Place, a nursing home, works to maximize supports in the institutional environment for Mrs. Brown, a 78-year-old widow who was admitted to Rafferty Place directly from the local hospital where she had been treated for a stroke she suffered six weeks earlier. Mrs. Brown had been living alone for the past ten years, had been in relatively good health, and had never planned to enter a long-term care facility.

> The admissions material on Mrs. Brown said she was alert and oriented to person, place, and time, and that her memory had not been affected. It said she had minimal speech difficulty, but use of her left arm and leg was severely limited. She uses a wheelchair. It was additionally noted that she is very unhappy to be here but does realize she can't live alone right now. So I went to her room to see her.

I entered Mrs. Brown's doorway and knocked on the door. I saw that she was lying in bed with her back to me. She moved when I knocked but she didn't say anything. I asked if I could come in, and she replied with a very weak "Yeah."

ME: Hi. My name is Sam Garr. I'm your social worker and I work here at Rafferty Place.

MRS. B: (No answer. She looks at me. I have pulled up a chair and sat down near her bed at a right angle.)

ME: It can be lonely being in a room by yourself.

MRS. B: (Closes eyes, pulls legs up to chest in a semi-fetal position).

ME: (silently sit and wait a few minutes): It can be scary to be in a new place, not knowing what to expect next.

It is important to notice the respect the worker accords Mrs. Brown —knocking on the open door, waiting in the doorway, asking permission to enter. In all too many instances, professionals and paraprofessionals alike feel free to walk right in on patients as if illness gives everyone else a license to invade the sick person's territory at will. It is also important to notice that as soon as the worker positions himself, he starts attending to the client's feelings; and he continues to engage her feelings as their work proceeds. Note, too, that the worker checks out his inferences about the client's feelings.

MRS. B: (opens her eyes and looks at me): My daughter brought me here. She said it was a good place . . . My mother was in a nursing home. She died there.

ME: Are you afraid you'll die here?

MRS. B: No, not really (and she begins to cry).

ME: You're crying.

MRS. B: Oh, this is all so new to me. A couple of months ago I was so active. I was involved with my church, my card groups, my gardening. I took care of my apartment and all of my affairs. Now look at me . . . I'm in a nursing home and my family doesn't think I'll be able to go back home.

ME: Do you think you'll be able to go back home?

MRS. B: Well, I hope so. I want to. But . . . .

ME: But you're afraid you won't be able to?

MRS. B: Yes; I'm afraid I won't be able to go back home. Oh, damn it, why did this have to happen to me? Why did I have to have this stroke? Why do I have to be here in this empty room? You know, I had a beautiful apartment. It had all the comforts of home—my green Lazy-Boy chair, my magazine stand, my new color TV. . . .

ME: Did you know you could bring things from your apartment here, to your room, while you stay?

MRS. B: No. Can I really bring those things in?

ME: Yes. You can bring in your chair, your magazine stand and your color TV. You can also bring in some pictures to be hung, and those shelves over there, those are yours, too.

The worker continues to deal with the client's feelings and begins to *give information,* a skill not as simplistic as first glance might suggest. In this computer age, information has become synonymous with data, but in the helping process, data is only information when the client does not have it already, and when it is specifically relevant to the client's present concern. If too much is presented at once, or if it is not immediately pertinent, it can overwhelm and hinder rather than enlighten and empower. In the practice excerpt above, it is when Mrs. B talks about missing her personal furnishings that Mr. Garr tells her which of them she may bring to Rafferty House. As the process continues below, he reaches for information, reaches for feelings several more times, then gives information about the Newcomers Club and "Resident Sponsors" precisely when Mrs. B is thinking about old friends and new ones.

MRS. B: Well at least that might brighten things up a little. I'll talk to my daughter about bringing some things in. But . . . what about that empty bed over there—is someone coming in soon?

ME: I'm not sure who will be coming to this room. What kind of a roommate would you like?

MRS. B: Oh, I don't know (and she takes a deep breath and sighs and closes her eyes for a minute, then opens them and looks at me and says) . . . someone like me, I guess.

ME: And what would someone like you be like?

MRS. B: Someone with all their marbles. You know, I'm not crazy like some of these people.

ME: I'll try to find a roommate for you "with all of their marbles." It can be scary to think of getting someone who's confused for a roommate.

MRS. B: Yes, it is scary. I had a roommate in the hospital who cried all night for her mother. She was in her 90s. She never remembered my name and she made me nervous.

ME: Well, I'll do my best to find you an appropriate roommate. I'll introduce her to you if I can before she comes.

MRS. B: Yeah, that would be nice (she pulls her knees down from her chest and smiles at me).

ME: You're smiling.

MRS. B: Yeah, I am. I think I'm feeling better (then she closes her eyes again and takes another deep breath and sighs. Then she says) You know, all my friends live on the other side of town. I doubt I'll be able to visit with them.

ME: It can be sad to be separated from friends you've had for a long time.

MRS. B: Yeah, (she starts to cry but stops abruptly) it is sad, especially when I don't have any friends here.

ME: It can be lonely when you don't have any friends.

MRS. B: (looks at me, wipes her eyes): Yeah, it can be lonely. But I've always made friends rather easily before. In a few weeks or so I'll find a friend here.

ME: Do you know we have a "Newcomers Club" here at Rafferty?

MRS. B: No. What's a Newcomers Club?

ME: Well, it meets twice a month and all the new residents who are able to come, come to meet each other and get acquainted with Rafferty. Then there are "resident sponsors," and they'll take you on a tour of the building, to some of the favorite activities you might like, and introduce you to other residents. In fact, one of the "resident sponsors" will be coming down to see you later today. Would you like to go to this group?

MRS. B: Yes, I would. It sounds like a good way to get to know other people. Now, when does it meet next?

ME: It meets tomorrow morning at nine in the lounge. Your "sponsor" will tell you more about it later today and they will come and get you after breakfast and take you to the meeting.

MRS. B: That sounds good.

ME: O.K. Now, you said you were worried about the type of roommate you might be getting and I said I would try to find someone for you who isn't confused, that I would introduce them to you if I could before they came; you said you were afraid you might not be able to go back home and that your room was empty looking. You're going to talk to your daughter about bringing in some things from home while you stay; and, you said you were lonely and wanted to meet other people and would attend the "Newcomers Club" tomorrow. Does this sound like what we worked on together?

MRS. B: Yes, it does. When will you be coming back to see me again?

ME: I'll stop in to see how you are getting along later tomorrow afternoon (then I got up, put my chair back where it came from, and left the room).

At the end of the session the worker *summarizes,* recapping the facts *and* feelings of their transaction. This summary not only pulls the work together, but outlines the terms of the contract as the worker understands them to be. Summarizing is a skill that is also useful at the start of a session in order to 1) refresh memories about where work stopped at the end of the prior session, and 2) lay a foundation for setting the focus of the session that is beginning. Also, if talk strays from the purpose of a meeting, summarizing can be used to help refocus.

Later the next day, after the "Newcomers" group, I went to see Mrs. Brown to see how she was doing, how the group went for her, and if she got to know any of the other residents. I knocked on her door and asked if I could enter.

MRS. B: Yeah, come on in. I've been waiting to talk to you!

ME: <u>You look angry.</u>

MRS. B: Yeah, I'm angry all right. Those snobs in that group you sent me to ignored me most of the time and then they made plans to go and play cards afterwards. They didn't even ask me to go. Of course I couldn't play anyway—with the left hand hanging down limp like this.

ME: <u>It can be upsetting to be ignored.</u>

MRS. B: Yeah, you're right. I'm upset because I was ignored by those women. That one lady, Mrs. Sykes, she ignored me the whole time. I wonder what I did to her? Can you ask her what's going on?

ME: <u>No, I think that's something you need to talk to her about.</u>

MRS. B: Well, I thought you were my social worker.

ME: I am your social worker, Mrs. Brown. However, <u>I think you're able to ask Mrs. Sykes what's going on.</u> I wasn't there to know what happened.

The worker reaches for feelings as Mrs. B describes her painful experience. Then she asks him to speak with another person for her. The worker refuses, *not* because he does not care, but because he cares very much that the client take her difficulty to the proper place where she may get results. This is an example of *redirecting a message,* asking people to speak directly to whomever their message is actually intended. In using this skill, the worker conveys a belief that the client is competent to manage her interpersonal relationships even though it is sometimes difficult and uncomfortable to do. Although the "reason" the worker gives the client in this instance is somewhat misleading, redirecting messages implies recognition that it is through direct involvement that people can discover real and lasting resolutions to their struggles with each other. It is to this end that, a short while later, the worker offers to try and arrange opportunity for direct talk between the two parties involved.

As the process continues below, the worker uses another skill, *confronting distortion,* providing accurate information to replace the client's partial, skewed, or otherwise erroneous statements. In this instance, the accurate information which the worker presents entails the existence of highly pertinent resources—potential environmental supports—that can be brought to bear in reducing the client's current limitations.

MRS. B: Well, that's true. You weren't there. I think I know why they ignored me anyway—it's because I had a stroke. You know; I can't do things for myself anymore like I used to. I can't tie my shoes, I can't play cards, I can't . . . (she stops talking and turns her head).

ME: No, Mrs. Brown, you may be not able to do those things now; however, you may be able to learn to do some of those things again. Are you aware of some of the adaptive devices you could order which would help you with those things?

MRS. B: No, I'm not. What are they?

ME: Well, I know Jane, our physical therapist, has a catalogue she can order specific items from, such as a plastic card holder so you could play cards again. Would you like to talk to Jane?

MRS. B: Yes, I would.

ME: All right. I'll go down and talk to her after we're finished and let her know you'd like to talk to her about this.

MRS. B: (smiles and says): That will be fine.

ME: Now, about the group. Did you meet any other people besides Mrs. Sykes?

MRS. B: Yeah. There were a couple of nice people there, but I didn't catch their names.

ME: Will you go to the next meeting so you can learn who they are?

MRS. B: No! I won't be going back to that group until I've had it out with Mrs. Sykes. I won't be ignored by her again!

ME: Would you be willing to meet with her and discuss how you were feeling, what happened, and what could be done to help the situation?

MRS. B: Well, I'll meet with Mrs. Sykes if she'll meet with me.

ME: I'll talk with Mrs. Sykes and see if she'll be able to meet with you and then I'll get back with you and let you know.

MRS. B: That'll be fine.

ME: Now, back to your feeling that you were ignored because you've had a stroke. Can you tell me what leads you to think that was the reason?

MRS. B: Well, I know I look like a cripple, that I can't do things I used to do, that I can't get around too easily.

ME: That can be frustrating to face.

MRS. B: Especially when others don't understand!

ME: Yeah; that is upsetting. Have you heard of the St. Louis Stroke Club?

MRS. B: No. What's that?

ME: It's a group that meets once every month at the Senior Citizens Center downtown. They have outside speakers in to talk about issues which people who have had strokes must face. They also have refreshments and a get acquainted time. Would you like more information about the club?

MRS. B: Yes. Especially after that last group I went to.

ME: Another resident here at Rafferty, Mrs. Lynford, is a member of the Stroke Club. In fact, she lives two doors down from you. Perhaps you've met her already.

MRS. B: No, I haven't met her. Could I talk with her before I go to any meetings?

ME: I'm sure she'd be happy to talk to you. How about the next time you're up and about you go over to her room and ask her to tell you about the group.

MRS. B: I'll give it a try.

ME: And in the meantime, I'll call the Stroke Club and ask them to send out some literature for you and find out what the topic this month is or who is speaking.

MRS. B: Yeah; that's a good idea.

ME: O.K. Mrs. Brown, when I came to see you this afternoon, you were angry and feeling you had been ignored by Mrs. Sykes. Now I'm going to speak to Mrs. Sykes and see if she'll meet with you and I to discuss what happened. Then we talked about some adaptive devices you might benefit from and I'm going to talk to Jane so she can come up and discuss these items with you. Then we talked about the

Stroke Club, and you're going to talk to Mrs. Lynford about it and I'm going to get some information from the club for you. Right?

MRS. B: That's right. I need to talk to Mrs. Sykes; I'm going to go over to Mrs. Lynford's and talk about the Stroke Club, and I want to talk to Jane about the devices so I can do more for myself.

ME: O.K. I'll stop back tomorrow to see how things are going.

Initially, the social worker kept in close contact with Mrs. Brown, but also from the beginning, he connected her with other residents, other staff persons, and other programs outside the nursing home. He did not borrow the physical therapist's catalogue in order to show her the adaptive devices he mentioned. Rather, he arranged for the physical therapist to get together with Mrs. Brown. Also, he did not find out about the Stroke Club and give her the information. Rather, he suggested she talk with another resident who is a member. Thus, in accord with the Principle of Maximizing Supports in the Client's Environment, the social worker was gradually working himself out of a job.

The Principle of Least Contest

This principle directs the worker to exert the least pressure necessary to accomplish the client task. In the first place, force tends to generate counterforce. The amount of pressure that the worker brings to bear on a target system is directly related to the amount of counterpressure that the target system is likely to exert. And since low-pressure interventions tend to evoke minimum resistance on the part of the target system, low-pressure interventions are more likely to result in successful task accomplishment. Moreover, when low-pressure interventions are not successful, greater pressure can then be exerted.

The initial use of forceful intervention behaviors precludes the use of less forceful behaviors. It can be likened to "putting all the eggs in one basket," for in the event that the forceful intervention does not result in task accomplishment, alternative interventions are severely limited. To maximize the probability of task accomplishment, the worker should not act so as to preclude alternative actions. This suggests that the worker should serially order the possible interventions along a power dimension, from the least forceful to the most forceful.

With respect to types of activity, when task accomplishment demands a change in a particular procedure in a given agency, such as a lengthy intake procedure, the worker should try D-type activity prior to B-type activity. In other words, the worker should try to work with agency staff before organizing a client protest. The worker's own efforts with agency staff are likely to be less threatening than a client protest, and therefore less likely to generate the counterpressure than the more threatening client protest is likely to evoke. Further, in the event that D-type activity does not succeed, the worker can then move to B-type activity. The reverse is not possible, however, for the worker who has organized a client protest is no longer credible as a person who wants to help the agency.

Role-taking behavior is governed by a similar rationale. The worker should take the role of broker prior to the role of mediator, and the role of mediator prior to the role of advocate, for brokerage is less threatening than mediation, and mediation is less threatening than advocacy. Moreover, the worker who has attempted to mediate the client-agency engagement can, in the event that complementarity of interest cannot be implemented, shift from the role of mediator to the role of advocate. Again, the reverse is not possible, for the worker who has taken the side of one of two parties to a conflict has lost credibility as a "neutral," or as a person equally concerned with both parties.

The same rationale holds for selecting a point of intervention into a bureaucratic system. An issue is of less moment when it is raised, and remains, at lower levels of the hierarchy, and increases in importance as it moves upward in the hierarchy. Therefore, the worker should escalate issues slowly, initiating action at the lowest possible hierarchical level, and proceeding upward until a concession is obtained. This process gives personnel at lower hierarchical levels an opportunity to contain the issue at the lower level by granting the concession, an opportunity which personnel in the highly political public welfare agencies are likely to seize. And if personnel at lower levels cannot or do not grant the concession, the worker can then escalate the issue to the next hierarchical level.

The principle of least contest, then, directs the worker to rank the interventions along a power dimension, and to use less powerful interventions prior to using more powerful interventions. Specifically, the worker should engage in D-type activity before B-type activity, take the role of broker before taking the role of mediator and the role of mediator before the role of advocate, and escalate issues slowly by intervening at the lowest possible hierarchical level in a bureaucratic organization and proceeding upward until a concession is obtained.

The Minimax Principle

Sometimes, even though the demands of the client task have been fully and appropriately followed and every effort has been made to maximize supports in the client's(s') environment, the needed resources are not forthcoming. It is at this point and in this situation that the Minimax Principle should be applied. It is not an intervention of choice. It is a last resort.

The Minimax Principle directs the social worker to identify, reinforce and/or increase the client's(s') repertoire(s) of strategic behaviors for minimizing pain and maximizing positive outcomes and satisfaction. This is not an effort to remediate, to make up for deficits in the client. To the contrary, consistent with the orientation of structural social work practice, 1) clients are seen as adequate people who accurately construe reality, and 2) the behaviors of concern are for political struggle between self and withholding others, struggle that ought not to be necessary. The social worker arms clients and provides them with opportunities to practice so that they can, consciously and deliberately, use behaviors that maximize the probability of eliciting positive responses from an unyielding community which provides needed resources reluctantly or not at all.

It should be noted that the value society places on the myth of rugged individualism and self-sufficiency leads to a victim-blaming mentality even among persons who are themselves social/political victims. Ergo, to the extent that clients attribute their inability to obtain resources they need to their own internal, personal inadequacy, it is important to include some consciousness raising in the Minimax process, consciousness raising that challenges and dispels the fallacious attribution and recasts the client's plight as political rather than intrapersonal in origin and operation. To illustrate, in the practice sample below a social worker attempts to raise the consciousness of a new member in a group of Adults Molested as Children (AMACs).

> Then Maryann started to cry and said she should have said no to her father and she should never have run around the house in those tight jeans. She said her mother will never forgive her for luring her father out of her mother's bed. I said, "Maryann, your father deserves the blame, not you. You were a child and you deserved to be protected. Tight jeans is no excuse for a man to molest his child. And if your mother knew about it, she should have put a stop to it. You were the victim of criminal behavior, and you have a right to be very angry about what they did to you!" Then I asked what other group members thought. Lucy said she used to feel guilty and blame herself for wearing tight jeans and make-up, but all the kids wore tight jeans and make-up, and their fathers didn't rape them. She said she's furious at her parents.

Another practice example of conciousness raising as part of the Minimax process is provided in "The Conferee and Minimax Principle," a section of Chapter 5.

The Self Principle

This is a unique practice principle and an essential addition to social work practice. The Self Principle directs social workers to apply Principles one through five to themselves. With respect to the Accountability Principle, workers should develop contracts with colleagues and supervisors. In terms of the Task Principle, workers should look beyond themselves to see which colleagues are dealing with the same or comparable situations or are bothered by common situations or personalities.

Also, practitioners should engage in A-, B-, C-, and D-type activities. They should:

A. work in their own behalf, as, for example, in the development of professional support groups and continuing education opportunities.

B. work for themselves and colleagues in social work and other disciplines in behalf of themselves and all persons in the human service professions, as, for example, in developing and modifying state licensure laws.

C. work with others, such as legislators, in behalf of all social workers, as in drafting a bill registering the title, "social worker."

D. work with others in behalf of themselves, as in speaking to other professional associations.

Workers should work with different numbers of colleagues at different times according to the demands of the situation. They should take different roles at different times. As brokers, workers can connect colleagues of different disciplines, or can encourage participation in professional and continuing education activities through giving information or accompanying others to particular events. Workers can serve as mediators in conflicts among colleagues. They can advocate for greater accountability, for more resources, for higher quality services, and for just working conditions. The practitioner can also take the role of conferee as needed with colleagues and supervisors.

With respect to the Environmental Supports Principle, workers should bring to bear, change, and/or create agency structures to humanize the workplace and increase opportunities for professional development.

As for the Principle of Least Contest, social workers who notice a problem in the agency should try D-type activity before B-type activity. That is, they should talk with decision-makers before organizing colleagues to protest. Similarly, they should take the role of broker before mediator and mediator before advocate. They should assume an orientation of collegiality first. If collegiality is obstructed, then they can mediate the difference with the parties involved. And if mediation does not result in a resumption of collegiality, then it would be appropriate to advocate for the issue at stake. Finally, workers should escalate issues slowly, reluctantly, and only when the issue is of such

TABLE 3.1. Structural Social Work Principles and Procedures

1. Be accountable to the client	Develop a service contract
2. Follow the demands of the client task	Look beyond client to see if others are in the same plight Work in all four quadrants of activity Take all four different roles as needed Work with different numbers of people at different times
3. Maximize supports in the client environment	Bring to bear, change, and/or create structures Do not occupy the central position in the helping process unless it is not possible to locate sufficient supports in the environment
4. Proceed from the assumption of least contest	Engage in D-type activity before B-type activity Take the role of broker before mediator before advocate Escalate issues slowly
5. Identify, reinforce, and/or increase the client's(s') repertoire(s) of strategic behavior for minimizing pain and maximizing outcomes and satisfaction	Accept the client's(s') construction(s) of reality Identify, reinforce, and/or increase the client's(s') repertoire(s) of strategic behavior Suggest additional strategic behavior Provide practice opportunities
6. Apply principles one though five to yourself	Develop contracts with colleagues and supervisors Look beyond self to see which colleagues face the same task Use all four quadrants of activity within the social agency Work with different numbers of colleagues at different times Use all four roles with colleagues Change structures to humanize workplace Minimize obstacles and maximize opportunities Engage peers before supervisors and supervisors before administrators Assume collegiality until there is conflict, and mediate conflict before taking sides

import that it would be wrong to continue containing it at the staff level. Workers should discuss staff-level dissatisfactions with colleagues before their supervisor, and with their supervisor before the administrators.

To pursue the Minimax Principle, workers should increase their repertoire of strategic and tactical behavior for minimizing organizational obstacles and maximizing opportunities to work in behalf of client interest.

An overview of all six principles and the procedures that operationalize them appears in table 3.1.

4. Intervention Principles and Procedures: A Process View

The cross-sectional model described in chapter 3 identifies the key elements of structural social work practice and depicts the interrelationships among them. Such a perspective provides social workers with a way to understand what they are about. But social work is not merely something one understands. It is something one does. And one must do it one step at a time. Therefore a second, complementary model is needed, a process model that indicates what to do first and what to do next, a process model that tells workers every step of the way what to ask themselves and what to do contingent upon the answers. This chapter provides workers with a process model that translates the principles and procedures of structural social work into sequential practice behavior. Whereas the cross-sectional model was explicated in terms of guiding principles, the process model is explicated in terms of guiding questions.

The Contract Phase

The process model of structural social work has three phases: the Contract Phase, the Task Phase, and the Termination/Reentry Phase. The Contract Phase begins with the social worker in Quadrant A. The worker takes the role of conferee and talks with clients about the pressures they are experiencing. Usually, the worker asks an open-ended question such as "What's happening?" then listens to the client's response. Perhaps the client will talk about how lonely he has been since his wife died. After the client has spoken and, in this instance, after the worker has communicated empathy, the worker is at the first decision point, the point at which to ask herself the first key question:

Has the client described the pressures on him? In this example, the client did describe the pressure he feels, so the answer is "yes"; and, as indicated in figure 4.1, a "yes" answer signals the worker to translate the pressure the client says he is experiencing into tasks which, when accomplished, will alleviate that pressure. A task to alleviate loneliness, for example, might be structured contact with other people on a regular basis, the sort of activity often offered by settlement houses, YMCAs, and senior citizen centers. If, on the other hand, the answer to the first key question is "no", the worker must continue to seek information and feelings about the pressures with which the client is struggling. When the client responds to the worker, she again asks herself "Has the client described the pressures on him?" If the answer is still "no," the worker stays within this loop, probing further until the answer is "yes."

Once the worker has translated the pressure described by the client into tasks to alleviate those pressures, she reaches the second decision point and must ask herself the second key question: are the tasks she formulated agreeable to the client? If the answer is "yes," the worker tells the client what she can and will do to help accomplish the tasks. For example, she may indicate that she can and will contact the local YWCA and one or two settlement houses that are nearby to gather information about the programs they offer. If the answer is "no," however, indicating that he is not interested in the tasks the worker has mentioned, the worker needs to ask another question: does the client think the tasks she suggested are not appropriate?—a question some of us often forget to ask when a client appears "negative" or "dissatisfied." Yet this question may be critical to increasing the probability that a satisfactory contract can be developed and that appropriate service is rendered.

Clients tend to be the best consultants about their own pains and needs, and good social work includes maximizing opportunities to use clients as consultants in their own behalf. For example, the client who is lonely may not be looking for on going contact with others through discussion groups. His need may be more specific, as the need of an elderly Polish man to speak Polish again with others. Sometimes lonely people are, despite their loneliness, afraid of social contact. So if the answer to the last question is "yes," meaning that the client does not see the proferred tasks as pertinent to his need, then the

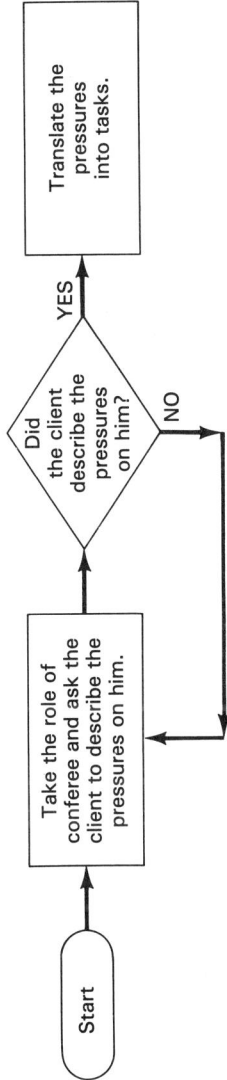

FIGURE 4.1. Phase 1. Contract: Identifying the Task

worker must begin again, asking the client for additional, more pre-
cise, and/or elaborated information about the pressures he is experiencing. If, on the other hand, the answer is "no," meaning that the
client recognizes and agrees that the proffered tasks are appropriate,
but he does not wish to involve himself in them, no service contract
can be developed at this time, and the worker-client relationship
terminates. There are times when people do not want to alleviate their
pressures, particularly when they believe that by doing so, they will
be exposed to other pressures that are even harder for them to bear.

After the worker tells the client what she can and will do, she
stands at the third and final decision point of the Contract Phase and
must ask herself the third key question: are the actions she has
proposed agreeable to the client? If the answer is "yes," a service
contract has been developed, and the process moves ahead to Phase
Two. If the client does not agree to the worker's proposed actions, on
the other hand, the worker has to ask herself another question: does
the client have ideas about how the worker might be helpful?—ideas
that are acceptable to the worker? If the answer is "yes," meaning the
client had ideas that are acceptable to the worker, a service contract
has been developed and the process goes into Phase Two. Should it
turn out that the client does not agree to the worker's proposed actions
and does not have an alternative proposal that is acceptable to the
worker, then no service contract can be developed at this time, and
the worker-client relationship ends. There are times when people
want to alleviate their pressures but choose not to do so, especially
when it seems that the requisite tasks do not fit them well.

The entire flow of the Contract Phase is shown in figure 4.3. To
illustrate this flow, consider the following transaction between a school
social worker and a new student at the junior high school. Note, too,
that this social worker meets students in their situations rather than
sitting in an office and having students come to him, devoid of all
natural contexts.

> I went into the 9th-grade math class like I usually do on Wednesday
> and sat next to the new boy. I twisted my body so I was at a right
> angle to him. I introduced myself as a social worker and asked,
> "How's it going for you?" He responded nervously, "Okay, I guess."
> He then asked what does a social worker do. I told him we help

FIGURE 4.2. Phase 1. Contract: Specifying Worker's Intended Actions

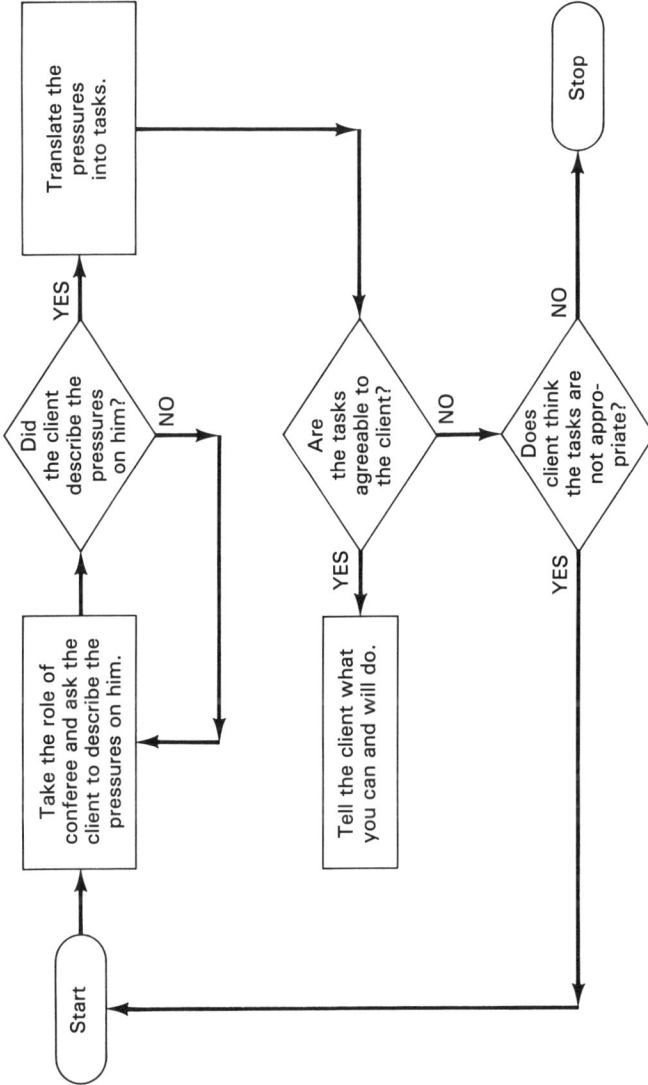

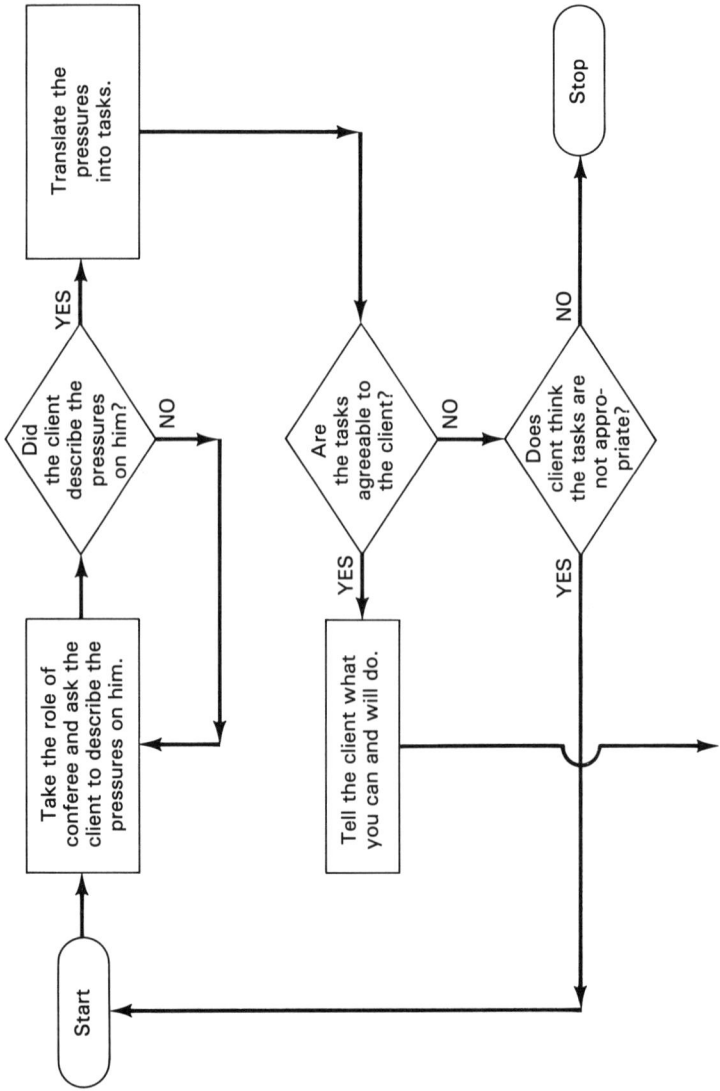

FIGURE 4.3. Phase 1. Contract

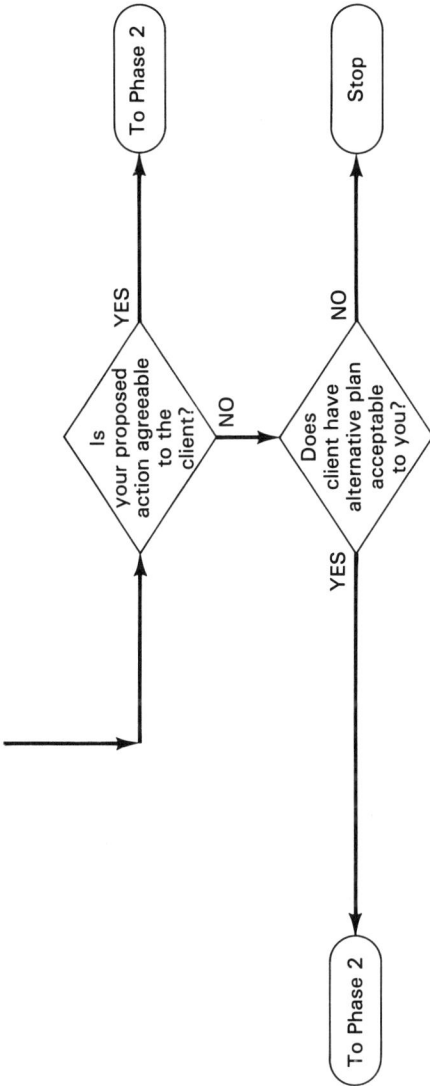

Is your proposed action agreeable to the client?

YES → To Phase 2

NO → Does client have alternative plan acceptable to you?

NO → Stop

YES → To Phase 2

75

people with their problems. Like here, I help students get what they need from the school. "Is there anything you need?" He hesitated, almost spoke, but then just slumped in his seat. (I also slumped and twisted in my seat so that we were both facing the front of the room.) I waited. He seemed to be struggling but then hung his head and stared at the floor. I said, "You look like you have something to say, but can't." He sat up and said, "You help people with their problem, right?" I answered, "Right, I help people with their problems. You want me to help you?" He nodded his head meaning yes. I nodded also, saying "Yeah." He said, "These kids keep bugging me." "In this section?" I asked. "No, in my section," he responded. "You're not in this section"? I asked. He said no, that he was just kind of observing it. I said I didn't know that the school had a procedure like that. He turned his head away and his body seemed to tense up. I said, "You turned away from me." There was some silence, so I waited. Then he explained that he had been in this class the preceding period and since he liked the math teacher, he stayed rather than continuing on with his regular section schedule. He said he really didn't like his roster or any of the kids in his section, and that he wanted his section changed to this one. I saw this as the pressure he was feeling (not liking his roster and the kids he was put with) and switching to this section, which he suggested, as the appropriate task. So we both agreed.

I then asked. "Have you asked your counsellor to change your section?" He said that he had tried, but had been unable to see her on several attempts because she was always too busy. I said, "That can be a hassle." He shrugged. I asked "Do you want me to help you get your section changed?" (my way of telling him what I could do and seeing if it was okay with him). He assured me he would, so we had a working contact.

In the example above, the worker employed seven different skills introduced and illustrated in chapter 3. Initially, despite the stationary seats, he positioned himself. This was followed by alternately reaching for information, giving information, and reaching for information again. He then waited as the student seemed to struggle, apparently drew an inference from the struggle he perceived, and appropriately checked out his inference. In response to the boy's question, he gave information, then reached for three different pieces of information himself.

When the student said that he was "observing," an unlikely, but not impossible, practice in junior high schools, the worker did not challenge him, a move that could well have destroyed the beginning rapport. The worker was not there to uncover infractions. Priority was on helping the boy have a good beginning in his new school. Therefore, the worker gave information instead. He told the boy that he was not aware of the procedure—and even *that* seemed to generate tension! So the worker wisely reached for the feelings that seemed to be building, then waited.

When the boy began to talk about the problem that he was experiencing, the worker listened, accepted the boy's description of his need as the appropriate task to be accomplished in order to resolve the problem, reached for consequential information, reached for the boy's feelings once again, and ultimately reached for the information which, when given by the student, resulted in the contract between worker and client.

In the practice episode below, a contract gets developed between a social worker and a group of older adults. The worker convened the group because she noticed that many of the older people sat around the lobby, but did not interact with each other, and many always seemed to be sad. She begins by telling the group what she perceives to be some of their pressures and proposes weekly group meetings aimed at alleviating them.

> I was introduced to the older adults during their weekly luncheon. I told them that the Center was starting a new group called the Human Relations Workshop. I said that I probably didn't even have to tell them because they certainly know that it isn't easy to be old. I said that I understood how hard it was and how many problems they had to face and how hard it was to face them. I said that they knew what I was talking about—problems like living all alone, or living with their children in their children's homes after running households of their own for so many years; problems like feeling that nobody needs them anymore and feeling useless or lonesome or like there's nothing left for them. (At this point I became very aware that all side conversations had stopped). I said that these

were really tough things to live with, and I imagined that sometimes it must be very frightening. I said that this new group was a place to get together and talk about all this and maybe get some help with some of their problems. I said that my job would be to help them talk to each other and work on their problems. I then said that anyone who is interested could meet me in room 110 right after lunch.

As I was leaving the auditorium, Sarah stopped me and asked me to tell her about the group again. I told her, and her eyes filled up. She said she had lots of problems and that she would join the group. Another woman showed me what she said was her "calling card": in the middle it said "RETIRED," and on each of the four corners it read "NO BUSINESS," "NO MONEY," "NO PHONE," and "NO ADDRESS," respectively. I nodded and said it looked like what we were talking about. She said, "Yeah."

When we got into the room, Ruth and Milton immediately put their chairs next to mine. Sarah stood between Milton and me. Blanche told her to go around to the other side of the table where there was more room. Sarah told everyone in that row to move down. Nobody moved. Ruth told me to tell Sarah to go to the other side so the group could get started. I said that where people sat was up to them and the group, not up to me, and suggested that if Ruth wanted Sarah to go elsewhere, she could tell her. She did. Sarah said she was alright where she was and sat down at the corner of the table between Milton and me. Milton, Blanche, and Bea moved down, and Sarah put her chair where Milton's had been.

I began by saying that I knew, and they certainly knew even better than I, that it's hard to be old. I said there are so many problems to face: loneliness, ill health, the illness of a husband or wife, the death of family and friends, etc. I also said that many of them had told me at different times that nobody wants to listen to their troubles. I said that if they wanted, this group could get together with me every week and talk about some of the problems they were facing in their daily lives. I asked if this was okay, and everyone said it was. I said that my job would be to help them talk about the problems and get help from each other. This was okay with them, too, so we had a beginning contract and the work could start.

The Task Phase

Once a service contract has been developed, the social worker has the right to practice and the process flows into phase two, the Task Phase. As in phase one, selection of worker behavior in phase two is contingent upon the answers to a series of key questions. The first two questions are: 1) Is there an existing organization that should alleviate the client's plight? and 2) Are persons other than the client in the same plight?

These two questions combine to determine which of four possible actions should be selected as the initial step in following the demands of the client task, the second principle of structural social work practice. As shown in figure 4.4, the origin of the four choices can be identified in a two-by-two table where the above questions form the

FIGURE 4.4. Phase 2. Task: Activities Contingent on the First Two Questions

Is there an existing organization that should alleviate the client's plight?

	YES	NO
YES	yes–yes Change organizational structure.	no–yes Create self–help network.
NO	yes–no Refer client to the organization.	no–no Create resource network.

Are there persons other than the client in the same plight?

two dimensions and the answers "yes" and "no" constitute the categories on each.

In the yes-no condition (lower left-hand cell), there is an organization charged with meeting the client's need and no other persons seem to have this need. The social worker discovers the latter when, in accord with the Principle of Following the Demands of the Client Task, she looks beyond the client to see if others are in the same plight. Finding that others are not in the same plight suggests either that people are able to get that need met through the existing organization, or that this is a special case. In either event, the worker should initially take the role of broker and refer the client to the existing organization. If a client needs dentures, for example, and other low-income or no-income people have had free access to them through the local Bureau of Vocational Rehabilitation, the worker should refer the client to that agency.

If, however, the yes-yes condition exists (upper left-hand cell), there is an organization presumably mandated to meet the client's need. Yet, when the worker looks beyond the client, she finds that many others have the same unmet need. In this instance it is reasonable to assume that the policies and/or procedures of the organization responsible for meeting the need in question do not adequately recognize and/or respond to persons with that need. This tells the worker to direct efforts toward structural change. Guided by the Principle of Least Contest, the worker should begin the effort by taking the role of broker and moving into 'Quadrant D' to initiate joint problem-solving with key staff members of the relevant organization. If, in the above example, the worker looked beyond the client and discovered that there were many people needing dentures, she would need to approach staff at the Bureau of Vocational Rehabilitation in order to learn what obstacles prevent that agency from providing dentures. Perhaps dentures are not perceived as vital to obtaining work. If this were, in fact, the obstacle, the worker could take the role of advocate in Quadrant D and argue that appearance plays a major role in who gets hired and who does not—especially when there are more job seekers than there are jobs. Perhaps cutbacks in funding are at fault, and dentures for cosmetic purposes have become a low priority. Given such a situation, the worker as advocate in Quadrant D could point to the illnesses people suffer from improperly chewed foods. In any event, the worker's efforts would be directed toward opening or re-opening the channel through which people in need of dentures can obtain them with relative ease.

In the no-yes condition (upper right-hand corner), many people have the same unmet need, and there are no organized arrangements to alleviate it. For example, there are mothers who are forced into part-time jobs as opposed to the full-time jobs they would prefer because there is no one to care for their children after elementary schools dismiss at 3:00 or 3:30 p.m. In this instance, the worker is directed to take the role of broker in Quadrant A and to create a self-help structure such as a child care cooperative whereby high school students are engaged to play games with the children between the time school dismisses and the mothers arrive at approximately 6:00 p.m. Money to pay the teens would come from the mothers whose incomes will increase as they take the full-time jobs they want to take. It should be noted that the creation of such cooperatives is consistent with the Principle of Maximizing Environmental Supports.

In the no-no condition (lower right-hand cell), there is neither an agency assigned to meet the need of the client, nor are there others with a similar need. One mother, for example, needs child care so that she can work full time to support her family. This suggests that the worker create a special resource such as a core of neighbors who will take turns baby-sitting—another instance of maximizing environmental supports.

As shown in figure 4.5, following performance, in the role of broker, of the differential activity indicated by each of the four conditions described above, the social worker must ask: was the task accomplished through brokerage? Is client need now being met? If the answer is "yes," the process moves directly to phase three—Termination/Recontracting. If the answer is "no," however, and the unsuccessful effort had been directed toward creation of a self-help structure or a special resource network, the worker is directed to take the role of conferee, move into Quadrant A, and engage the client in the five-step Minimax Process described in chapter 3. In all instances, application of the Minimax Principle is followed by movement to the Termination/Recontracting Phase.

If the task was not accomplished through referral (prescribed by the yes-no condition in figure 4.4), or through efforts at joint problem-

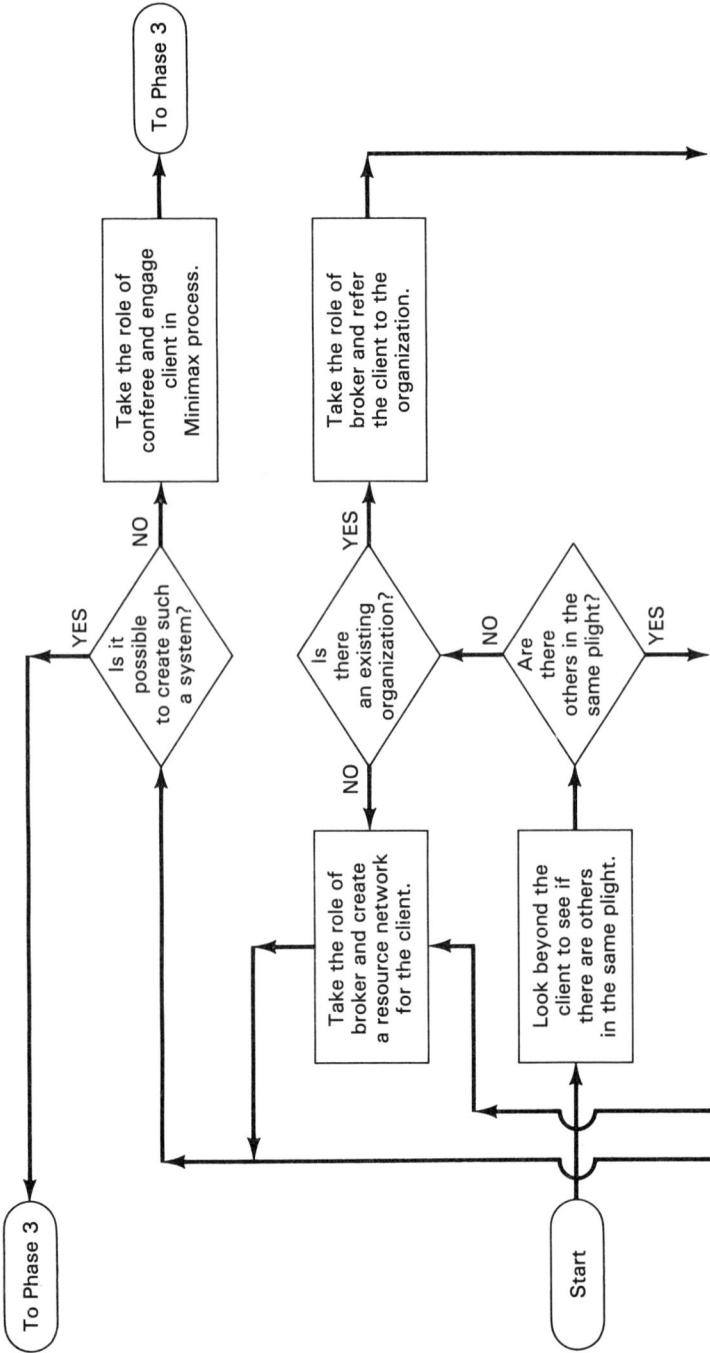

FIGURE 4.5. Phase 2. Task

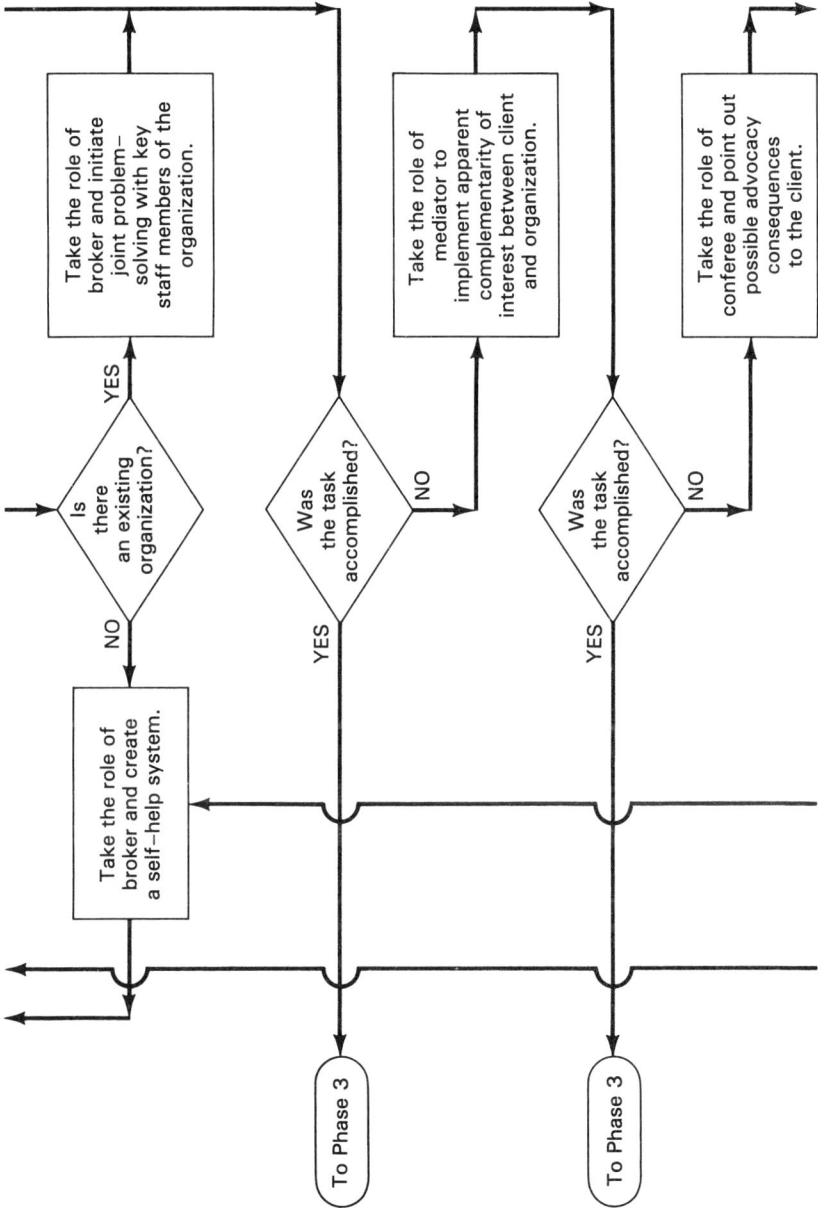

Take the role of broker and initiate joint problem–solving with key staff members of the organization.

Is there an existing organization?

YES

NO

Take the role of broker and create a self–help system.

Was the task accomplished?

YES

NO

Take the role of mediator to implement apparent complementarity of interest between client and organization.

Was the task accomplished?

YES

NO

Take the role of conferee and point out possible advocacy consequences to the client.

To Phase 3

To Phase 3

83

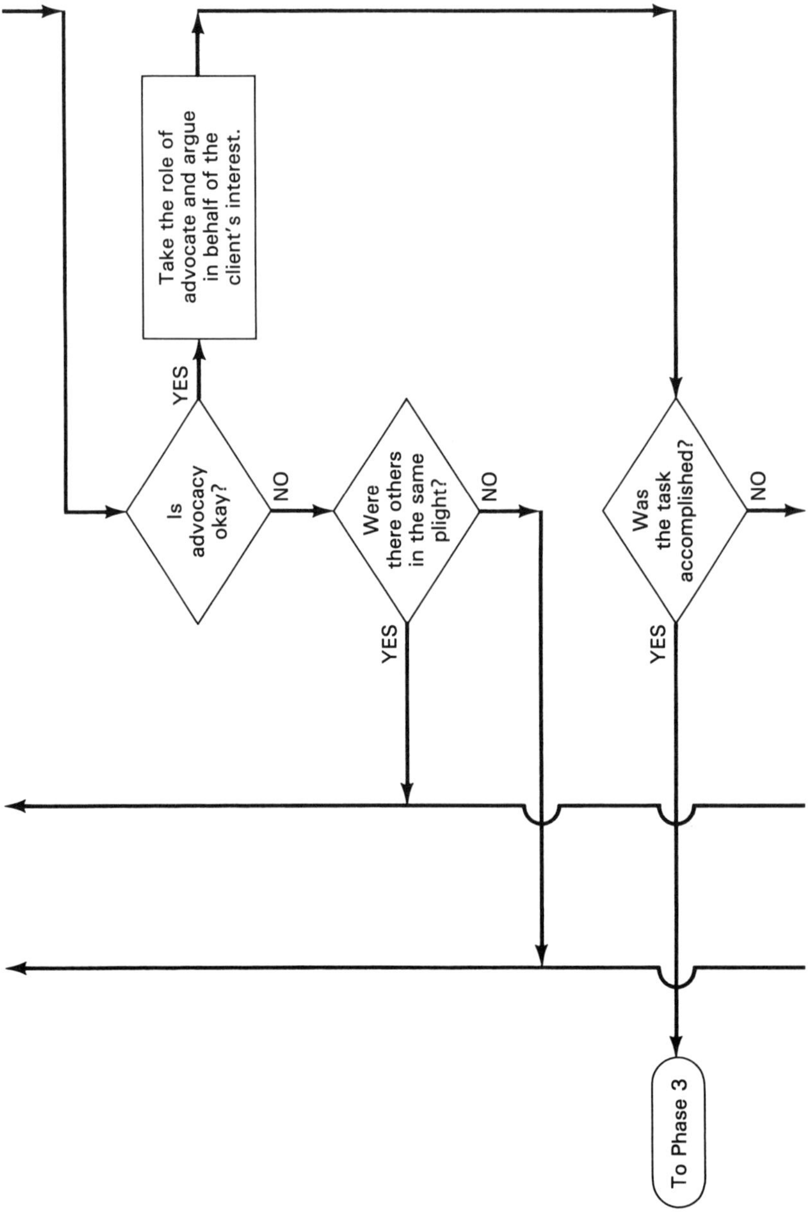
Take the role of advocate and argue in behalf of the client's interest.
YES
Is advocacy okay?
NO
Were there others in the same plight?
NO
YES
Was the task accomplished?
NO
YES
To Phase 3

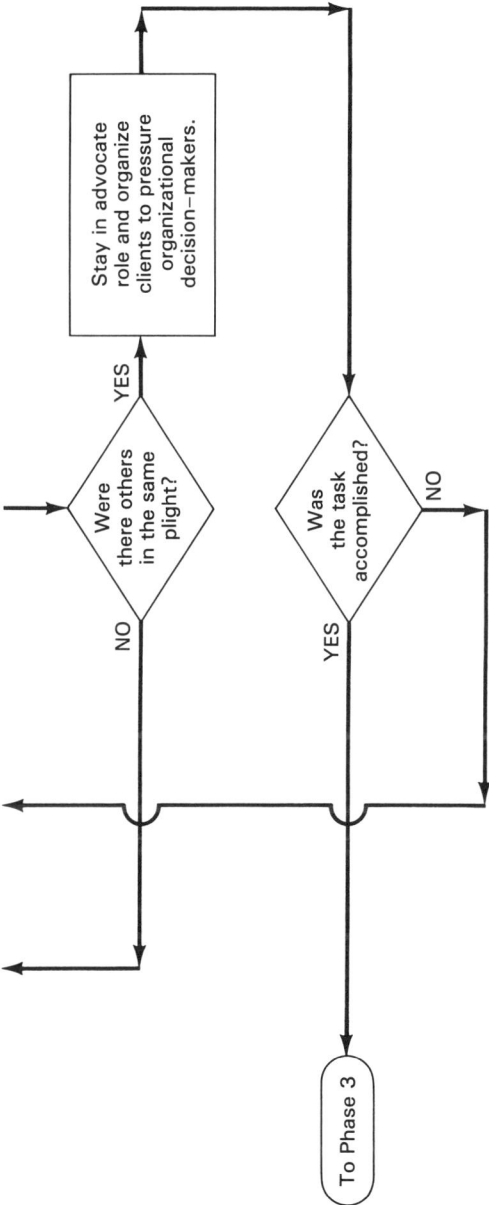

solving with the staff of an existing organization (prescribed by the yes-yes condition in figure 4.4), then, in accord with the Principle of Least Contest, the worker should take the role of mediator and straddle the line between Quadrant A and Quadrant D. In the role of mediator, the social worker brings the client with his need for service face to face with a representative of the agency with its need to deliver service and asks them to talk to each other, with her help, in order to arrive at a mutually beneficial resolution, that is, a resolution by which the agency serves, as it should, and the client receives the service, as he should. Because the role of the mediator is a particularly difficult yet frequently necessary role for social workers to use, it is described and illustrated at length in chapter 7.

Mediation is followed by the fourth question: was the task accomplished? Is client need now being met? If the answer is "yes," the process moves to phase three. If the answer is "no," however, and client need remains unmet, then, as shown in figure 4.5, the worker is directed to take the role of conferee, move back to Quadrant A, and thoroughly discuss with the client or clients the possible consequences of advocacy for them, since, with the informed consent of the client(s), the role of advocate in Quadrant D is next in the worker's progression from least to greatest contest. As indicated in chapter 3, the discussion of possible consequences is essential because advocacy can result in retaliatory action by the target persons, and it is the client who must bear the effects of such retaliation should it occur. It is imperative that the clients fully understand the possibilities and choose whether or not the possible gain is worth the risk. Because it is the client who must bear the consequences, it is the client who must make the decision. Therefore the fifth question for the social worker to ask herself is: is advocacy agreeable to the client? If clients indicate that the possible gain is not worth the risks involved, which is to say they do not wish to go ahead with advocacy, then the worker must take the role of broker and try to create a structure—a self-help structure if others are in the same plight, or a special resource network if the client's plight seems to be unique. If the worker succeeds in creating such a structure in accord with the Principle of Maximizing Environmental Supports, and client need is being met, the process moves to phase three. If the worker is not able to create a satisfactory structure, she must engage the client(s) in the Minimax process and then proceed to the third phase.

If clients indicate, after thorough discussion of the potential consequences of advocacy, that the possible gains are worth the risk, then the social worker takes the role of advocate, enters Quadrant D, and, consistent with the Principle of Least Contest, argues with the person, persons, or organizational representatives for the goods or services needed by the client(s). After this, she asks herself: did arguing for the clients accomplish the task? Is client need now being met? If her argument did, in fact, accomplish the task, the process moves to Phase Three. If the task is still not accomplished, however, if no others appear to be in the same plight as the client, the social worker should procede as if no agency existed, take the role of broker in Quadrant D, and attempt to organize a special resource network of non-sufferers to help alleviate the client's pressures. If it is not possible to develop such a network, the worker is directed to engage the client in the minimax process, then move to phase three.

If arguing in behalf of the client did not produce the needed resources and there are persons other than the client in the same plight, on the other hand, then the worker is advised to stay in the role of advocate, move into Quadrant B, and try to organize some of the people in need to join together in a concerted effort to bring pressure to bear upon organizational decision makers and/or other key persons who may have influence with them. Following this, the social worker must ask: did organizing those in need and pressuring the decision-makers result in task accomplishment? Is client need now being met? If the answer is "yes," then the process moves to Phase Three. If the answer is "no," however, the worker should take the role of "broker," move to Quadrant A, and try to organize the persons in need into a self-help structure. If this effort is successful, the process can move to Phase Three. If the effort is unsuccessful, then the worker is obliged to engage the client in the Minimax Process before moving to the third phase.

To illustrate the process of structural social work practice in the Task Phase, recall the contract developed by the school social worker in which he was to help a new student change his section and his roster. Once that contract was made, the worker recorded the following.

Under ordinary circumstances I would have taken the role of broker in Quadrant D and referred Jarrod to his guidance counsellor. Since he already tried to see her several times on his own and she was too busy whenever he tried, I figured I should follow the Principle of Least Contest up one notch and try to mediate the situation. To do this, I first took the role of conferee with Jarrod (in Quadrant A) and pointed out to him that I would try to get the counsellor to sit down and talk with him, but that he would have to convince her. He said that was okay with him, so I took my conferee role into Quadrant D and spoke with the counsellor. She told me that Jarrod's records showed poor scholarship and sporadic attendance. She also had reservations about dealing with the situation because she vaguely remembered him as a discipline problem and didn't trust his motives for wanting to change sections. In addition to that, she said the two sections he was interested in were already large classes. She said something else I tucked away for later: she was afraid that granting Jarrod's request would result in a deluge of section change requests. I decided that later I would check into student satisfaction with sections and rosters and if many felt like they were not where they thought was best for them, I would try to engage in joint problem-solving with the counsellors and the vice principal. For now, though, I had a contract with Jarrod, and it didn't look like his counsellor would be willing to sit down and talk with him.

I was all set to be Jarrod's advocate, when I remembered that his counsellor had a stake in talking with him. She hated to see kids drop out of school, and lots of kids here drop out as soon as they can. So I pointed out her stake—that she doesn't want kids to drop out, and Jarrod was quite likely to unless the school seemed to care about him and be responsive to him once in a while, like making some adjustments to meet his needs. She reluctantly agreed to talk with him, and when they did, Jarrod promised to improve his grades and attendance if his section was changed, and she agreed to recommend the change to the vice principal. I was afraid to let this get lost in the shuffle, so I suggested that all three of us go see the vice principal right then and there, which we did. Both the counsellor and I recommended the change, then the vice principal wanted to talk to Jarrod alone. When he came out about five minutes later, his section and his roster were changed.

Later, the social worker followed up on what he discovered to be a widespread problem of mis-rostering in that and other schools, and he initiated discussions with teachers, administrators, and counsellors to investigate the causes of the problem in order to recommend realistic and effective changes. The worker also followed up with Jarrod. Three months later, the counsellor reported that his attendance, deportment, and grades had all improved markedly.

The Termination/Recontracting Phase

The third and final phase of the process model involves terminating the contract on which both worker and client had focused their attention, and recontracting to alleviate other pressures if the client so wished. Therefore, as can be seen in figure 4.6, part of this third phase looks like the Contract Phase.

The process begins with the social worker taking the role of conferee in Quadrant A. First the worker engages the client in summarizing their work together and assessing the outcomes in terms of the task specified in the service contract. This brings the worker to the first question in the Termination/Recontracting Phase: was the task accomplished? If the answer is "yes," the work is done, and the worker-client relationship ends. If, on the other hand, the task was not accomplished, the worker must ask herself: is there an alternative task? Can the pressures the client originally described be alleviated by accomplishing a different task? If the answer is "no," then the work is done, and despite lack of success, the engagement terminates. To continue beyond this point is to wander aimlessly, frustrating the worker, the client, and everybody on the waiting list. When the social worker's best efforts fail to accomplish the task and there is no alternative task, it is time to stop.

If there is an alternative task to alleviate the pressures the client is experiencing, the worker should ask herself a third question: is the alternative task agreeable to the client? If it is not, the work stops and the relationship ends. If the client agrees that the alternative task is valid and valuable, the worker indicates what she can and will do to help accomplish it, then asks herself the fourth question in phase three: are the actions she has proposed agreeable to the client? If the

90

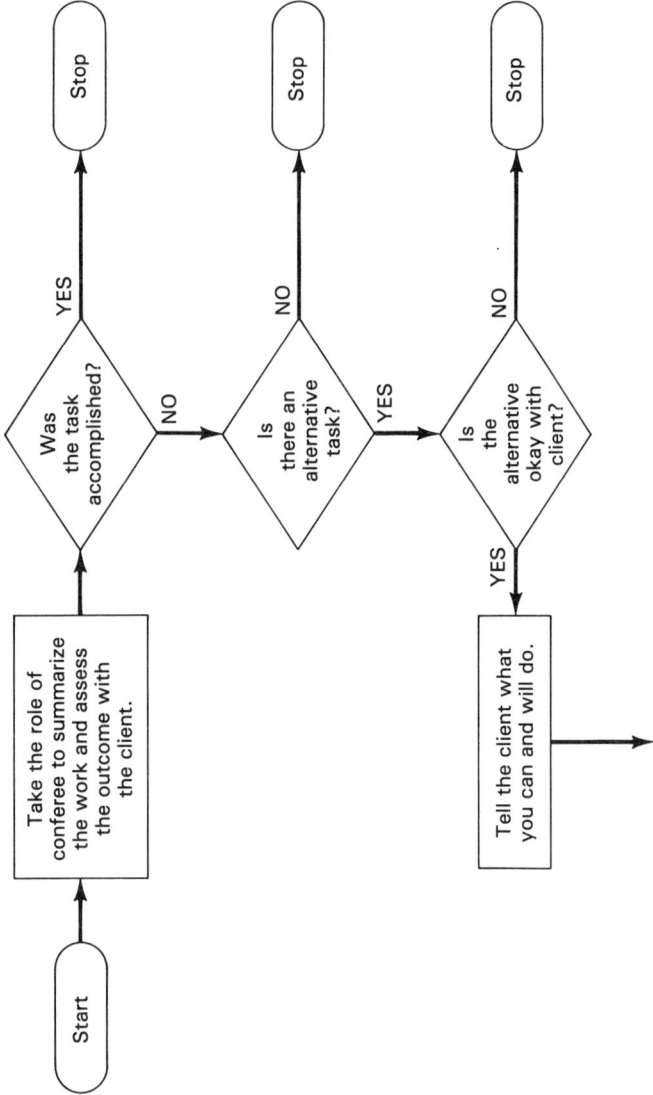

FIGURE 4.6. Phase 3. Termination/Recontracting

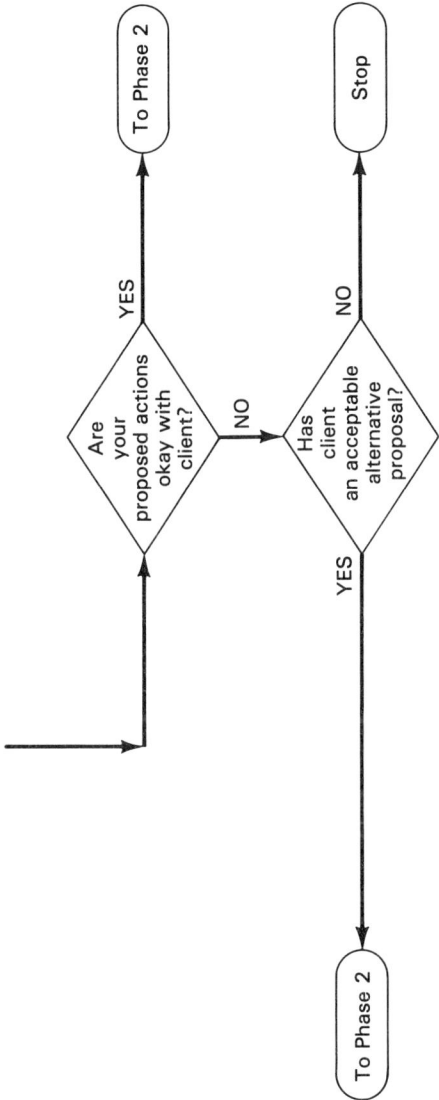

To Phase 2

Stop

YES

NO

Are your proposed actions okay with client?

NO

Has client an acceptable alternative proposal?

YES

To Phase 2

91

answer is "yes," a new contract has been developed and worker and client reenter the process at the beginning of phase two, the Task Phase, in order to work on the new task. If the client does not agree to the actions the worker had proposed, however, the worker asks herself one more question: does the client have a proposal regarding possible worker activity, a proposal that is also agreeable to the worker? If the answer is "yes," there is a new service contract and the interventive system is reentered at the start of the Task Phase. But if the client neither agrees to the worker's proposed actions nor offers an alternative acceptable to both, the process terminates.

The following example from practice illustrates social work in the Termination/Recontracting Phase. The worker enters Phase Three with a group of Hispanic parents.

> I took the role of conferee in Quadrant A and started summarizing where we had been and where we are now. (I'm not fluent in Spanish, but I try, and they don't seem to mind that I talk slowly sometimes and sometimes ask them to repeat what they say.) I said we started working together when some of them got upset that their children weren't learning much in school, and I found out it was because everything was taught in English even though this is a Spanish neighborhood. We agreed I should talk with the teachers and the principal to change the situation. But when I talked to the teachers, they said they didn't want to learn Spanish. They said the children are going to have to learn English in order to get jobs later, so they should start learning it now. So I talked to the principal about getting some bilingual teachers, and he said it wouldn't be fair to get bilingual teachers and fire teachers who had been at that school for years and years. Then we all went to the School Board hoping to pressure them into sending at least some Spanish-speaking teachers, and all they said was that they'd look into it. So we didn't get anywhere. I said I was sad and I knew they were. One of the men shook his head and said America isn't supposed to be like this, and lots of others nodded. I nodded, too.
>
> Then I told them I had another idea and I wanted to see if it was okay with them. I said maybe we could get the school board to hire some Spanish-speaking aides who wouldn't be replacing any of the teachers, just helping the children understand what the teacher

was saying. I also said maybe I could get someone to teach the children English after school a few days a week. I told them I thought they deserved better than this, but since we couldn't get bilingual teachers, would this be okay to try for? They were pretty enthusiastic about it, even though I wasn't, so I agreed to look into it for them. I assumed this was a new contract, and I went back to the beginning of the Task Phase to work on it.

WHY TWO TYPES OF MODELS?

The cross-sectional model of structural social work, described and illustrated in chapter 3, sets the boundaries for practice. It tells the worker the nature of the outcomes to be sought, the types of activity from which to select in each instance of the search for such outcomes, and the roles that are available. But it does not answer the social worker's important, ongoing questions: what should I do first? What should I do next? For this, the process model provided in this chapter is necessary. A cross-sectional model sets the stage for practice, while a process model provides a basic script for the play that will unfold on that stage.

PART THREE

Social Work Roles

A ROLE IS A set of expectations for behavior. To the extent that these expectations are clearly specified, behavior in accord with them is reliable, that is, consistent and stable. Prerequisite to systematic role taking and role enactment in social work, then, is a definition of the expectations for each of the roles the social worker must perform.

In this section, the four roles basic to structural social work are described. The expectations organized under the roles of conferee, broker, mediator, and advocate are defined, and the assumptions which underlie each role are elaborated. These assumptions are the organizing principles for role expectations and constitute the criteria for determining the appropriateness of a given role in a given situation. That is, a role is appropriate to the extent that the situation meets the assumptions underlying that role. For example, the role of advocate is not suitable in a situation in which interests are complementary and that complementarity is operational. In such a situation, broker is the role of choice, for brokerage presupposes an operational complementarity of interest. Advocacy, on the other hand, presumes a basic conflict of interest. The role of mediator presumes a non-operational identity or complementarity of interest.

The sequence in which the role chapters are presented reflects the Principle of Least Contest. Within each chapter, interactions among roles, principles, and quadrants of activity are discussed and illustrated.

5. The Conferee

The label "conferee" distinguishes a set of expectations which social workers fulfill in certain situations. "Conferee" stems from the notion of the conference, that encounter where two or more persons consult together, compare opinions, deliberate, and devise actions to be taken after the conference. A basic assumption underlying this role is that all parties have an equal opportunity and obligation to determine subsequent action. Key concepts inhering in such a role, then, are mutuality and partnership. When the social worker assumes the role of conferee, the reciprocal role which the client must assume is also that of conferee.

The social worker, with the special knowledge and skill acquired through professional education and experience, and the client, with special knowledge of his life situation and all that it takes to live his life, consult together to decide what ought to be done and what each can and will do to reduce the pressures which the client is experiencing. To insure the integrity of the conference, the social worker must take the role of conferee through behaviors which clarify for clients that they too are conferees, that they are not in a one-down position even if they expect and have had more experience with a one-down position. In other words, it is the responsibility of the social worker as conferee to initiate and maintain through all that she says and does that the client too is a conferee. It is the social worker who must set this role relationship in motion.

Earlier it was suggested that every instance of social work in direct practice begins in Quadrant A, that is, in work with specific clients out of concern with their plight. At this point it should be noted that in every instance of social work in direct practice, the worker begins by taking the role of conferee. That is, the worker starts with the client, listening as the client describes his situation, the pressures he feels, and what, if any, part of it he may want help with. Clients do not ask the worker to "be my broker" or "be my advocate." They talk about what is going on in their lives, how they feel about their life situations, and what they think will make a difference for them.

Thus, when client meets social worker, their relationship is that of conferees who will engage in activities surrounding task specification for each, pursuing the work to be done together and separately, and will conclude their contact with each other when the mutual work is over. The conferee role with any given client may be brief and may lead quickly to the social worker's assumption of the broker, mediator, and/or advocate roles as determined by initial exploration of the plight of the client. As the work proceeds, the movement back into the conferee role may punctuate task accomplishment as various facets of the client's situation are engaged. As such, the conferee role has a linkage relationship to the other roles and threads through the rest of the work, prominent mainly at the beginning and at the ending phases of the contact. In other words, the conferee role may be the primary role, particularly when the major concern or pressure upon the client is the determination of what action(s) he wishes to take to resolve his difficulties.

The conferee role, like the other roles discussed, is operative in all quadrants of activity, but we shall emphasize here the conferee role in Quadrant A. In Quadrants D and B the behavioral expectations for the social worker as participant with others in conferences guided by the assumptions of mutual and equal responsibility for involvement are quite familiar, as for example in team meetings, collaborative meetings, case conferences, and the like.

In Quadrant A, then, the social worker as conferee must set the stage and clarify with the client how they will work together. Rather than social worker being one-up and client one-down, their positions are side by side. Often the transaction occurs by means of an interview, which, if taken in its meaning, sheds light on the nature of the interaction; to interview is to see each other, to have mutual sight. A significant difference bound up in the conferee designation resides in the partnership implied in its execution, in contrast, for example, with the role labels of "counselor" or "therapist" which specify a different power balance: knowledgeable worker and less knowledgeable client.

Three major expectations comprise the activities of the social worker as conferee: 1) translating pressures into tasks; 2) exploring alternative courses of action and their consequences; and 3) determining when the work is over and concluding the contact with the client. These same expectations are equally applicable to the client, who is also a conferee.

Translating Pressures into Tasks

In some instances the social worker is but one more in a long line of social workers who have touched the life of the client and/or his acquaintances. In this event, it is likely that the client has already formed a picture of what social workers do or do not do. It is likely, too, that the client has an elaborate set of attitudes about social workers in general, and that he brings these attitudes to the first encounter. In the role of conferee, the social worker may need to help the client sort out and claim the preconceptions and previous experiences that condition what he thinks and feels about the possibilities of their work together prior to the more specific work of agreeing on the tasks to be accomplished and establishing a service contract.

Thus the first expectation for the social worker as conferee is to help translate the pressures on the client into tasks to lessen them. Preliminary within this expectation are those orienting and stage-setting activities geared to acknowledgement of preconceptions and prior experiences which condition the client's view of the situation. This is not to imply that the social worker builds a relationship first and then works on determining the tasks to be accomplished next. Rather, as part of that process, the possible barriers to such work are engaged in order for the conference to proceed. The following example recorded by a social worker in the probation office of the county court is illustrative: the worker checks out a powerful inference which precipitates talk about what might otherwise remain an unacknowledged, underlying obstacle.

A client came into the office saying that he had been told by the secretary in the front office to report to either K or T (Last names only were used.) As Mr. K was speaking with another client, I got

up, walked over to him, and introduced myself. The client looked a
bit startled. I asked if he would like to have a seat and I proceeded
to get out his file. The client sat down rather rigidly without remov-
ing his coat. A look of disgust came over his face, and he began to
stare straight ahead, avoiding all eye contact. He mumbled an "umph."
"Mr. J," I said. He responded again with another grunt. Again I
tried, "Mr. J, you look uncomfortable. Does it bother you that I am a
woman?" Mr. J did a double-take and immediately looked at me. He
responded, "Yes. I'm used to reporting down here, but I'm not used
to speaking with a lady other than a secretary."

Obviously, this kind of exchange is necessary in order for the social
worker to earn the right to work with the client. The need for such
stage-setting activity is apparent at the outset for any new engagement and is especially highlighted with nonvoluntary clients or in
instances when the social worker meets clients or potential clients on
their home territory.

As part of the first phase of the work, the establishment of the
service contract, the social worker attends to the atmosphere of the
exchange, to the climate that surrounds the initial engagement. The
activities involved in establishing the service contract have been discussed in chapter 3, and these become the central focus in translating
client pressures into tasks for client and social worker to pursue.

Exploring Alternative Courses of Action and Their Consequences

A second expectation for the behavior of the conferee is that of exploring with the client a range of alternative courses of action and their
possible consequences. It is out of such deliberation between worker
and client as conferees that the service contract is initially established,
subsequently changed, and finally terminated.

Central to this phase of the work is the decision-making process
which contains both rational and emotional elements. Throughout the
conference process, the worker should encourage the client to make
his own decision rather than a decision which others may want him
to make. The worker should encourage the client to consider alterna-

tives in light of the possible consequences of each, the client's own feelings about what he can and cannot bear, his own assessment of what is and is not congenial to his cultural and individual values and life style, and to choose the course of action that he considers best for himself, irrespective of what the decision might be. The social worker as conferee does not attempt to influence the client to choose the alternative which she (the worker) thinks is best, nor does she judge the client from her own frame of reference. She does not evaluate the client's ability to make decisions based on how similar the client's decision is to the worker's own preferred course of action or personal values. Rather, the worker recognizes that the decision belongs to the client and only the client, because the consequences are the client's and only the client's to bear.

Included in this phase of the work is the determination of what part of the client's pressures need to be considered first, the running out of possible actions the client wants to take or wants the worker to take, and the anticipation of possible outcomes of various separate and/or joint actions. And as the conferees think about and take steps to act in a series of possible moves, they are testing out action against the backdrop of the client's social reality and making decisions that will affect the client's social situation. As part of this process, the client gains confirmation from the worker, through their joint deliberations and actions, that he is not alone with his problems or feelings.

In the following example, a social worker in a hospital takes the role of conferee to help a woman explore alternative courses of action and their consequences. Encountering a tearful Mrs. Case in the corridor, the worker gets with her feelings and reaches for information with an open-ended question in order to explore the situation. She suggests a place to talk, positions herself, and waits out feelings. When Mrs. Case indicates that she is ready, the worker reaches for feelings, reaches for information, and attends while the client describes what is going on. When Mrs. Case seems finished, the social worker reaches for and gets with her feelings.

> When Mrs. Case stepped out of her husband's room, I could see that she was crying. I walked over and touched her shoulder. "You look upset", I said; "What's happening?" She shook her head. "Why don't we go down to the family room where it's a little more private?"

I said. She nodded wordlessly and we walked around the corner to the unit's family room. I pulled two chairs at a 90-degree angle to each other and handed her a box of tissues. We sat silently for a few minutes while she cried and tried to compose herself a little bit. I said, "Please don't feel you need to stop crying." She said, "No, I really need to talk." I said, "You seem terribly discouraged." She wiped her eyes and said, "Well, I'm afraid the news isn't very good according to some tests that have just come back." I said, "What's happening?" She sighed and said, "All of his blood counts are really low even though they've given him blood transfusions. The results from the biopsy also show that the cancer cells are now in his bone marrow. Dr. Willis said that he just doesn't have the strength to undergo any more treatment. The treatments themselves would make him feel worse and break his body down more quickly than the disease." I said, "I'm so sorry. This must have been such a blow —he seemed to be doing a little better." She said, "I know. He's really got the doctors confused. First he'll do real poorly and then he'll perk up and his fever will go down and he'll eat again." I said, "That must be doubly hard on you." She said, "Well, you know, it really is. I keep thinking maybe this time he really *will* pull through and I get my hopes up and then the next day he gets worse."

As the work continues below, the social worker facilitates the client's consideration of alternatives and consequences. In doing this, she reaches for two pieces of information, draws an inference from the client's responses, and checks out that inference. When the client acknowledges that the inference is accurate, the worker provides relevant information about self-incurred consequences. She waits out the clients feelings, draws and checks out two additional, salient inferences, and continues to draw and check out inferences by way of speculating with the client about more of what may be going on. The social worker then reaches for a feeling link between Mrs. Case and her husband, gets with Mrs. Case's feelings, and gives her more relevant information.

"How much does he know about his condition now?" I asked. Mrs. Case said, "I've been afraid to say anything to him—he wants to go home so bad. That's all he talks about." "What about the rest of your family—your son and daughters?" I asked. "I haven't told them anything either," she responded, "I'm afraid to. It'll just destroy them." I said, "It sounds like you're trying to protect them." "I am," she said. Then I said, quietly, "But that also means you have to keep all this painful knowledge to yourself. That can be an incredibly heavy burden." She began to cry again and said, "I know, but I just can't bear to see all the people around me feeling so bad—it just tears me up inside." I remained silent for a minute or two, then I said, "Do you think your husband and your family might suspect things might be getting worse—or not getting better?" She said, "I think so. Sometimes he talks about how I need to talk to the accountant to get some tax things straightened out for next year—as though he won't be there to take care of it. But he never asks the doctors how he is! I'm always the one to sneak away and talk to the doctor." I said, "I wonder if he might be trying to protect you from hurting too much." "Maybe", she said. I said, "Maybe you're both trying to protect each other by not talking about some very important things. It seems to hurt you very much not to be able to talk about it to him or anyone else. Do you think he might be feeling a little bit of that hurt also?" She responded, "I guess I hadn't thought of it that way." I said, "It's painful and frightening for both of you. Maybe both of you could reach a point where you could talk to each other about the fears and hurts you're each feeling. It won't make it go away, but it might make it a little easier to bear the burden if you share it." "That sure sounds like a good idea", she said, "but I need to think about it."

We talked about some other things, then I walked her back to her husband's room. She asked me if I'd be there tomorrow, and I said that I would be and that I'd come see her in the afternoon.

Because decision-making is never a purely rational process, it must be understood that feelings and attitudes will arise to distort, elaborate, and modify facts as work on the contract proceeds. Thus the social worker as conferee must be prepared to engage her own attitudes and feelings, and to help the client do the same. More specifically, the worker must raise both the positive and the negative feelings that the client may be experiencing, although not expressing. The worker may need to help the client understand that it is all right to have feelings and that facing these, whatever they are, will be neces sary in deciding on some action, hard as this is sometimes. And if the client expresses only one side of his feelings, the social worker should raise the less known ones that might also be there, for these become part of the information on which the client can ultimately base his decision.

All decisions are heavily influenced by attitude, past experience, emotion, and even intuition and hunches. Recognizing and facing these influences that lie in the emotional realm proceed along with recognizing the problems and possible actions. For example, there may be eagerness yet fear involved in taking a new job or in trying a new attitude with others, and both elements involved in a new shift would need to be faced and explored as part of the client's choice.

Concluding the Work

The third expectation ordering the behavior of the conferees is the determination of when the work is over and their contract concluded. Much as they begin their work together by mutual consent through the conference process, so do they end their work together by mutual consent through the conference process, and each goes his separate way. The ending is apparent when the tasks are accomplished and/or when the parties agree that the work should be concluded.

As with all other aspects of the conference process, the mutuality is central to the ending phase, but the client plays the primary role in signalling the end. As the client is central in defining the pressures upon him at the outset, so is he central in determining the need to conclude. And while, in some instances, the social worker may see much more that could be engaged and worked on, she takes her cue from the client's perception of the degree and scope of involvement he sees for himself, and adjusts her view to the client's vision.

In the following illustration from practice, the social worker and the client meet to conclude their work together. The instance is unique in that the client, a stroke victim, is still suffering from aphasia, limiting her ability to convey her thoughts in words that can be understood. She is leaving the rehabilitation center to live with her sister, so she will not be seeing this worker again.

Mrs. Walsch motioned for me to come sit by her, which I did. "I know you'll be leaving tomorrow," I said. She just looked at me and nodded. I said she had made a lot of progress in the four months she had been here. She nodded again, then she reached for my hand, pressed it, and started to cry. I held her hand. She had a difficult time getting the words out for her next thought, so she just said, "Oh, Lordy," and looked at me. I said we had become fairly close during our work together. She nodded. I said that I had seen her really improve and I would miss her very much. She cried again, and I got teary, too. She said she was going to her sister's for a while, but that as soon as she could walk the stairs a little better she wanted to go home. She showed me how well she could walk with just a cane. I said that was fantastic. I told her she was a strong lady. She joked that she sure could lift fifteen pounds now (she lifts a hand weight as part of her therapy). We talked a little more and then I had to leave for an appointment. She cried a little when we hugged goodbye, but then she smiled and said she was on her way. I agreed that she did a lot of hard work and that it really paid off.

The worker began by giving information, then got with the feelings nonverbally. She summarized both facts and feelings, and again got with feelings nonverbally. Later, when there was more talk, the social worker got with feelings verbally. Ultimately, she gave the client some final positive feedback and took her leave.

THE MINIMAX PRINCIPLE AND THE CONFEREE ROLE

There are times when all efforts to help a client fail to produce the desired outcome(s); the needed resources are not forthcoming, social agencies cannot or will not modify their practices to accommodate the client's needs, the informal community service network is already stretched to its limits. Although suitable programs ought to exist, there are none. For example, some states do not provide "general assistance." Financial aid is limited to families with dependent children. A woman or man without children is not entitled to any public welfare money, despite the fact that they are unemployed because not enough jobs are available, and therefore do not have any money. They are not even entitled to unemployment compensation, a program reserved for people who *did* have jobs. How, then, can a person find a place to live? Consider the following instance.

> I saw Mr. Planck at the Mental Health Center, and despite his claim that he needed to be an inpatient, there was nothing wrong with his mind or his affect. As we continued to talk, I learned that he had no money and no home. His days were spent walking to a church that offers a sandwich at lunch time, then to a mission 'soup kitchen', and finally to a shelter that provides a bed between 9 P.M. and 6 A.M. He never had a job. He told me several of the places he tried to get one but was turned down at all of them. He would still be looking, but doubts that if they turned him down then, surely they would turn him down now that he has no clean clothes, no deodorant, no toothpaste. . . . (Note that the Food Stamp Program is a Department of Agriculture thing and not a welfare service for the poor. That is why nonfarm commodities such as toothpaste, toilet paper, soap, deodorant and the like cannot be purchased with food stamps.) Even given the limitations of the Food Stamp Program, however, Mr. Planck does not qualify for the program anyway because he does not have an address!
>
> I made a lot of phone calls. One drug store would provide him with a basic toiletries kit if I promised not to call them again. No, they would not replenish it when it was used up. Public Housing, I learned, was not available for a single adult. Families only. Through a friend who works in the prisons I was able to get one pair of jeans, one sweatshirt, and one pair of socks. The man was so pleased with this pittance that it made me sick. Surely human beings are entitled to the basic necessities of "civilized" life.

Because people deserve better even though nothing better exists for them, the Minimax Principle is necessary. And it is in the conferee role that the social worker engages the client in a process aimed at helping him to understand that the problems are not inside him. The community should provide for all of its people, though it does not. He has been excluded through no fault of his own. Because we know that people who are treated badly tend to see themselves as having little or no worth and not deserving of anything, as conferees, social workers must do some consciousness raising. Social workers have to help clients to see that their plight and the plight of many others is a political, not a personal one.

To raise consciousness, it is necessary to start with the client's own personal experiences of deprivation, then show him how many others have had and continue to have the same deprivation as he has had. That is, he can begin to see that the deprivation he experienced as unique to him and attributed to a flaw inside of him is neither unique nor his fault. He comes to understand that he is one of many others who have been systematically excluded in order for some other group of persons to benefit. He should not be grateful for getting what is far below his entitlement. He has a right to be angry. He is a person of worth who has been led to believe he is worthless so that he will settle for less than is his due while others benefit from his oppression.[1]

While grand-scale consciousness raising such as the women's movement requires much time, the sort of consciousness raising needed in the instance described above can often be done rather quickly, by getting with feelings and giving relevant information, as in the piece of work described below.

> I went to see Mr. Gardner to tell him the final bad news. We reviewed our work together, then he said in a defeated tone, "I should have figured it would never happen." I nodded sadly. "Real frustrating, isn't it!" I said. He nodded. "Look," I said, "You're entitled to go to college. We have the scholarship money, and you and I both know you'd do just fine in your classes. It's not fair for you to have to settle for correspondence courses. It's not fair and it's not right. And I think it's important for you to know that your disability isn't the problem. The problem is that the people who run the college in this town are keeping you and other people in wheelchairs out by keeping doorways narrow and not building ramps and installing elevators. It's a political and economic issue and it has to be dealt with at the legislative/political level. There has to be a law that mandates wide doors, ramps, and elevators in all public buildings so that disabled people like you are not systematically excluded!" "If they widened the doors I *could* go to college," he said angrily. "Yeah," I said; "You and a whole lot of other disabled people."

6. The Broker

The aim of brokerage in social work is to link clients with community resources. Brokerage presupposes a complementarity of interest between the client in need and the agency or persons able to provide the needed service. Ideally, the social worker taking the role of broker uncovers and clears the access routes between clients and the resource distributors, whose purpose is to meet various needs. In this role, the social worker operates at the level of least contest; for assumedly, service providers must have populations in need to receive the services just as the populations in need must have some place to turn for particular services that the broader community has determined to disperse.

The role of broker is perhaps the oldest and best-known social work role, dating back to the friendly visitors and settlement house workers of the turn of the century. The early caseworkers were experts in finding, interpreting, and creating resources for the needy. In fact, these activities comprised so much of the work that it hardly seemed necessary to attach a special theoretical importance to them. In large part, this was what any "good" caseworker did. Imbued with the spirit of social reform, the settlement house workers brought immigrants to English classes, alerted young adults of the ghetto to upcoming civil service tests, described the advantages of day nurseries and credit unions to the poor, and provided vacations in the country at the "milk farms", with lots of food, rest, and clean air for the mothers and children of the tenements. These early social workers also found "angels" to sponsor an aspiring young talent, told the ladies' auxiliaries where to distribute the holiday dinners, and worked with politicians to get garbage removed, streets lighted, and clinics established.[1]

With urban life becoming increasingly complex, brokerage—concerned with exchange and transactions—performed either as a total occupation or as part of an occupational interest can be found in many areas of society. The purpose of these intermediaries, go-betweens, or agents is to connect seekers with offerers in the worlds of commerce, business, and industry much as in social welfare. The cadre of experts who provide knowledge and resources in affairs of doing and being includes, for example, the public accountant who understands the tax requirements, the investment counselor, the real estate agent, the travel agent, the bridal consultant.

Within social work's relatively brief history, brokerage functions probably predominated until the 1920s when casework shifted primary attention from the social realities to the internal dynamics of client problems.[2] Today, this role possesses least status in the eyes of many in the profession, probably since the mainstream interest of the profession from the 1940s to the mid-1960s was in "professionalizing" itself. Greater energy and theoretical interest surrounded "intensive" casework or "specialized" group work than the more mundane activities of referral or resource creation. Often, brokerage is the first role to be given away to others or to be sloughed off in the social worker's busy workaday schedule. With the exception of hospital discharge planning, brokerage is barely discussed in the professional literature, minimally supported in funding, and hardly legitimated or sanctioned by the community through institutionalized, visible service components within the network of services.

However, the need for brokerage is today more acute than in the past. Hunger is rampant in America. The population of homeless persons, including homeless families, increases daily. The AIDS virus threatens to reach epidemic proportions. To meet some demands of the urban scene emergent forms of brokerage include "hot lines" to reach the drug user, the suicidal, or the unmarried, pregnant teenager, for example. Many of these are staffed by volunteers devoted to a particular cause; others may employ professionals with specialized skills and a commitment to the validity of this role. In various communities trailers bring the broker to alienated teenagers, Vietnam veterans, and the people on skid row[3]—populations that might not take themselves to the offices of community agencies. The needs of people for goods and services have been and continue to be a major concern in social work.

If resources were available in abundance, well-known to all segments of the community, accessible without question, and offered without stigmatization, the role of the broker would be relatively easy. The practitioner would merely tell the resource seeker where the distributor is located. Since present social arrangements do not meet these conditions, however, the complexities of the broker role are enormous.

The supposed complementarity of interest between client need and agency service often has broken down or has never existed in today's world of burgeoning social needs where the economic arrangements are based upon scarcity. Thus, brokerage must demand more than merely linking needs with resources. Within the reality of current social arrangements for service delivery, we propose three expectations for the behavior of the social worker taking the role of broker: 1) knowing the resources, 2) cultivating these resources, and 3) creating resources where now there are none.

Knowing the Resources

Knowing the resources of the community is more complex than may initially appear. Involved here is knowing what services are offered, how and to whom they are available, what demands are made upon the seeker, and other formal aspects of the service delivery pattern. In addition, social workers need to have an informal reading of the delivery system. That is, they need to know what actually happens when people try to avail themselves of that resource. Moreover, it is not enough to know the range of resources available within the network of social service agencies. If brokers are to be effective, they must be familiar with resources offered under political auspices, by religious institutions, self-help organizations, schools, storefront programs, through health delivery systems, and all other enterprises in both the public and private sectors of the community. In short, workers should have the pulse of the community and access to the formal and the informal resource networks at their fingertips. And they should constantly revise their inventory of resources and distributors in accord with information learned in day-by-day contacts.

Knowledge about the diverse access routes to each resource is especially important, be this a generalized notion of the reception procedures or the name of a key individual. Such detailed information cannot be obtained merely from a directory of services. Entailed here is firsthand knowledge amassed from actual contact with the distributing agents and their resources. This means that one priority for social workers is that of becoming personally acquainted with related service centers so that they know exactly what they are talking about when they suggest various resources to clients.

Cultivating the Resources

In addition to having up-to-date knowledge of community resources, the broker must attend to and cultivate them in the long-term interest of clients. Brokers should maintain contact with responsive systems and work to effect more responsive procedures in difficult systems at times when no client is in need and no particular crisis demands an immediate response. In the first place, such noncrisis-precipitated intersystem collaboration facilitates the efficient connection of client need to community resources in terms of the amount of time between a client's initial expression of need and service to meet that need. The broker confronted with a critical need for a particular resource can tap previously established channels rather than begin, at the point of crisis, the time-consuming search for, and effort to open up, a connection for the first time. Moreover, noncrisis-oriented intersystem collaboration can be approached from a universalistic perspective. That is, the collaborative work can focus on developing structures that will endure beyond any single client and any single moment.

Intersystem contact that is limited to points of crisis, on the other hand, must, of necessity, seek and settle for exceptionalism, for a special arrangement, so that only this particular client can get only this particular service at only this particular time. By implication, the client's need is an exceptional one and could not have been predicted. And while this may be the case in some instances, human needs are largely universal and predictable, although programs to meet human needs are more often than not predicated on the fallacious assumption of exceptionalism.[4] If social workers are to avoid perpetuating the myth of exceptionalism in their own practice, then, they will take the role of broker when they are not confronted with a client in crisis, in order to create access roads through the network of community services — roads that will be open when any client needs to use them.

Creating Resources

The third expectation for the social worker as broker is that of developing resources where none exist. That a particular resource is needed may occur to the social worker in relation to a particular client's problem, or as a more generalized insight in the course of pursuing the professional assignment in a particular place within the service delivery network. Rather than dismissing the idea as impractical, impossible, too time-consuming, or an interesting notion for someone else to pursue, social workers can and should lend their efforts to implementation of the idea. Since the brokers stand at the interface between client need and community resources, they must do what needs to be done to induce the forces within the environment to produce resources. In other words, if there is no resource to serve the client, then part of the brokerage role must include the creation of a resource.

As suggested, the creation of a new resource begins with an idea about need and how it might be met. Once the idea has occured to her, the broker must consider who else might be interested in it, and how those who are interested can be engaged as co-implementers, allies, or both. In some instances the clients themselves can be mobilized in their own behalf, as illustrated in the formation of the telephone network described in chapter 3. In some instances the worker can organize others in the community to provide systematically a particular resource, such as the corps of community doctors cited in chapter 1, who were enlisted to write prescriptions for community mental health center clients. In still other instances the workers can interpret the need to their own colleagues, organized groups in the community, legislators, and/or other funding sources in the interest of providing resources to meet client needs.

If the social worker's orientation includes helping others to provide resources for themselves and helping move potential allies to provide resources, new possibilities are immediately open. For example, one consultant was engaged by a school district to offer three sessions to school counselors from several high schools as part of upgrading their skills in using groups. In the final session, it was obvious that the training was just taking hold and the counselors were operating as a group, enthusiastic about their learning experience. The impending end of the sessions was viewed with dismay by the counselors, who expressed grief and apprehension that they now had to "go it alone." In the final session, the consultant helped the group plan to meet independently as a self-help seminar. The final part of the training session was devoted to helping the group organize itself, distributing responsibilities for conducting the next meetings, planning a sequence of content to move into, and developing some new morale in anticipation that they could keep learning by means of certain additional structures and ground rules suggested by the consultant.

In taking the role of broker, social workers must know both the formal and the informal aspects of obtaining resources from various agencies; they must cultivate these resources, maintaining contact with responsive agencies and effecting more responsive procedures with difficult agencies; and they must work to create resources when there are needs but no services to meet them. But let us assume, now, that the social worker knows of a suitable resource to meet a client's need and has maintained a working relationship with the agency. When the client is referred to the service, it is incumbent upon the one in the brokerage role to stay by that client until the linkage with the service is accomplished. In some instances, this new connection will spell the end of the brokerage and the work with the client. Sometimes there are other tasks that require the attention of both client and worker at the time the client also moves to another service. In such instances a new contract is made, and the worker continues to meet with the client and/or others in the client's life who are important to the ongoing tasks. In other situations, the clients return with their version of what happened or did not happen when they sought help from a specified resource. Perhaps the agency was unresponsive. The social worker's role might now shift to mediator in order to explore the blockage to an effective contact or to an advocacy role to bring pressure upon the resource to be more responsive.

Clearly, brokerage implies analysis of the situation after the referral is made, for the work is not over until some response from the other distributors of services is made. Perhaps alternative resources may be proposed if the first referral failed; or increased pressure may be applied to an unresponsive resource. In the brokerage role, the social worker can gather data that can be gleaned only from operating at the interface between persons in need and community response. Such data can be used to inform the policy-makers of the plight of all those who slip through the holes within the network of resources and thus lead to the creation of systems more prepared to accomodate those who need services. In fact, being skillful and thorough at this level might bring about a lessened need for activity by social workers in roles of increased pressure.

The Broker and the Environmental Supports Principle

The Principle of Maximizing Supports in the Client's Environment, described in chapter 3, requires social workers to meet client need by finding community resources, finding and modifying community resources, and/or inventing resources, developing structures in the community, structures that can exist and operate independent of the social workers and continue to exist after the social workers have gone on to develop and deliver yet other needed services. And it is primarily in the role of the broker that social workers perform such activity— ferreting out needed resources, modifying existing services to meet client need, and creating services where none currently exist. Thus the role and the principle go hand in hand.

For example, when the social worker takes the role of broker, moves into Quadrant D, and refers a client to a particular resource distributor in accord with the Environmental Supports Principle, the worker not only follows up to be sure the client received the needed service; in addition, the social worker tries to engage the resource provider in developing, maintaining, and *advertising* a direct channel to that resource for those who need it. Thus persons in need of the service would no longer have to go to other agencies to hear about it and/or be referred to the agency that actually delivers it. Rather, persons who need that resource can go directly to the distributor— self-referred, with no unnecessary run-around.

The following example of practice in Child Protective Services illustrates the social worker's use of the broker role to create a needed resource, one that would be able to exist independent of the worker who conceived it and set it in motion. The work began in Quadrant A, with the social worker taking the role of conferee. Note the sensitivity the worker demonstrates as she reaches for and gets with the angry and deeply painful feelings that the interaction generates in the client.

I got to Ms. J's about 9 a.m. and knocked on the door. There was no response. I knocked louder, then waited. After several minutes Roberto peeked his head through the door and said "Hi" (sheepishly). I walked in and Roberto ran back to the couch beside his brother, watching TV. Ms. J was in bed (I could see her bed from where I was standing).

While I waited for Ms. J to get out of bed, I asked Roberto if he was sick today (because he was not in school). He shook his head, no. At this point Ms. J came into the living room with a scowl on her face. She marched over to where Roberto and Esteban were sitting on the couch, passing me very abruptly. She stood between the TV and the children and raised her arm as if she were going to hit them, but didn't. Instead she began to shout at Roberto, "You little S.O.B., I told you never to turn on this TV before you go to school in the morning! Why aren't you in school? You're going to get me in all kinds of damn trouble." Roberto cringed and placed his arm over his head as if to ward off any blow that his mother might deliver. His face looked frightened. Then Ms. J turned to me and said, "He makes me so damned mad! He knows he's supposed to be in school! But there he sits in front of that damned TV." Drawing closer to her and the children, I looked at her and said, "It is frustrating when children don't do what you tell them to." Then I angled my body into the couch and sat down. Ms. J sat down in a nearby chair. I asked her if this happens often and she said yes, that these little brats know that they are supposed to be in school but they just won't go. I asked if they had trouble getting up in the mornings, and she said no, that they get up and get dressed to go, but then they sit here and watch TV instead. Then I asked if she were able to get up with the boys in the morning, and she said that she didn't see why she should be expected to get up when she's tired from taking care of the girls all day and night (ages one-and-a-half and three). I said,

"Two little ones can really keep you hopping!" "They do," she said, "I'm always tired."

The worker begins by getting with the powerful feelings Ms. J has expressed. She then positions herself and begins to reach for information. When her third question seems to trigger more strong affect, the worker temporarily abandons her quest for information and reaches for the client's feelings. As the interaction continues below, worker attention to client feeling continues. When her checking out of an inference prompts Ms. J to verbalize some painful childhood memories, the worker listens, then reaches for that pain. After the client acknowledges the hurt she still feels, her nonverbal behavior suggests the need for "time out," a subtle cue that does not escape the worker's notice. In response, the worker waits silently until Ms. J indicates that she is ready to move on.

After a brief silence I said that it seemed like the boys needed some help getting out in the morning. Immediately, Ms. J said "I didn't have anybody to help me when I was little and I did the things I was supposed to do. If I didn't, I got the shit beat out of me." She grabbed her cigarettes: her body got rigid and her facial expression was taut. "Just remembering that can make you feel hurt and angry!" I said. "Yeah," she said, "and I'll never forgive them for it either." There was a long silence while she stared off in space. I waited.

When she turned her head back to me I said that since caring for the little girls was so exhausting, maybe we could get a morning helper to come in for an hour each school morning and see the boys off. She looked kind of wary and asked me what I meant. I said that maybe I could get a high school girl to volunteer. Her look changed from wary to surprised. When I called attention to that she laughed and said all her other workers figure she's just lazy and threaten to take the boys away from her. I told her she didn't seem lazy to me, that it seemed to me that she has an exhausting schedule and could use some help with it. Then I asked her if she wanted me to see if I could get someone and she said that would be great. I said, "No guarantees, but I'll do what I can and get back to you as soon as possible." She asked me if I'd like some coffee before I left.

When the client seemed ready to move on, the worker gives some speculative information, which, when clarified, seems to surprise the client. Still very attentive to feelings, the worker reaches for that surprise and gives the client perhaps the most important kind of opinion-type information that social workers can give, the kind that can begin to restore a sense of dignity where too many self-righteous feet have trampled it almost to death. And it is only after this that Ms. J tentatively reaches out.

Having developed a contract with Ms. J, later that afternoon the social worker proceeded to follow the demands of the client task. She looked beyond Ms. J and identified some other families in her caseload that may need morning help, so when she called the local high school she was looking for at least one, and hopefully several more than one, volunteer. She arranged to meet with the vice principal the next day.

The social worker, now in Quadrant D, took the role of broker and described to the vice principal both the need for "Project Morning Help" and the potential benefit for student volunteers—colleges like to see community service on application forms. Then both the social worker and the vice principal spoke to an assembly of juniors and seniors after which 16 students committed themselves to volunteer as morning helpers. Since many other students expressed a desire to help with things later in the day, especially minding children after school, the worker told them she would look around, see what was needed, and get back to them. Eventually, a second group of students formed a "Latch Key Kids" program which gave some peace of mind to many working mothers and enabled many mothers who did not go out to work to get out of the house one afternoon each week.

Following the Environmental Supports Principle, the social worker enabled the vice principal to coordinate both volunteer projects, thereby working herself out of a job.

THE BROKER IN QUADRANT D

In the example above, the social worker moved into Quadrant D, took the role of broker and created a resource. Although brokerage is necessary in Quadrants A and B, as will become apparent in later sections of this chapter, most brokerage takes place in Quadrant D. And some of this brokerage involves checking out resources before making linkages that may not be in the client's best interests. In the following example, the social worker goes to a potential parolee's proposed home placement in order to see if the people there want the man to live with them and to see if the situation seems as though it will help the man stay out of jail. In this instance, the person offering a home is the man's wife of one and a half years. They met through a local "biker" organization while the man was still in prison. She offered him his last home placement, and they were married immediately following his release. He was returned to prison after only two weeks out because he was charged with a new offense.

> After some introductory remarks. I told Ms. D that her husband listed her as his home sponsor and her home as his placement. She said, "Yeah. Johnny lived here before and everything went okay." "No, it didn't," I said, he ended up going right back to prison, and according to the records, part of the reason was that he didn't stay here during his curfew when he was supposed to." "Well, yeah; you're right," she said, "But I mean Johnny and I got along all right. You see, I know Johnny, and he's got a bad drinking problem," she continued. (I nodded that I knew.) She said that Johnny would never do well until he gets help and that he had already been through D & A (a local drug and alcohol abuse program), and A.A. before she even met him. "So I don't know what to do to help him," she said. I said, "It sounds real frustrating.""Yeah," she said, "What are we supposed to do if Johnny's got a problem but there ain't no place that can help him?" I told her I would talk to him and if he wanted treatment for the drinking problem I'd try and find a program for him. She said that she goes to see him all the time and she knows he wants treatment.
>
> We then went through a question and answer period where she wanted to know about curfew time, travel restrictions, etc. She asked a couple of questions about whether Johnny had to stay at her home or if, once out, he could change his home placement. After she raised that several times, I said, "Ms. D. the way you keep asking me about him moving out . . . You're trying to tell me something, right?" "Well," she said, "I think after he's out he's gonna wanna move." I asked her what made her think that and she said, "Ya see, he can stay here and all, this is a legit home placement, it's

just that he already told me he wants a divorce. He's got this girl that comes to see him at prison and that's who he was going to see when he missed them curfew checks last time." "Whew," I said, "That hurts." Then she started to cry.

The social worker begins the interview by giving information, then confronts distortion as Ms. D begins to misrepresent what had occurred. He listens as she talks about her inability to help her husband with his drinking problem, then reaches for her feelings of frustration. As she continues to talk, the worker gradually infers that Ms. D is both trying and not trying to tell him something, so he gently checks out his inference, and the whole story comes tumbling out.

Although Ms. D was not a client, the social worker responded to her pain and was able to refer her to a mental health center for counseling and grief work. It should be noted that, because so much of brokerage is done in Quadrant D, usually with the persons who most closely affect and are affected by our clients, it behooves us to be available to them in at least a limited way. In social work, good brokerage involves respectful concern for all members of the client's resource network.

THE BROKER IN QUADRANT A

Whether by choice or by default, whether preferred by clients over alternative service systems or necessitated by the lack of alternatives, there are times when the needs of people can be served in self-help groups and/or mutual aid networks. At these times, the social worker brings the requisite systems into existence, and because of this, the worker's activity can properly be called brokerage. In forming these groups, the worker engages clients in their own behalf, therefore the worker's activity is located in Quadrant A.

The following is an example of brokerage in Quadrant A. The context is a high-rise apartment building for the elderly. The social worker is from the senior citizens program of a nearby settlement house. As in all instances of direct practice, the worker initially takes the role of conferee.

I went to see Mrs. Carter about the place I found that gives free eye examinations, and while I was there, she told me about another problem—shopping for groceries. Her legs had gotten worse so that now she had to use crutches. With crutches in both hands, she couldn't even take her fold-up shopping tote with her, let alone pull it when it was full of groceries on the return trip. She knew about Meals on Wheels, but said she is not an invalid and doesn't want to feel like one. She's capable of and likes to do her own cooking just like she's always done. I asked her what other people in the building with canes or walkers, or even wheelchairs, do about shopping. She said she used to shop for some of them and she thought maybe relatives did it for some others. But mostly, she thought, people relied on asking a neighbor to bring back one or two items for them next time they go to the market. She said she wouldn't ask anyone though; she didn't want to be a burden to her neighbors.

I asked her if she knew of others who wanted to do their own shopping but were similarly hampered. She knew of several and told me about them. She also said there were some in wheelchairs, perfectly able to take care of themselves except for marketing. And then there were the people who just weren't steady enough on their feet.

I asked her if, instead of using crutches, she could hold onto and push a wheelchair. She said she certainly could. So I said that maybe we could get her and some others like her together with some people in wheelchairs, and they could take each other shopping. She seemed delighted with the idea, adding to it that the ones who can stand can get the items from the shelves and freezers, and the ones in the wheelchairs could hold and balance the bags. She gave me a list of people who might be interested, and I started knocking on doors that evening.

In three days we had a meeting in the community room with more than fifteen enthusiastic people. When one of the "walking people" sadly noted that they outnumbered the "wheelchair people," one of the "wheelchair people" said she didn't mind making two trips—in fact, she said, the second time she could get what she forgot to get the first time. All of the "wheelchair people" agreed that two trips was no problem. They decided to meet in the community room on Monday morning and pair off for the first trip. I said I'd go with them the first few times if they wanted me to, and they said they didn't need me, that they would do just fine by themselves.

A few weeks later, when I was there helping some new residents fill out social security forms, Mr. Taggart, one of the "wheelchair people," told me they were doing just fine with the "shopping brigade" and were now even getting together and having dinner parties on Saturday nights. He also said he hasn't felt this good about life in a long time. He patted my hand. I said I was real glad for all of them.

A special form of brokerage in Quadrant A involves the creation of "trade units," informal, two (or more) person bartering structures through which participants meet each other's needs. The creation of such structures is predicated on the social worker's recognition that every client is not only a person in need. Every client is also a person with resources. It is further predicated on the assumption that social workers make it a matter of course to know what resources their clients have to offer, thereby making it possible to identify potential need-meeting linkages. For example, if the worker knows that an elderly man who needs some general repairs around his house happens to be a good cook, and if that worker can identify a person capable of doing the needed repairs who would enjoy some good home-cooked meals, the worker can link the people to each other, maximizing environmental supports by creating a mutually beneficial "trade unit."

"Trade units" need not be limited to pairs of persons. One structure which a social worker created involved a woman who needed three things: transportation to medical appointments, access to less expensive food purchasing than the neighborhood grocery, and a source of clothing alteration so that her younger children could wear outfits outgrown by her older children without feeling bad about themselves and how they looked. The worker knew that this woman enjoyed children and was good at child care. The worker also knew of three women who worked outside the home and needed child care between the time school was over and the time they got home from work—three women, each of whom could meet one of the first woman's three needs. Mrs. Felton, an expert seamstress, could cut clothing items down to whatever size was needed. Ms. Clark could offer transportation to medical appointments, and Ms. Washington, who did her own weekly shopping at a warehouse outlet market on the other side of town, could easily take the first woman with her. Thus a "trade unit" comprised of three bartering pairs with one person belonging to all three structures was created, and the pressing needs of four persons were able to be met.

THE BROKER IN QUADRANT B

In Quadrant B, brokerage involves the development of resource cooperatives intended to benefit both the clients involved in creating and maintaining them *and* others with similar needs. A classic example outside of social work is the volunteer fire department common to small cities and towns across the nation. Within social work, the best known instance of this sort is the food coop, an enterprise in cutting food costs through bulk purchasing from wholesale distributors. Ordinarily, a food coop is developed and run by a small cadre of families who make the goods available to the larger neighborhood. If the families that did the work involved were the only ones to benefit from their efforts, the creation would more properly be called a self-help system and the social worker's activity would properly be placed in Quadrant A. When the intended beneficiaries extend beyond those persons with whom the worker is directly engaged, the project can be considered a resource cooperative and the workers activity is rightly placed in Quadrant B.

Resource cooperatives can be developed for many different goods and services. In the following example, a social worker helps some of the residents in a subsidized housing project develop and run a "block watch" for the protection of everyone who lives there.

> Somebody stole Mr. Collier's TV set and he was really upset. He told me he'd been robbed three other times that month but this time it was the worst, because he relies on the TV for company as well as entertainment. I told him I'd try to get him an unclaimed one from the police and he said he'd be real grateful for that.
>
> I asked him if he knew what a "block watch" program was. He didn't, so I described it to him and he thought it was a good idea. Then I asked him if he thought some of the people who live there would volunteer to patrol one night a week, and he said not him because he's too old. He told me to talk to the young ones. I asked

him to give me some names and addresses, but he said he didn't want to get involved.

On the way out I saw some little kids playing, so I asked them where they lived and I went to the door one of the little boys pointed to. I told the woman who I was and she said she had seen me around there before and what did I want with her. Without using his name, I told her about Mr. Collier and what "block watch" was all about. I told her the police lend you the walkie-talkies and the base stations, and that they teach you what to do and what not to do. I asked if she or her husband and any others she knew might be interested. She said she didn't have a husband, but her brother lived around the corner and he was a big strong guy.

By the time I found her brother, Mr. Williams, and told him everything too, it was beginning to get dark and I wanted to leave and come another day. Mr. Williams wanted me to tell some other men he knew about the "block watch" idea, though, so he told me he'd walk me to my car later and see that I got off all right. I agreed to stay, and he phoned up some friends and invited them over.

Not everyone he called could come, but three men did come and two of them had wives and children they wanted to be sure were safe. All four men were interested and they talked about some others they might be able to get. I asked them when they thought they could get all the people together, and since they weren't sure, I gave them my number so they could call me to arrange for the police to talk with them and lend them equipment. About a week later they called me to set it up, which I did.

By the time the meeting with the police was over, they were all organized and ready to patrol about a six square block area, and I agreed to talk to residents outside that area about getting together and doing the same thing.

7. The Mediator

Another set of expectations for behavior which has gained increasing recognition over the last two decades is the role of mediator. Generally associated with its primary formulator, William Schwartz,[1] mediation is based on the concept of mutual aid from the social philosophy of Peter Kropotkin.[2]

Whereas advocacy, discussed in the next chapter, presumes a basic conflict between individual and social interest, mediation presumes a common bond. The common bond may be a complementary one, as the bond between client need and agency service, or it may be an identical one, as the bond between construction workers who need each other in order to obtain wage increases. Consistent with this, conflict is viewed as a sign that one or both parties to the encounter have lost sight of the need each has for the other, and signals an occasion for the performance of mediating behaviors.

It is the aim of the mediator to help the parties in conflict to rediscover their need for each other, thereby freeing them to contribute to each other's welfare. Mediators position themselves between the conflicting parties to help each reach out to the other for their mutual self-fulfillment.[3] In other words, the basis for mediation in social work is implementation of the identity or complementarity of individual and social interest where it breaks down or grows obscure.

The role of mediator can be defined in terms of five expectations for behavior: 1) identifying the common ground on which the two parties with their conflicting perceptions of self-interest can meet; 2) identifying the obstacles which are obscuring the common ground, such as authority problems, and challenging both parties to find a way around or through the obstacles; 3) defining the limits of the situation; 4) providing information; and 5), projecting an image of oneself as a person who stands for the welfare of both parties.[4]

Identifying Common Ground

Common ground is a point of reference belonging to more than one person. It is an area of overlap between the self-interest of one person and the self-interest of another person. Where it can be recognized, it constitutes the basis of their need for each other and the motive for cooperative interaction.

In a corporate society where every person is part of a complex network of demand and relationship, the bond between individual and social interest grows diffuse and can easily be obscured in any particular instance of the individual-social encounter. When social workers take the role of mediator in order to implement the mutuality of interest between parties, therefore, they must begin by recognizing the point at which their apparently different self-interests converge. Having noted that point of convergence, mediators talk with each of the parties individually, pointing out the stake each has in instituting a cooperative relationship with the other, and asking each to engage the other in order to effect such cooperation. They offer to help each party talk to the other, and should this be agreeable, establish service contracts with both.

The second step involves a joint meeting in which the mediator points out the common ground on which the two parties can meet and establishes a service contract with them as a unit. The worker then clarifies her stake in their engagement, indicating that she will help them do what they came together to do, that her interest is in their engagement rather than in any particular outcome. In other words, she sides with neither one party nor the other, but stands between them, equally concerned about both, and placing her faith in their engagement.

Identifying Obstacles

As two parties work to effect cooperative interaction, many obstacles can arise to block valid communication. Variables such as culturally based ethics, norms, and personal needs, for example, can intervene and obscure the common ground. Norms against comparing salaries can prevent employees from discovering and substantiating the existence of inequities, thereby hindering united action to rectify them. Likewise, norms that prohibit the open communication of emotion prevent essential information from being exchanged and can render a potentially meaningful relationship sterile. This is frequently a problem in marriage counseling, and much of the counselor's effort is directed toward increasing the flow of affect between husband and wife.

The prevalence of a win-as-much as-you-can ethic in our society poses a constant threat to the integrity of cooperative efforts to obtain mutual self-fulfillment. It is not unlikely that either or both parties to the encounter will lose sight of the potential for mutual gain to the extent that each will consider losing some of what he already has won, so long as the other party loses more. Problems of authority also become obstacles to valid communication and mutual aid when they operate just beneath the surface. Manifest efforts to cooperate both hide and serve as the medium through which a counterproductive game of who's-on-top[5] is played.

When obstacles such as these subvert authentic efforts to cooperate, the mediator should indicate the obstacle and challenge both parties to deal with it openly and honestly. She should again point to the common ground and ask each if his need for the other is sufficiently strong to motivate him to find a way around or through the obstacle. In other words, the mediator forces underlying issues to the surface where they can be tackled with purpose and with affect.

A somewhat different but highly pervasive obstacle to arriving at mutually satisfying conflict resolutions involves reputational concerns —primarily loss of face. People can go to great lengths in order to save face, even when the costs to them are very high. So the strategy in and of itself may not suffice. If someone is reputed to be a person who never backs down, for example, and if that person places a high value on this reputation, motivation to save face may well outweigh motivation to cooperate, if cooperation is construed as backing down. In situations like this, the social worker as mediator can help to release a person who wants to cooperate but is caught in a reputational bind by finding a "higher value"—such as "for the sake of the children" if the persons in conflict are school teachers—to which that person can subscribe; a higher value that can justify a shift in position without the usually accompanying loss of face. Given such justification, instead of construing the person's cooperative behavior as an instance of backing down, it can be considered a forward arabesque, worthy of a rational and reasonable person. In the broader political arena, a favorite "higher value" that is frequently paraded out to allow persons in high levels of government to back down yet save face is "in the interests of national security."

Defining Limits

Every instance of the individual social encounter occurs within and is influenced by an institutional context. Contextual forces external to the particular encounter, such as time, money, and the demands of other relationship systems, impinge upon both parties and limit the nature and extent of their potential agreement and the conditions under which it can and cannot operate. If a student who wants to learn and a teacher who wants to teach recognize their need for each other, they can come to grips with and work through such an obstacle to their mutual self-fulfillment as problems of authority. But they cannot extend the teaching/learning time to include Saturdays, for example, without producing consequences for their respective family systems. Both parties must be aware of the boundaries beyond which their agreement produces consequences for other systems in their social networks in order for them to make choices and exercise some measure of control over their individual and mutual destinies. In order to guard the right of self-determination of both parties, the mediator should ask them to recognize the boundaries explicitly and to make their decisions in light of all foreseeable contingencies.

Providing Information

Because people formulate issues based on the information (facts, opinions, ideas, feelings) they possess and choose actions from available alternatives, information is critical to decision making. That is, the extent to which persons can make critical decisions about their own lives depends upon the amount and kind of information which they possess about the situation in which they are involved and the conditions under which that situation can be changed. In other words, information is a resource and, like any other resource, when it is differentially distributed, it produces power differentials.

When one of two parties to an encounter possesses relevant information which the other does not, the social worker in the role of mediator should help establish parity either by asking the one party to share this information, or by providing it for the other herself. What if the worker has access to relevant information which neither party to the encounter possesses? In this event, the mediator should provide both parties with the information so they will be neither dependent upon her every step of the way nor forced to make decisions without considering all possible data.

When mediators provide information, particularly ideas, feelings, and opinions, it is important that they present it as their own rather than as established "truth," and they should only provide information which has direct bearing on the issue at hand at the time it is at hand. Opinions presented as facts serve to distort and manipulate, and information that is not relevant, if it is heard at all, can divert the attention of the two parties from the particular piece of work in which they are engaged. If information is presented honestly and in a suitable manner, it can increase the power of people to exercise some measure of control over their relatedness to others and the outcome of this relatedness to their individual lives.

Projecting an Image

As indicated earlier, mediators stand for the welfare of both parties to an encounter. They position themselves between the parties and act to implement their presumed identity or complementarity of interest. In siding with neither one party nor the other, but with the engagement itself, mediators announce their faith that the outcome of open and honest communication between people who need each other will be to their mutual benefit. And when they ask both parties to deal with the obstacles that block communication, they project an image of themselves as persons who believe that such obstacles can be overcome, and that the need of people for each other is a sufficient motive for doing the hard but necessary work to overcome them. This is the image which the social worker as mediator must project, and this image is inextricably bound to the assumption of identity or complementarity of interest between parties. In other words, social workers can take the role of mediator if they presume common ground. If they presume a basic conflict of interest, on the other hand, they properly take the role of advocate.

MEDIATING IN QUADRANT A

In all instances of mediation, the social worker stands at the interface between persons. Mediation that takes place entirely in Quadrant A can be understood as a form of group work in which the social worker helps all of the persons talk to each other with purpose and feeling about real issues that affect their lives together. Mediation solely in Quadrant A is appropriate in situations where an *identity* of interest is obscure; where social complexities, prejudices, and the like prevent people from banding together to take concerted action in order to get collectively what none of them can get if each acts alone.

In the following example of mediating in Quadrant A, the social worker meets with the SWS Club, a group of teenage girls with troubled lives who came together, at the worker's suggestion, to help each other stick with school. The group meets three times per week, during study hall, and the excerpt below is taken from the first meeting of the fifth week.

Jane and Lois came in together talking about a vocabulary test they had just taken. Ann, Lisa, and Sally arrived next, but hung around the door talking with some boys. When Pauline and Linda got here, the girls at the door came in and everyone sat down. Margie ran in last and said she almost didn't come because she was so upset. Lois asked her what happened, and she said she just called her Mom to see how the baby was, and her Mom was drunk, so that meant nobody was taking care of little Timmy and she figured she'd better go home and see to him. But then she ran into Lloyd (Timmy's father) in the hall and told him she wanted to come to this meeting so he'd have to see to Timmy until she could get home. But Lloyd said he couldn't on account of basketball practice. "And that's the way it's always going to be," she said. "And I can't just sit here in school worrying about him and have him maybe crying and wet or hungry and not getting what he needs. I just can't keep going to school. You know I want to," she said, "but I just can't." I said, "Hey, that's a real tough spot to be in." "Yeah," she said, "but I knew it was going to happen." Margie stood up and started putting her coat on when Ann looked up and asked her where did she think she was going. Ann told her that that's what this club is all about, helping each other, not just talking about it. "So you sit right back down and we'll try to figure out what to do." Lisa asked what about day care, and Margie said he's too young, that they don't take kids that age and they won't even take an older kid if he's not toilet trained. Lisa suggested baby sitters, maybe some older lady in the neighborhood who likes little babies and wouldn't mind making a couple of extra dollars. "Who's got a couple of dollars?" Margie asked in a don't-be-silly-voice. "Well, I do," Lisa answered. "I spend about a dollar for lunch every day, but I could pack my lunch instead." Sally said she could, too, and her mother would be so happy that she's finally going to eat right. Everyone but Pauline laughed, and I noticed that her eyes were red and puffy.

The social worker listens and responds to Margie's feelings. As soon as group members begin to help, in accord with the Environmental Supports Principle, the worker moves out of the central position in the helping process and listens quietly.

When the worker notices nonverbal behavior that other group members apparently did not see, she amplifies the subtle message (below) so that group members can respond to it if they wish. Again, as soon as the group responds, the worker's intervention appropriately stops. In fact, when one member, Jane, directs to the worker a message intended for another member, Pauline, the worker redirects the message so that the self-help and mutual aid process among members can continue.

When the laughter subsided, I told the girls that Pauline's eyes were red. "And she's shivering, too," Lois added, passing her sweater to Pauline. "What's the matter?" Pauline said it wasn't anything important and she'd rather the group continue putting money together so Timmy can be taken care of and Margie keep coming to school. Pauline also said she can put in about twenty dollars a week since money is the only thing her father's not stingy with . . . money and his hands. "What did he do to you?" Linda asked with an angry look on her face. "Nothing," Pauline said. Jane looked at me and said that wasn't fair, that they all agreed to tell whatever it is. I told her to tell that to Pauline. She nodded, turned to Pauline, and said "we're all here to talk about the stuff we can't talk about anywhere else." "And we said we'd help each other too," Margie added. "Look what everyone is doing for me!" Her eyes filled up when she said it. "It's not like that," Pauline said. "Spit it out, girl," Linda said. "Okay, okay," Pauline said, and tears started flowing down her cheeks. "My father caught my little brother with some pot and he beat him up so bad we had to take him to the emergency room. And I'm scared to death he's going to beat me, too. He's been after me about hanging out with boys, and I don't let boys touch me or nothing, but what if he doesn't believe me? And nobody can help, because he'd beat me to death if he knew I told anybody." She continued to cry, the sobs much deeper now. Nobody spoke.

Suddenly Sally said that if Pauline's father is anything like her father, he wouldn't do anything while anybody else was around. "Yeah," Pauline said, still sobbing, "so what?" "Oh, yeah," Lois said. "I think we're all going to be having big tests for the next couple of weeks and we'll have to study together at Pauline's, right?" "If I study late, I'll have to sleep over," Jane said, "won't the rest of you?" "I will," Lisa said. Everyone was nodding. Pauline stopped crying and tried to smile. "Thanks," she said, "but nobody can stay with me forever, you know." "So what," Lois said, "in a couple of weeks he'll be cooled out. Then, if he starts making threats a few weeks later, we'll do it again. And all that studying sure isn't going to hurt us any." "It won't hurt me, either," Pauline said. "Maybe it'll pull my grades up and keep my father off my case longer."

MEDIATION AT THE INTERFACE OF QUANDRANTS A AND D

As suggested earlier, mediator is an interface role. The social worker as mediator stands at the interface between persons whose need for each other seems to be obscure. In addition to interfacing between persons whose need for each other is identical, which is the case for mediating in Quadrant A, in instances where complementarity is at issue, the mediator also stands at the interface between clients and others, between Quadrant A and Quadrant D.

In the following example of work at the interface of Quadrants A and D, a social worker in a prison takes the role of mediator to help an inmate and a volunteer who teaches hairdressing to rediscover their complementary need for each other and arrive at a mutually beneficial resolution to their conflict.

The social worker opens the interview by reaching for information with an open-ended question, then gets with the feelings the client expresses. To explore what happened, the worker again asks an open-ended question. After the client describes the situation, the social worker gives her some relevant information, asks a closed-ended question to obtain an important detail, then gives information again, this time outlining what it is that she can do to help.

> Chris came in and sat down. "Hi," I said, "What's up?" "Things are all coming down on me," she said. I said, "That's terrible!" "Yeah," she said. "I just messed myself up but good." "How?" I asked. "I blew up at Mrs. Geery and she threw me out of the hairdressing program. I really *need* that license to make parole, and I only have a month and a half to go before I qualify to take the test. Can you get me back in it? I really need it!" "It's up to Mrs. Geery, not me; so I can't get you back in it . . ." "Then what am I going to do?" She started to cry. I waited, then I asked if she had talked to Mrs. Geery since the blowup, and she said, "How could I? She doesn't want any more of me after the names I called her. I was hoping you could talk to her."
>
> I told Chris that what I can do, if she wants me to, is ask Mrs. Geery to sit down and talk with her about what happened and how badly she wants to get back in the program. "Then," I said, "If you're both willing, I can set up a meeting between the two of you and try to help you talk to each other." I'll do *anything* to get back in," she said.

Next, the worker speaks with Mrs. Geery. In the interaction below, the worker starts by giving relevant information, then listens suppor-

tively. Although initially averse to it, when the worker reminds Mrs.
Geery of a potential motivation for agreeing to talk with Chris, and
challenges her to act on it, Mrs. Geery agrees.

> I went to see Mrs. Geery and told her about Chris coming to me
> and what I said to her, "Look," Mrs. Geery said, "I come here
> without getting paid, and I work hard to help these girls learn a
> vocation they can count on when they get out. I even get most of
> them licensed. But I don't put up with abuse, and that's what Chris
> was doing to me when I kicked her out. Did she tell you the names
> she called me?" "Not exactly," I said, "But she told me she called
> you names." "She did, huh," Mrs. Geery said with eyebrows raised
> in a surprised look. "She's got quite a mouth on her!" "Yeah," I
> agreed, "And you've worked with a lot of the angry women we've
> had here over the years." "That's right," she said. "And you turned
> a lot of them around as I hear it," I said. "That's right, too," she said,
> then, "Oh, I see what you're getting at. Well, it won't work." "You
> mean your pride in turning around angry women and sending them
> out with a vocation isn't strong enough to get you to just sit down
> with Chris and talk about what happened and how it happened and
> what you were feeling and what she was feeling?" I asked with a
> smile. She smiled too and said she'd talk with Chris but that I
> shouldn't expect her to take Chris back. I assured her that was
> entirely up to her, that my concern was that they talk together, not
> what they decided.

Following these individual meetings, the social worker arranged a
joint meeting. The excerpt below shows the process of that meeting
and the way in which the worker mediated the engagement. As you
read through the work, note the way in which the worker connects
the two persons on a feeling level and how that feeling link seems to
lead quickly to a solution that is apparently satisfactory to both. More
will be said about this later.

The social worker starts the session by summarizing the reason
each participant agreed to meet with the other, and asks if these
reasons are accurate. When talk between Chris and Mrs. Geery begins, the worker redirects their messages from herself to the other,
and listens while they interact. At an appropriate moment, the worker
reaches for Mrs. Geery's feelings and redirects her affective expres-

sion to Chris. She then reaches for a feeling link from Chris, and redirects Chris's acknowledgment to Mrs. Geery. Chris and Mrs. Geery do the rest.

I set up a meeting, and when all three of us got together <u>I looked at Chris and said, "You're here because you wanted a chance to talk with Mrs. Geery about the blowup: what you were thinking and feeling and some of your thoughts and feelings since then. Is that right?"</u> She nodded. Then I turned to Mrs. Geery and said, <u>"And you agreed to come and listen to what Chris has to say, mainly because you've turned around a lot of angry women since you've been here and that means a lot to you."</u> "It certainly does," she said. "And this is the first time any of my women called me vile names, and in my own classroom, in front of everybody there!" She was looking at me when she spoke, so <u>I asked her to tell that to Chris.</u> She turned to Chris and said, "I don't take abuse from anybody!" Chris looked down and said in a small voice, "But you yelled at me first." "Yes, I did," Mrs. Geery said. "You were making the same mistake you made all last week—after I spent more than an hour going over it again and again with you. But I never called you names and I never cussed at you." Then there was silence.

Chris broke the silence. She looked at me and asked, "What am I going to do? That's my future down the drain." <u>"I told her to tell that to Mrs. Geery.</u> She turned to Mrs. Geery and said that the hairdressing program was all she had. Mrs. Geery told her she should have thought about that before she started cussing and calling names. <u>I looked at Mrs. Geery and said, "Being called names can really hurt."</u> "It did hurt," she said to me. "I felt this big" (holding her thumb and forefinger about an inch or so apart). "Tell Chris," I said, nodding. Turning to Chris, she said, "You cut me down to nothing." <u>I asked Chris if she ever felt like Mrs. Geery did, chopped down to nothing.</u> She looked at me and nodded. I motioned her to tell Mrs. Geery, and she did. She told her that her husband used to cut her down bad and smack her around, right in front of her parents and her children. Instantly, Mrs. Geery looked at Chris and said, "Don't you ever let him or anybody else do that to you again!" Chris looked a little startled. "Nobody has a right to humiliate you," Mrs. Geery continued. "And that's what it is, being humiliated." Chris got a little teary and nodded. There was another silence.

This time Mrs. Geery broke the silence. She said, in a kind of sarcastic tone, "So now you expect me to take you back in the program." "I hope you will," Chris said softly. "Well, I'm not going to do that. I've got my pride and I don't want anybody to get the idea they can treat me that way. The only way I'll take you back is for you to spend the next month washing heads and sweeping up. If you're willing to do that, and you do it well, when the month is up I'll take you back in the program." Chris nodded and said, "I'll do it; thanks . . . and I really am sorry."

Many of the mutually satisfactory outcomes of mediating, such as in the example above, seem to flow from the social worker's use of all or a part of a particular sequence of skills.[6] Ordinarily the sequence begins with the worker reaching for the feelings of Person A. Since the worker was the one who invited A to express feelings, A understandably directs the feeling statement to the worker. At this point, the worker does not get with A's feelings as she would do if she were meeting with A individually. Rather, the worker directs A to express the feelings to Person B. Once A has done this, the social worker immediately reaches for a feeling link from B. For example, she may ask B if B ever felt the way A was feeling. When B starts to talk about an instance in which she had feelings similar to A's, B would tend to respond to the worker, again because it was the worker who questioned B. So now the worker asks B to tell the story to A. This sequential pattern of reaching for feelings, redirecting them, reaching for a feeling link and redirecting the response is then repeated with regard to B. The worker reaches for B's feelings, redirects B's response from herself to Person A, reaches for a feeling link from A, then redirects A's reply from herself to Person B.

For all intents and purposes, people seem more responsive to each other when their own feelings are attended to with genuine concern and their capacity for empathy is tapped. Perhaps this is what at least partially accounts for the apparent success, in many instances, of the skill pattern described above. To date, the evidence is impressionistic. If further study supports the efficacy of the pattern, the need for advocacy, the role elaborated in the next chapter, may well be reduced in frequency—to the benefit of all concerned.

In the following episode, the feeling-oriented skill pattern described above is again demonstrated. In this instance, a social worker tries to help an AIDS victim and his estranged parents talk to each other about their pain.

Nick's parents haven't spoken to him since he told them he was gay about six years ago. Now he's dying and he thinks that maybe if they know that, they'll come to say good-bye. When I asked him if he's tried to call them over the years he said yes, but when they heard his voice, they hung up. He said that once he tried from the hospital, but they hung up before he could tell them he was in the hospital. He asked me if I'd call and tell them. I said I would.

When I called his parents, his mother burst out crying and his father told me not to call and upset Mrs. Wayne again; then he hung up. About 40 minutes later, though, his mother called me back and said they'd come on Sunday. I told Nick the whole thing: the call I made, his parents' responses, and his mother's call back. He seemed excited, but scared, too. I commented on that, and he agreed. He asked me if I would be there with him when they came and I said I would, that what I'd do is try to help him and his parents talk to each other about what they are thinking and feeling. I didn't have to ask the elder Waynes if it was O.K. for me to be there because Mrs. Wayne already told me on the phone that they'd like me to be there if I could.

The worker accepts Mrs. Wayne's request that she be present as her contract with the Waynes. But she neither told them what her role would be, nor did she explicitly check any of it out with Mr. Wayne. And as the reader will see, this latter omission becomes problematic as soon as the transaction begins.

I met the Waynes in the lobby and showed them to Nick's room. They both seemed a bit nervous. Just outside the door, they hesitated. "A first meeting after six years of silence can be frightening," I said, quietly. Mrs. Wayne nodded, swallowed hard, and pushed the door open. I held the door for Mr. Wayne and followed him in. For a few moments there was dead silence, then Nick said "Hi." They looked at him, but said nothing. I motioned them over to the three chairs I had put in a semicircle to Nick's bed. Mrs. Wayne sat down. When I motioned Mr. Wayne over a second time, he said, "No; this is *her* visit. I'll just stand back here." "Dad," Nick said to him. Mr. Wayne looked down at the floor and didn't respond. I made a quick decision to let that be for now and dragged one of the chairs over to the door so Mr. Wayne could sit. Then I sat down next to Mrs. Wayne. "You're thin," Mrs. Wayne said to Nick. "Yeh," Nick replied. Silence. Mrs. Wayne turned to me and said, "I don't know what to say to him." "Tell him that," I replied. She gave an embarrassed smile, then told Nick she didn't know what to say to him. He told her she didn't have to say anything, that just being here was enough. He extended his hand. "Is it O.K. to touch him?" she asked me. "Yes," I said, "You won't get AIDS from holding his hand." "I wouldn't ask you to do anything that would hurt you, Mom," Nick said. "The hell you wouldn't!" Mr. Wayne shouted angrily from his spot near the door. He was standing up now. "Bud . . .," Mrs. Wayne began. "No," Mr. Wayne interrupted. Then there was a long, loud silence while Mr. Wayne and Nick stared at each other.

The worker reached for the Waynes' feelings as they hesitated outside their son's door, and once inside, she moved to position everyone for the interaction to come. But her oversight during the contract phase came home to roost. She could not hold Mr. Wayne to any prior agreement since she did not have a contract with him. Apparently recognizing this, she quickly assessed the potential consequences of the intervention choices remaining open to her and decided to allow Mr. Wayne to be present, yet physically distant. And at least up to this point, she chose not to engage him. The worker restricted her attention to Mrs. Wayne and Nick, redirecting the former to the latter, and providing information.

When Mr. Wayne sat down again, Nick turned to his mother and asked her how she'd been keeping. She said she'd been well, even doing aerobics at church. This was followed by some talk about Nick's condition and what the various physicians had said. Then Mrs. Wayne said, "There's no cure, is there?" Nick shook his head "no." Her eyes filled with tears. "You're crying," I said to her. "Yes," she said; "I don't want him to die." "Tell Nick that," I said softly. "Oh, Nicky," she sobbed, "I don't want you to die." There was more silence.

Nick broke the silence. "I was afraid you wouldn't come, Mom," he said. "I was afraid you stopped loving me." She looked at him. "You can't imagine what you did to us. We thought we knew you. We had such dreams." Her voice broke a little. Shattered dreams can be so painful," I understated. She nodded. "Nick," I said, "Have you ever felt a little like your mother has—pain when a dream falls apart?" Nick nodded. "Tell her about it," I said. "Mom, remember I was first in my class in med. school?" he began. "How could I forget?" she said. "Well," he continued, "I didn't get the residency at Crawford-Lyons. Even St. Andrews turned me down. I felt betrayed, Mom. I still do. The pain hasn't gone away." She looked at him sadly. "I'm sorry, Nicky. You wanted that so much. . . . And my pain, it never goes away either," she said.

At that moment, Mr. Wayne started to walk out of the room. "Dad," Nick said, "Please don't leave." Mr. Wayne pushed the door open and turned to go. I asked him to wait a minute. "Nick," I said, "Tell your father how his walking out makes you feel." "I feel like he can't . . .," Nick began. "Tell him", I interrupted. "I feel like you can't stand me, and it hurts more than I can ever say," Nick said. "Mr. Wayne, how does what Nick just said make you feel?" I asked. "There's nothing he could say that matters to me," Mr. Wayne said. "But you're here!" I said to him. "Only to bring my wife," he replied. "You could have waited in the lobby," I said. "Or just outside this door. But you chose to be in this room." "I'm here for my wife," he said; "That's all." "Dad," Nick said, "I think you came to see me . . . and I'm glad you did. I want you to know I love you." "You don't know what love is!" Mr. Wayne responded, and left the room.

In the sequence above, the social worker reached for Mrs. Wayne's feelings, and when she responded, the worker redirected her message to Nick. Shortly thereafter, the worker again reached for Mrs. Wayne's feelings, but this time, after Mrs. Wayne responded, the worker reached for a feeling link from Nick, then redirected his message to Mrs. Wayne. A moment later, Mr. Wayne started to leave; Nick spoke to him, and the man did not respond. The worker then reached for affective information from Nick, and in the same statement, redirected Nick's message to his father. She followed this by reaching for affective information from the father, confronting his distortion, and confronting it a second time when he continued to deny the reality.

Below, the social worker reaches for Nick's feelings, then redirects his message to his mother.

> As soon as the door closed, Mrs. Wayne said, "You have to forgive him, Nicky. He's still so hurt and angry. . . ." "I know he is, Mom," said Nick. "How about you?" "I guess I am, too," she said. "What about you, Nick," I said. "Being rejected by parents can hurt a lot . . . and make you angry." "I used to feel that way," he said. "Tell your mother," I said. "Mom," Nick said, "I don't have time to be angry."

Nick died five days later. Both of his parents were in the room.

8. The Advocate

From the earliest efforts of social reformers committed to the social justice movement, from Dorothea Dix, Lillian Wald,[1] Jane Addams,[2] and Jacob Riis,[3] to present-day centers for battered wives, rape victims, the homeless, and other vulnerable populations, social work has always been concerned with obtaining and guarding the rights of people. Heightened political consciousness of the late 1960s and early 1970s generated the desire to translate this concern into action. That persons at risk should have the basic necessities of life became an imperative for social workers. During these years the dimensions of the advocate role were articulated with increasing specificity,[4] resulting in the emergence of a clearly recognizable set of expectations for the behavior of social workers when it was important to challenge inhumane conditions. With the advent of the conservative 1980s, however, with enormous budget cuts in the social welfare arena, the role of advocate became even more necessary yet less likely to be played. Social workers, themselves, were at risk. Advocacy for oppressed persons never endeared the advocate to the larger community!

According to Richan,[5] the basis for advocacy in social work is protection of the clients' rights. That is to say, "the advocate steps in to help the individual victim or the class of victims obtain their entitlement."[6] In practice, that is largely an effort to make service systems (hospitals, housing authorities, schools, social agencies) more responsive to clients and their needs, but it could also include the unresponsive slumlord, the harried schoolteacher, the overprotective mother, or the corner grocer.

The role of advocate is predicated on the assumption of a conflict situation. Given that role-taking is reciprocal,[7] that people choose roles to complement the roles others have already taken, action on this assumption invites the target of action to take the role of adversary. If the target of advocacy accepts the role of adversary and plays it well, however, the goal will not be realized. This is the advocacy paradox. Social workers take the role of advocate because they presume the other to be an adversary, and in taking the role they initiate a process which could end in a self-fulfilling prophecy.[8] The encounter can quickly become a contest in which neither side can bear to lose. And it is the client who gets lost, as each of the warring parties seeks total defeat of the other.

If social workers are to maximize clients' opportunities to obtain their entitlement, the workers should take the role of advocate only if their activities in other social work roles (broker, mediator) have failed to produce the desired outcome. And when workers do take the role of advocate, they must compensate for the reciprocal role message to reverse the self-fulfilling prophecy. Richan and Rosenberg allude to the need for compensation and provide some heuristics:

> An important principle in advocacy is making it easy for the target system to say "yes." For instance, the put-down—humiliation of a decision-maker—may be personally gratifying to the advocate, but it is the surest way to build a wall of resistance. The advocate needs to be prepared to help the target system save face. Related to this is the need of the target system to justify its actions. The advocate can help in supplying the rationale for a positive response.[9]

In a bureaucratic organization, the power of the advocate is the potential power to escalate the problem, to raise it to higher levels in the hierarchy. Thus the point of entry into the target system is critical. To maximize this potential power, the advocate should enter the system at the lowest possible hierarchical level and proceed upward until a concession is obtained. The problem should be escalated slowly, with personnel at each succeeding level recognized and afforded ample opportunity to contain the problem at that level by making a positive response. This is consistent with the principle of least contest discussed in chapter 3. In addition to maximizing the social worker's bargaining power, this procedure minimizes alienation of, and consequent subversion and/or retaliation against the client by, line workers who have to implement whatever concessions are obtained at higher levels.

When a concession is made and the benefits to which the client is entitled are obtained, it is imperative that the social work advocate shift her stance. She should engage the other as a partner in outrage over the violation of client rights rather than as a defeated adversary. While this is directed toward helping the other to save face, it is neither gimmickry nor manipulation. To the contrary, it is a human response to the human feelings which concession engenders. Goffman has elaborated an array of strategies that are employed to help losers keep their self-image intact and adjust to situations following defeat or concession.[10] Implicit in this discussion are such activities as listening, helping them get out their anger, helping them preserve the illusion that they wanted the change, and so forth.

Such deliberate shifts in the advocate's behavior not only help the ones who have conceded to maintain their status, but they pave the way for important cooperative action to modify or create a structure through which all present and future clients can obtain their entitlement without needing an advocate. This is consistent with the principle of maximizing supports in the client's environment. From a structural perspective, the aim of advocacy is always universalistic as opposed to an exceptionalistic aim of obtaining this concession for this client at this time.

The Other Side of Advocacy

In general, the clients of the social work advocate are relatively powerless. That is, their resources (money, political influence) are not equal to those of the withholding party. In fact, clients are frequently dependent upon the resources doled out by the more powerful party. Thus, while the consequences of not receiving withheld benefits may be deleterious to the social welfare of the clients, the consequences of opposing that powerful system upon which they are dependant may be even harder for them to bear. The tenant who engages in a rent strike against a slumlord who refuses to have faulty plumbing or wiring repaired, for example, may get the plumbing or wiring repaired, but may then have to live with such retaliatory measures as no heat, or eviction should a single rent payment be late. Worse yet, the strike may not be successful, and the tenants may have to bear the landlord's retaliatory action in addition to the faulty plumbing or wiring.

Since the social worker can never promise a successful outcome without repercussions, the client is often faced with what amounts to a Hobson's choice. And this is the basis for ambivalence on the part of the client in response to the social worker's offer of advocacy. There is a fearful "no" beneath the most enthusiastic "yes," and a "yes" beneath the most adamant "no." And because it is the client who must bear the consequences, it is the client who must decide whether or not to oppose the powerful other. It is therefore incumbent upon the social worker to raise the other side of advocacy. That is, the social worker should take the role of conferee to help the clients entertain the possibility of defeat and recognize their ambivalence. The worker should provide them with information regarding alternative actions from which they might choose and the possible consequences for themselves of each. The young adult who wants to move away from domineering parents, for example, has to entertain the possibility of needing money and having the parents refuse to provide it, or needing to move back in and having to bear the "I-told-you-sos." The social worker is ethically bound to engage the client in a full discussion, even if—especially if—through the process of that discussion the client decides "no." Perhaps this is the hardest part for the enthusiastic and idealistic social worker, but it speaks to the heart of client self-determination, to a genuine respect for the rights of people to decide their own destiny.

Should the client decide "yes," social work advocacy can be done in Quadrant D, Quadrant B, or both. In Quadrant D, the social work advocate argues for the client's entitlement. That is, the worker directly engages the party or parties presumably violating the rights of the client and intercedes in the client's behalf. In Quadrant B, on the other hand, the social worker organizes those clients whose rights in a given area have been violated and mobilizes them to press for their own entitlement. Whenever a situation calls for advocacy, the worker needs to choose either D-type, B-type, or some combination of the two.

Since the aim of advocacy is to obtain the benefits to which the clients are entitled, we propose potential for accomplishing this aim as the primary criterion for determining the particular form of advocacy the worker should take in any given instance. Like all social workers, we value the positive experience which people can have as they work together and take action in their own behalf, even if they do not succeed in accomplishing their manifest task. But when the rights of people are at stake, we do not value the psychological experience above task accomplishment. In other words, when situational factors and political reality make D-type advocacy (see the Principle of Least Contest) seem more strategic, we recommend that the worker use it, even though it may not promote the positive feelings associated with self-help. Moreover, we believe that the positive feelings associated with accordance of one's rights are more real and more lasting, irrespective of the extent to which one has obtained it through one's own efforts.

THE ADVOCATE IN QUADRANT D

As indicated above, advocacy in Quadrant D involves speaking in the client's behalf. And it should be noted that in some instances the process need not be rife with interpersonal conflict and confrontation. Sometimes, requisite change can be obtained with nothing more than a straightforward description of the perceived problems and suggestions regarding possible solutions. Consistent with the Principle of Least Contest, therefore, efforts to advocate in Quadrant D should start this way whenever possible. If description and suggestion are not sufficient to produce necessary change, the social worker can *then* shift to argument.

In the example of advocacy below, description and suggestion are sufficient. One can wonder if this is somewhat facilitated by the social worker's operating assumption that no malice is or was intended.

Mr. Davis, a deaf man who had been laid off work by a furniture manufacturing company several weeks ago reported on his regular day to sign for his unemployment check. Files called "Claims Records Cards" are kept on each claimant, and when a file gets lost,

which is not exactly infrequent, a duplicate card is made and marked
"DUMMY." When Mr. Davis came to the counter, I pulled his file
and found "DUMMY" written across the top in big red letters.

I'm sure the person who made that duplicate card didn't see any
connection between the claimant's deafness and the word "dummy"
on the card, but I am equally sure that Mr. Davis did. I made him a
new card marked "DUPLICATE," and at the next staff meeting I
described what had happened and we agreed that there would be
no more "DUMMY" claims cards in the office, only "DUPLICATES."

In the following example of advocacy in Quadrant D, description of
the problem and suggestions to alleviate it were not enough. So the
social work advocate shifted to argument. The episode began in the
Seniors Building of the Harrison Housing Development. While there
for other reasons, the worker became aware of the great concern
many residents had about security in the building at night. The worker
was surprised to hear it because the building is required to have a
guard on duty in the lobby twenty-four hours per day, and this was
the primary reason that elderly people chose to live there.

When I asked how long they had the night security problem,
Mrs. M explained that it had only recently come about, that the
evening guard "disappears" for long periods of time. Mrs. L asked
me to talk to the manager for them because when they tell him
about problems all he does is tell them not to worry, that he'll take
care of it. But he doesn't, they told me. And they also said he won't
even come to look at what's going on and talk with them about it.
Several other people verified this, saying many have called him with
various problems and all he says is okay, don't worry, you have my
word. "So what good is his word?" one of the men said. Many of
them thought that the manager might listen to them if I approached
him and told him how important their concerns were because I'm a
professional, and would I at least try for them. . . . I said I would
try.

The next day I visited and talked with Mr. F, the manager, in his
office. After my informing him of the senior citizens' concerns about
security, Mr. F replied, "I don't think they have any real problem,
but I'll come over just to pacify them." I said, "They don't want to
be pacified. They want to have the security they pay for and to

which they are entitled as tenants". He didn't say anything, so I added, "It's a pathetic situation when people who are elderly and in need of a safe place to live cannot look to management for help in providing it". Mr. F seemed somewhat taken aback. "I'm sorry I used the word 'pacify,' " he said, "but I've been very busy all day with tenants' problems." Then he told me Monday is the best day for him, and would I please post a notice on the bulletin board saying he'll be there to listen to them at noon. I said it would be beneficial if the officer in charge of the security forces could be there also so he would be able to personally hear their concerns and assure them of positive remedies that will be taken. Mr. F said he didn't think that would be possible, but he declined to elaborate. As there were several tenants waiting to see him regarding other matters, I did not press this point.

At noon on Monday, about forty residents were gathered in the arts and crafts room. Mr. F arrived and, much to my surprise, he was accompanied by the chief security officer, a Mr. S. I commented on this to Mr. F and he said, "After you left me on Friday, I thought about what you said and came to the conclusion that if anyone from the Development is in need of security, it should be the senior citizens". Mr. F added that he also thought that it would be important for Mr. S to be present, so even though he was off duty, he telephoned him at his home and he agreed to come. I then thanked Mr. F for his concern and told him that I know the tenants will appreciate both his presence and Mr. S's.

The meeting was very productive as many of the problems, especially the main one centering on the guard not being on duty at night, were made known to Mr. F and Mr. S. Mr. F told the group that if this situation ever occurs again they should feel free to call him at his home, the number of which is listed in the directory. Mr. S then informed the group that he is now instructing the guard on duty to lock the main doors whenever he makes the rounds of the fifteen floors and also will equip him with a walkie-talkie. Mr. S also reiterated Mr. F's statement that he should be contacted immediately if a guard is discovered to be absent from his post in the lobby and the doors are open.

Following the question and answer session I suggested that since the guards are not familiar with all of the senior citizens' relatives and friends who might come to visit, it would be a good idea for each tenant who has a phone to leave the number at the desk. That way the guard could telephone them prior to giving anyone permission to enter the elevator. This suggestion was approved wholeheartedly not only by the group but by Mr. F and Mr. S also.

Below is an example of advocacy in Quadrant D which highlights the use of subtle persuasion. It further demonstrates the Principle of Least Contest in a seemingly clear-cut adversarial situation, and illustrates the procedure of embracing the adversary as an ally just as soon as he changes his posture and agrees to help. Notice, too, that the social worker did her homework with respect to learning at least one of the major values of her opponent, and that use of this knowledge was probably the key to the outcome obtained.

Mr. and Mrs. Arnold, their four-year-old son, and two-year-old daughter, were made homeless after fire gutted the four-room house that had belonged to Mr. Arnold's father and grandfather before him. Both Arnolds worked for minimum wage at a fast food place in the neighborhood. To manage child care, one worked the first shift and the other the second shift. They "got by," but they couldn't afford insurance, so when the house went, it went. They found an apartment not too far from work that cost $300 per month and figured they could afford that if they were very careful. But the manager said they had to pay $200 security deposit plus the first and last month's rent before moving in. They told the manager they could pay the rent every month and gradually pay the security deposit, then the last month, but he said they can't do it that way. While they were looking, Mrs. Arnold missed her shift and lost a day's pay. She stayed at a neighbor's, with the children sleeping on the floor, until Mr. Arnold finished his shift. Then, carrying the children, they walked to the nearest shelter, three miles away. It was much too late. The shelter was full and closed for the night. So they went to an all night movie.

By the time I met them at Ryecross Shelter, only a week and a half after the fire, Mr. Arnold was still working—washing himself and shaving at a gas station bathroom—and Mrs. Arnold and the children looked tired and a little dirty. She said they look for apartments most of the day, but that without her working, they couldn't even pay $300 per month like they could have last week when they first looked. Besides, she said, when people with apartments see them looking like they do now, they won't rent to them anyway.

I called the place they found last week for $300 and told the manager what had happened since. I told him if he'd accept them, I knew they had the first month's rent to give him and they'd be able to pay every month because they had steady jobs—if he'd only suspend the security deposit and the last month's rent until they could save it up—about five weeks for the security deposit and about three months after that for the last month's rent: all told, about four months. I said that in four months they'd be all caught up and he'd have saved a family, including the physical and psychological health of two toddlers. "No way," he said; "and we don't want their kind." (I don't think I'm especially naive, but I felt so ashamed that a human being like myself could say such a thing about such decent people as the Arnolds!)

The following afternoon I called the manager back and told him how sorry I was for putting him on the spot like I did. I said it must be hard for him to have people doing that to him all the time. He agreed it was. I said I knew he was a churchgoing man because I'd seen him at St. Francis when I was there with Catholic children from a local shelter. I said it was unfair of me to lean on him, and I hoped he would understand that I was just doing my job. He said he did. He asked me about the children I sometimes brought there (to St. Francis), and I explained how hard it was for families on the streets to clean up their kids—clothes and all—let alone clean up themselves and their clothes, what clothes they have, in time for church. I said, "You know parents; no matter what, they want the best for their kids. So when I can on a Sunday morning, I go to one of the shelters and take the kids to a local church." I told him the great part was that no matter what church I took them to, the people always made them feel welcome.

Somewhat hesitantly, he asked me if the family I was talking to him about yesterday was Catholic. I said yes. I also said I'd found a place that would provide the $200 security deposit for them (I figured a couple of churches would kick in) and that since Mr. Arnold was still working, they had the first month's rent in the bank and wouldn't have trouble with the rent each month because as soon as they had a place to live, Mrs. Arnold could go back to work, too. But, I told him, they still can't come up with the extra $300 for that "last month's rent" stipulation, so the apartment at his place is obviously out. I guessed that, like many families these days, the Arnolds would soon join the chronically homeless. "They'll have to," I said. "It's rough on the streets, and Mr. Arnold cares about his family. So, soon he'll have to quit his job in order to stay with his wife and kids in order to protect them. And there's no way out of the hole after that. But there are lots of families in that situation," I said. "It's nothing new. Rotten shame, though, isn't it?" I said. He said it was criminal.

He said he wished something could be done about all the people in that situation. I said I wished so, too; that people like he and I really care about people. Then he said that at least he could try to help the Arnolds out. "How?", I asked. He said that with a security deposit and the first month's rent in advance, he could let them move into the apartment they had seen and liked. I told him it was fantastic that he'd be able to do that.

THE ADVOCATE IN QUADRANT B

Advocacy in Quadrant B requires social workers to organize clients to protest en masse the withholding of particular needed resources from them and a whole category of persons who share their plight; to challenge en masse policy that excludes them and a whole category of persons who share their plight; to pressure en masse local government officials for increased options and opportunities for them and a whole category of persons who share their plight; even to vote en masse as a bloc in order to impact the platforms of those seeking public office the next time around.

To some extent, working in Quadrant B tends to minimize the risks of advocacy for clients. As Germain and Gitterman indicate,

> Having greater visibility, group action gains institutional attention and concern, and militates against individual isolation and reprisals. Client groups can express their grievances through various forms of protest such as sit-ins, vigils, marches, rent strikes, picketing, the use of mass

media, and engaging the interest of a political figure . . . These actions are intended to increase clients' bargaining power to induce organizational responsiveness. At times, the mere threat of adversarial action and its potential consequences may be sufficient.[11]

A current example of the urgent need for advocacy in Quadrant B involves the exclusion of gay men afflicted with AIDS from most nursing homes and hospice facilities. At the moment, there are some social workers, straight and gay, who are trying to organize gay communities to protest the withholding of adequate care and challenge the policies that exclude them from the services they desperately need. To date, small inroads are being made. Obviously, this issue must also and ultimately be addressed at the macro level (Quadrant C). It is at the micro level, where people who hurt can be seen and heard, that each instance of inhumanity must be confronted via B-style advocacy.

THE ADVOCATE IN QUADRANT A

Often overlooked as a form of advocacy, giving information to clients can empower them when the information is consequential and not publicized. The more information people have that is immediately relevant to their situations, the better able they are to make informed decisions and exercise a measure of control over what happens to them. It is in this sense that the provision of information empowers clients.

For the most part, consequential information that is not widely known pertains to rules. Medicare, for example, has a "thirty-foot" rule, and social workers in hospitals empower clients for whom this rule is germane when they tell them that if they walk thirty feet or more, their Medicare benefits will end. Similarly, social workers empower teenage clients when they tell them what can and cannot be kept confidential before significant talk begins. Clients seeking food stamps are empowered by social workers who give them advance information regarding the range of pertinent eligibility requirements; and clients wishing to regain custody of their children after securing employment are empowered when their social workers tell them in advance the assessment criteria that are used to make such determinations.

Consideration and trial of empowerment via advocacy in Quadrant A moved one social worker in a parole office to write the following:

> I am not involved in clandestine acts, but then again, I've learned to keep my mouth shut . . . but by not asking, and not violating policy, I find I can share information with my clients which definitely opens up more choices to them. I let them know that any choice they make is their own and I try not to steer them in any one direction.
>
> I sit and laugh as I write this because during the past eight months I have become what some would consider an organizational radical. I usually have thought in terms of not biting the hand that feeds me. I now think in terms of reshaping the hand which touches my clients.

PART FOUR

Second-Order Work

9. The Case Manager

What is Case Management?

Case management has been described as both concept and process. As a concept, it is the system of relationships between clients, service providers, and administrators. As a process, it is the provision of services which facilitates a client's functioning at as normal a level as possible.[1] Case management has also been called both a problem-solving practice and the system that includes this practice plus all the needed administrative supports, the systemic arrangements, and the formal and informal community resources.[2]

We see these double-barreled definitions as indicative of the uncertain status of case management at the present time. Is it a policy-planner's dream? A management tool? A special kind of service delivery practice? Is it micro? Or macro? Or merely a new occupational title for what social workers always knew how to do? A recent descriptive article on case management claimed:

> At the level of service delivery, social caseworkers and social service workers are most directly involved with clients. Two sets of techniques constitute their technological base: case manaagement and *clerical* skills."[3] (emphasis added)

A typo? Close inspection of this statement and the article's Table 1 suggests the word should have been "clinical" rather than "clerical." Two letters. What a difference! Maybe it isn't an error!

With *clinical's* roots in medicine, tendrils into pathology, and adoption by the person-changing therapies, it now possesses a grand status and has crept into social work's vocabulary to stand for all of *direct practice*. There is more than semantic confusion here. There is turf.

Clinical (and clinical societies) connotes a specialized therapeutic orientation. Perhaps clerical *is* more to the point. Case managers have much accounting and paper work to do.

The case manager has been called the human link between the person and the system to ensure the provision of effective community support,[4] one who works to maintain a facilitative physical and social environment for persons in need. It may be the first field of mental health practice initiated and defined by administrators and policy planners instead of by clinicians.[5]

We see case management as *second-order work*. That is, it is a service orientation that makes use of the four roles we have already elaborated in other chapters—conferee, broker, mediator, and advocate. Its special distinction, as we shall discuss in this chapter, derives from its emergence in present day history as a versatile service response to the practice exigencies of these times. The case manager makes use of the orientation, practice principles, roles, and helping behaviors described as the structural approach. Thus the structural approach may be directed toward this particular, special purpose.

Case management is, in fact, the fastest developing direct service work of the 1980s. It encompasses a cluster of activities also claimed by nurses, vocational counselors, and others. The professions are competing at the present time, conceptually and practically, for major leadership in providing case management. One recent national survey of staffs of private case management firms for elderly clients found MSWs to be the major professionals employed.[6] The social work profession, with its history and societal mandate, its value base, its attention and commitment to person-*and*-environment, and its practice know-how should lead exploration, refinement, and evaluation of case management.

CASE MANAGEMENT FUNCTIONS

In the case management literature five functions are usually cited as critical: assessment, planning, linking, monitoring, and advocacy.[7] We shall describe them briefly.

ASSESSMENT. Assessment aims at appraising the client's current and potential strengths, weaknesses, needs, and interests. The worker must know the client's situation, level of functioning, strength of supports, resources, attitude toward services, and so forth. This information helps determine the direction of action for the work together, the goals, and the particular activities which may lead to attaining them.

PLANNING. A service plan developed with the client, and often requiring interdisciplinary team meetings, includes such things as a listing of needed services, short and long-term objectives, actions to take to reach goals, agencies to contact, time frames for activities, and identification of potential barriers to service utilization and delivery.

LINKING. Once a plan has been organized, the client must be linked with needed services or resources, with agencies, even with friends, neighbors, and relatives. Such connections involve more than referrals to an agency; many clients are unable to make necessary connections themselves. The case manager must do whatever is necessary to ensure that the client receives the service, e.g., take the client to the intake appointment. Perhaps the case manager can find a volunteer to help the client on a regular basis. For example, a high school student needed to have kidney dialysis three afternoons a week at a time when his father worked. With the worker's help and ongoing monitoring, a retired neighbor was recruited to accompany the boy. The linkage was "life-saving"—both ways! In chapter 6, "THE BROKER," a system such as this is called a "trade unit," predicated on resource bartering.

MONITORING. The primary goal of monitoring is assurance that services remain suited to the client. The case manager must maintain continuous contact with the client and service provider until all agree that service is no longer appropriate. Through the monitoring, the client's progress toward meeting the service plan's objectives or changing the plan may be evaluated.

ADVOCACY. Advocacy is described in the literature as interceding on behalf of an individual to assure equity, for a specific client or for any larger group or class to which the client might belong.

We prefer viewing advocacy as a separate special role, different from a function or set of tasks, since it rests on certain unique assumptions and is defined by specific expectations. This is elaborated in chapter 8, "The Advocate." Emphasis here is on power and pressure, on pursuit of particular outcomes through employing strategic thinking and tactical actions. Two different types of advocacy are

possible: case advocacy focuses on influencing folk-support and service systems on behalf of particular persons' needs, Quadrant D-type
advocacy; class advocacy focuses on influencing these systems in
relation to their general functioning, Quadrant B-type advocacy.

Other functions or roles for the case manager have been cited in
the emerging literature: diagnostician, case coordinator, expeditor,
community organizer, consultant, counselor, and therapist. Only
"therapist" has caused some controversy, especially in the community
mental health arena. It is seen by some as a threat to the traditional
mental health role of therapist, as a downgrading of clinical work, as
a cheaper service that requires less knowledge and a lower salary than
do "real" therapists.

It must be obvious by now that this newly emerging "cluster of
activities" is far from uniformly conceptualized in the literature. To
some persons case management may be a role or a function or a set of
functions, or a cluster of activities. We prefer to think of it (much as
we think of group work) as second-order work within the structural
approach, i.e., as an arrangement of the basic elements of the structural approach to accomplish certain goals.

THE "CASE MANAGER" TITLE

Case management work appears to be very like the case agents' and
settlement workers' work of a century ago. At least certain tasks and
activities seem comparable. Clearly, the community-based focus and
home visits are reminiscent; the emphasis on "social diagnosis," on
resource development, on linkage and filling in gaps in services, and
on client advocacy are not new. While yesteryear's worker saw to it
that the baby was taken to the Well-Baby Clinic, today's case manager
has to advocate that the patient not be discharged from the hospital
prematurely.

Yet, there are many additional complexities and requirements that
go with today's realities. While case management may have a focus
well known to social workers of other times, it is a new occupational
title and a newly conceptualized orientation which arose and received
increased emphasis in the aftermath of the Great Society of the 1960s.

As a response to the proliferation of categorical social programs,
case management evolved out of practical necessity. It was an effort

to have someone stay connected service-wise with the many individuals exited from institutions as part of the deinstitutionalization movement and the normalization mentality of the times. It was a recognition that someone was needed to coordinate services and assure continuity of care for the "transferred" mental hospital patient now in the community.

This someone might have been called: expeditor, primary therapist, continuity agent, service coordinator, broker, ombudsman, patient representative, advocate, systems agent, and—finally—case manager. The "new" role was born in the ambiance surrounding the rise of community psychiatry and community mental health centers, the growing awareness of a burgeoning aging cohort with its service needs, and hopes that monies would be saved (and individuals better served) if services were offered in the community rather than hospitals and nursing homes.

Some History

The need for coordination among services is as old as social work itself. In fact, the Charity Organization Societies (birthplace of social casework) arose in the 1870s partly in response to the lack of coordination among the services of the times. In subsequent years, the impact of urban industrialization with its accompanying demographic shifts, plus uncertain economic/social policies, affected systems-vulnerable persons and required new emphases for social work.

In the 1950s, case conferences became one means of coordinating services for clients, especially those regarded as "multi-problem families." During the 1960s and '70s, increased emphasis was placed on the activities relating to case management and on the social environment's continuing role in individuals' problems. Individual pathology received decreased emphasis. There was a move away from the medical model, and a move toward a legal mentality which emphasized client rights and treatment in least restrictive environments. Although neither a medical nor a legal posture was adequate, the rights emphasis marked a needed shift in the balance of power away from the worker and toward the client.[8]

Mandell recounts the social work profession's history from the

1960s to the 1980s vividly with what she terms "The Blurring Definitions of Social Services."[9] The shifts affecting social work include the federal Office of Economic Opportunity's funding of alternative agencies; the rise of the New Careers movement and community colleges; the federal support for Human Service Education through Title XX training monies; the deinstitutionalization of mental patients to the community and the contracting out of services to private agencies not necessarily part of social work's tradition; the declassifying of social work civil service jobs in many states and the development of job classification standards, clinical societies, and licensure in the states so as to qualify for third party payments from state and private insurance funds. She characterized social work as an old profession compared to the new human service field, as suffering from "hardening of the bureaucracies" yet rooted in a commitment to work with the poor, as having a social vision and a familiarity with social class, race, and gender issues beyond that of other disciplines.

In the 1980s, the pendulum has swung back again from the 1960s and 70s. There was a shift toward decentralized program authority with increased local responsibility for providing and funding human services, reduced federal spending, and the institution of cost containment measures. For the service providers, this brought cutback management, medicalization of community services (for reimbursement purposes), and an entrepreneurial, competitive service delivery system. Research on the impact of this changed federal role cited privatization of the most profitable services, targeting of services to particular clientele based on ability to pay, fragmentation, medicalization of social services (e.g., aging becomes a medical problem), and caregiving functions shifted from the formal delivery systems to home and family.[10]

At the macro or programmatic level, case management aimed at organization coordination and service integration, at dealing with fragmentation and inefficiency. At the micro level, the process emphasized the quickest, most effective, and cost-efficient means to restore the client to adequate performance in the community, or to as much independence as possible. It should achieve linkages between people and resource systems, and ensure service continuity for each client.

The case manager was expected to keep individuals from falling through the cracks of the system or, as Reagan would proclaim at a later time (to make huge social program cutbacks seem palatable), from sliding through the holes in the safety net (1981). This has not happened.

THE ENTREPRENEURIAL '80s

Government funding between the 1960s and 1980 protected the non-profit health and social service agencies so that they need not compete in the marketplace. Now, as nonprofit agencies begin to "sell" their services and operate on the basis of market principles, they are legitimating the system that ultimately will destroy a number of them, and threaten their philosophical orientation as well.[11]

With the increased complexity and vanishing accessibility of health care and social programs, and the experience that medication alone is no miracle for the deinstitutionalized mental patient, the need for more supports for vulnerable persons' survival in the community was obvious. These factors lent urgency to having case managers in the service networks—practitioners who would pursue client-centered goals and continually look out for client entitlements. Such a practitioner will suit well whether in domains of mental health or social care.[12] Both areas need the knowledge and skills known in social work.

To appreciate the complexity confronting case managers and clients in the service provider networks now in the late 1980s, a historical scorecard of the last two decades is needed. Such a review, describing the economic/political trends, reveals the gradual lessening of social work's hegemony over the provision of social services and the powerful influence of the medical profession. The turf struggles of the professionals (social workers, nurses, and other human service workers) which attended the medicalization and privatization of care are classic cases of power politics. Which profession would be salient, i.e., have most authority and responsibility, depended on the favor of the federal and state government planners and the insurance establishment's reimbursement policies. And the bottom line was what would cost least.

Fabricant describes the milieu for case management and social work, lamenting "The Industrialization of Social Work Practice" as assembly line practice. He claims that the situation in the large public sector agency drives toward increasing productivity (quantity) by making the work repetitive and mechanistic with less room for practitioner judgment and skill.[13] One research study of the declassification movement in public welfare agencies concludes that despite clients' preferences for trained case managers with their more "holistic" approach, an integrated service delivery system may be precluded in agencies where services are so compartmentalized among narrowly trained technicians.[14] Community mental health centers are responding to the policy and funding shifts and cutbacks by emphasizing business practices and enhancing efficiency.[15]

These MBA-type emphases and pressures hardly seem conducive to offering complex, quality services. And they take a professional toll. The major response is flight from the governmental bureaucracies by many trained social workers, a 10 percent drop of NASW members in local, state, and federal governments from 1972–1982.[16] With client accountability replaced by financial accountability, many supervisors and administrators are hired for their computer, statistics, and cost-benefit analysis abilities rather than social work expertise. They are more concerned with organization and bureaucracy than with client needs. A notable response to all this is burnout and alienation, a matter much discussed in the literature since the mid-'70s.[17] A recent study comparing job stress and burnout in private practice and mental health counseling centers found private practitioners experienced fewer psychological symptoms, less alienation, and greater satisfaction than did therapists in the centers.[18]

Another development: state human services systems contract with diverse private for-profit agencies to provide certain services, e.g., home health care, halfway houses. It now appears that some private providers form coalitions to eliminate other competing agencies. The craftiest, not necessarily the most quality-conscious, providers prevail in such marketplace service scrambles.

The mood is entrepreneurial now with fiscal binds on the public agencies, e.g., community outreach not being a reimbursable service. Only recently are "indirect services" beginning to be covered in some states by Medicaid and certain private insurance plans. For better or for worse, these contractual arrangements and restricted public services have spawned many new for-profit providers and have supported licensed independent social work practitioners who are ready to assume some case management activities as long as the time involved is reimbursable.

Case Managers and Clients as Partners

American medicine has been described as "oriented toward acute, high-tech care for people with insurance coverage, not toward schizophrenics and retarded persons who often need structured group homes where social and vocational skills are taught."[19] The stage is set for a caring social work case-management system attuned to the needs of such neglected ones.

Case managers and clients are partners facing tough circumstances that demand extensive knowledge, skills, and strategic maneuverings. While clients stand to learn system and support intracacies from case managers, case managers also find much to marvel at and emulate in clients' special savvy in "making-it" with marginal resources. The sharing and caring survival strategies among poor blacks, for example, and the "instinctive networks" of suburban mothers, the car pools and child-watching pools, are support know-hows useful for everyone.[20] One case manager in a public agency found a way for an AFDC mother to hold classes to instruct others on how to stretch buying power through planful use of free coupons.

Surviving The Bureaucracy

The Self Principle of the Structural Approach is crucial to helping case managers maintain a spirit of initiative and some control over their work, of preserving morale in the bureaucracies and other provider systems. Its use is consciousness raising for case managers themselves and is especially important in these times of ever shrinking resources and the mounting unmet need for human services.

While the other principles address the work with clients, related others, the community, and the extra-organizational environment, the Self Principle legitimates the worker's self-interest and concerns vis-à-vis colleagues and within-organization politics. It might also be called the Survival Principle, and should be an antidote to worker burnout.

Key Emphases

Case managers are concerned with outreach and client identification. They work to coordinate services, especially for those who need long-term care, for people who cannot, temporarily or permanently, pursue and coordinate needed resources on their own, and for the underserved. They are most valued in services for the chronic mentally ill client, the elderly, the developmentally disabled, those in health care systems, child welfare, rural communities, public welfare services, and other neglected people. Case managers also are concerned with reforming service delivery systems to make them respond to client need.

As a client sees it, the case manager needs to offer some or all of the following services:

COUNSELOR: I need someone to listen to me, to help me sort out my needs and feelings, to care about me, and to understand my hopes and fears.

COACH: I may need help learning survival skills: e.g., how to use a bus, how to buy groceries, how to get medical attention, how to pay rent, how to swap things and ideas with others.

FIRST AIDER: I have accidents made up of emotional bruises and fears that injure. I need first aid for these times when the world has been too much.

TRAVEL AGENT: I need to know how to get around, how to find the resources that make life possible. I need someone who knows where these things are and can provide the maps for getting there.

WATCHDOG: I need someone who anticipates trouble and steps in to keep it at bay. Is my medication forgotten? Is someone taking advantage? Are there rent or bills to be paid?

PARTNER: I need someone who will lend a vision, see what is ahead and help me find the safe direction so that today's problems might not become tomorrow's disasters.

LIBRARIAN: I need access to knowledge I don't have and don't know how to get. Know-how is precious, and often I can't get along without it. I need a "safe" someone I can ask to help me.

DETECTIVE: I often can't say what I need, perhaps because I don't know. Figuring out what is needed, when it can be done, and how it can be made useful to me is a big part of case management.

In general, the case manager should be community-based more than office-based. The service should be flexible. There is no set time pattern; and the ebbs and flows of provision should vary as needed. This is not "tidy" work. Nonetheless, it can be "tidied" somewhat, as the process guides at the end of this chapter suggest.

Much professional judgment is needed. Other agencies and resources must be used if they exist. Otherwise, new resources must be developed, and supportive people in the client's environment must be found. To the extent possible, the case manager must imagine new ways to bring the community to life, and must help make this happen by pushing away the obstacles and stretching the boundaries of rigid systems.

Determining the Work

The directives for the work can be guided by two questions: Is there an existing resource? and Are there others in the same plight? When a resource exists and no others are in this client's plight, presumably those in need are being adequately served. So the social worker can link the client to the resource. On the other hand, when a resource exists and there are others in this client's plight, presumably there are obstacles to service delivery that must be pushed away. When no resource exists and no others are in this client's plight, the social worker needs to find supportive people in the client's community. And

when no resources exist and there are others in the client's plight, it
is appropriate to help them help each other. The Window of Orientation (figure 9.1) summarizes the case manager's choices.

Ideally, the case manager makes use of four types of authority:
administrative (with clear policies and formal agreements within and
between agencies), legal (with a clear mandate, based in legislation,
to provide the services), fiscal (control over specific funds to purchase
specific services), and clinical (the understanding of clinical issues
facing the client and the ability to interact as a peer with other service
providers).[21]

Two kinds of skills are involved: 1) those required for doing the
work with the client and 2) those required for doing the work with
other delivery systems, and for dealing with one's own colleagues,
supervisor(s), and administrator(s).

The following case example will illustrate some of the intracacies
involved:

FIGURE 9.1. The Window of Orientation

Is there an existing resource?

	YES	NO
Are there others in the same plight? YES	Push away obstacles to service delivery.	Help clients help each other.
NO	Link client to resource.	Find supportive people in client's environment.

Marcia, twenty-eight years old, has been hospitalized ten times in the past two years, jailed twice in the past four months, treated in the mental health system for schizo-affective symptoms for the past six years although this diagnosis now appears questionable. Her true capabilities are not known, eclipsed by her street drug dependency, sexual promiscuity, enraged temper tantrums, and belief that everyone is against her. She has been "stable" for four months since release from the mental hospital and now shows signs of wanting to improve her life conditions, e.g., she is tired of the jail and hospital trips, longs for a relationship with her child, and values autonomy.

I first helped her plan how to spend and apportion her SSI checks, to find an apartment, apply for food stamps, and plan meals.

Here we see the case manager taking the role of conferee in discussing the SSI checks. The worker next takes the role of broker in seeking an apartment. Then it is back to the role of conferee for helping Marcia apply for food stamps and plan meals.

As the work continues below we see the worker continuing in the role of conferee as she helps Marcia get used to purchasing groceries. Note that the worker is appropriately circumspect regarding her hasty presumption that saving is possible from such a meager allotment!

I accompanied Marcia to the grocery twice a week while she selected her food, and helped her think about what she would do if she had monies left over at the end of the month, i.e., what were her priorities? I realize now that this was naive since she got only $360 a month and a $20 to $40 monthly food stamp benefit.

Meanwhile, I tried to find a drug rehab program for her. After talking with several drug rehab programs that "knew her," I was finally able to convince one to try her again, with the proviso that I would try to help her understand that medication, alone, would not do everything, and that she would have to work hard. I also reassured her that I would continue to stand by her.

In the role of advocate, the social worker convinced a drug rehab program to give Marcia another opportunity, and in the role of conferee, she assured Marcia of her continued assistance. It is also in the role of conferee that the social worker will discuss Marcia's behavior with her to help her stick with the drug rehab program she will reenter.

Also in the role of conferee, the worker accompanies Marcia to AA meetings, then shifts to the broker role to form a self-help group— creating a resource where none exists.

> We went to two AA meetings together weekly and I am coordinating the development of a small self-help group for her and other clients of the agency with similar dual-diagnosis problems. Another thing Marcia had told me was that she hated to be so "spread out" among five different workers so she was enthusiastic about the idea that I would coordinate the services and offer her some "in-house" support and direction with her alcohol dependency. She now has only two professionals in her life that she has to talk to regularly— the psychiatrist and me.
>
> I see my continuing work with Marcia as a combination of general counseling and teaching activities, giving feedback to her to foster productive behaviors, and efforts to give her messages of value and worth. I do not seek to be "best friend" but I do try to model friendship and demonstrate the significance of being connected to others as a way of maintaining self-esteem. I am hopeful this might counter some of her long-standing alienation—an attitude our culture conveys too readily to the out-of-step person. I hope to help her find some compelling reasons for staying well, to counter some of the seeming protections that sickness brings: fewer financial worries, more remote family tensions, and lessened aloneness in the hospital.

Process Guides

To assist the social worker in coping with the complexities of case management, the following process guides map out the basic flow of the work as it moves through four primary phases: assessment, planning, linking, and monitoring. Figure 9.2 depicts the Assessment Phase. In this phase, the primary role of the social worker is that of conferee and Quadrant A is the predominant locus of the work. The worker's interactional skills are directed toward reaching for information and attending to feelings as they arise.

Having performed an assessment, the social worker moves to the Planning Phase depicted in figure 9.3. Because the client must play as prominent a role as possible in planning to meet his or her needs, the social worker shuttles between taking the role of broker in Quadrant D and the role of conferee in Quadrant A, variously locating resources, then discussing them with the client. As the process guide for planning shows, it is also in this phase that the social worker will sometimes need to take the role of advocate if and when existing resources refuse to accommodate clients in need.

Once a plan consistent with the assessment has been made, the social worker moves to the Linking Phase, illustrated in figure 9.4. While linking occurs primarily in Quadrant D with the worker in the role of broker, there are times when the worker may need to take the role of mediator as well. Note, too, that at times it may be necessary for the worker to return to particular segments of the Planning Phase.

The Monitoring Phase, shown in figure 9.5, finds the social worker once again shuttling between two roles and two quadrants. As broker in Quadrant D, the social worker talks with service providers about how things are going. And in the role of conferee, talks with the client about how things are going. As in the Linking Phase, the worker must be prepared to take the role of mediator if necessary, and when circumstances warrant, to return to specific parts of the Linking Phase.

These process guides can help the social worker conceptualize case management in practice as well as actually practice case management—from the identification to the meeting of human service needs.

Conclusion

The customary environment of provision is now in flux as political decision-makers do major budget-cutting on the backs of the vulnerable. Add to this a new wave of volunteerism coming from the corporate world—guilty Yuppies.[22] The new perks in companies like IBM,

Xerox, and Wells Fargo Bank, "social services leaves," are "in"; the funding of necessary services is not! And Yuppie "service eagerness" can cloud the picture just enough to make it look as though needs can be met with reduced funding when in fact they cannot. With and without all of this, the case manager must manage to manage.

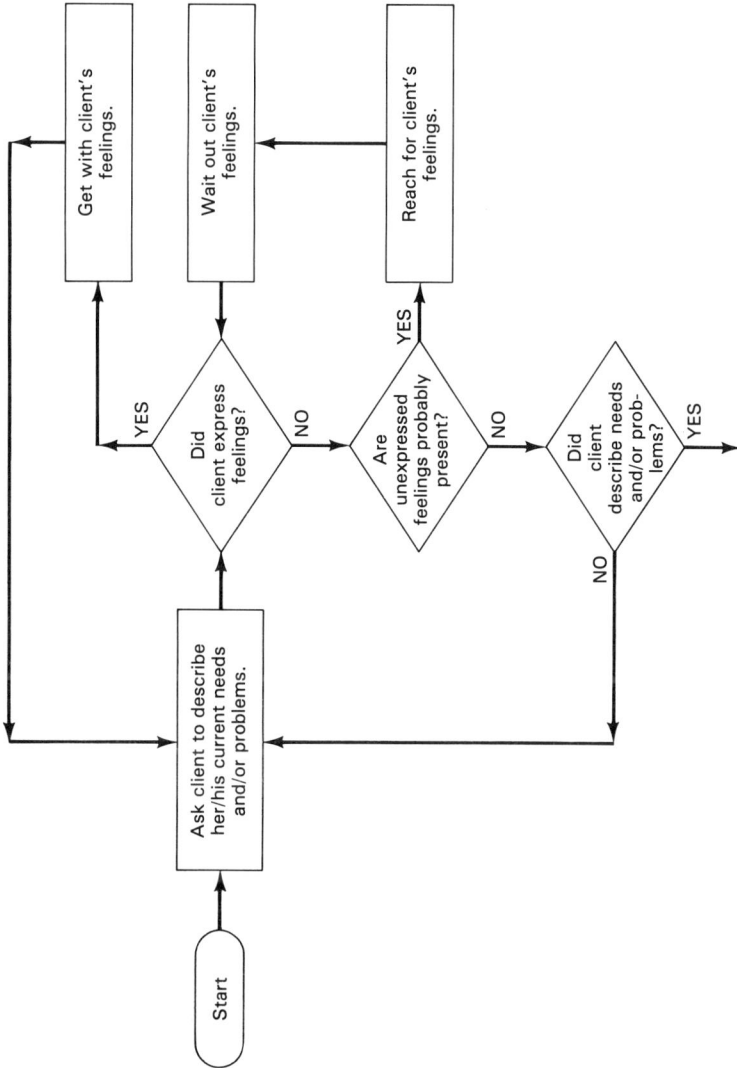

FIGURE 9.2. Process Guide to Case Management in Assessment Phase: Phase 1

171

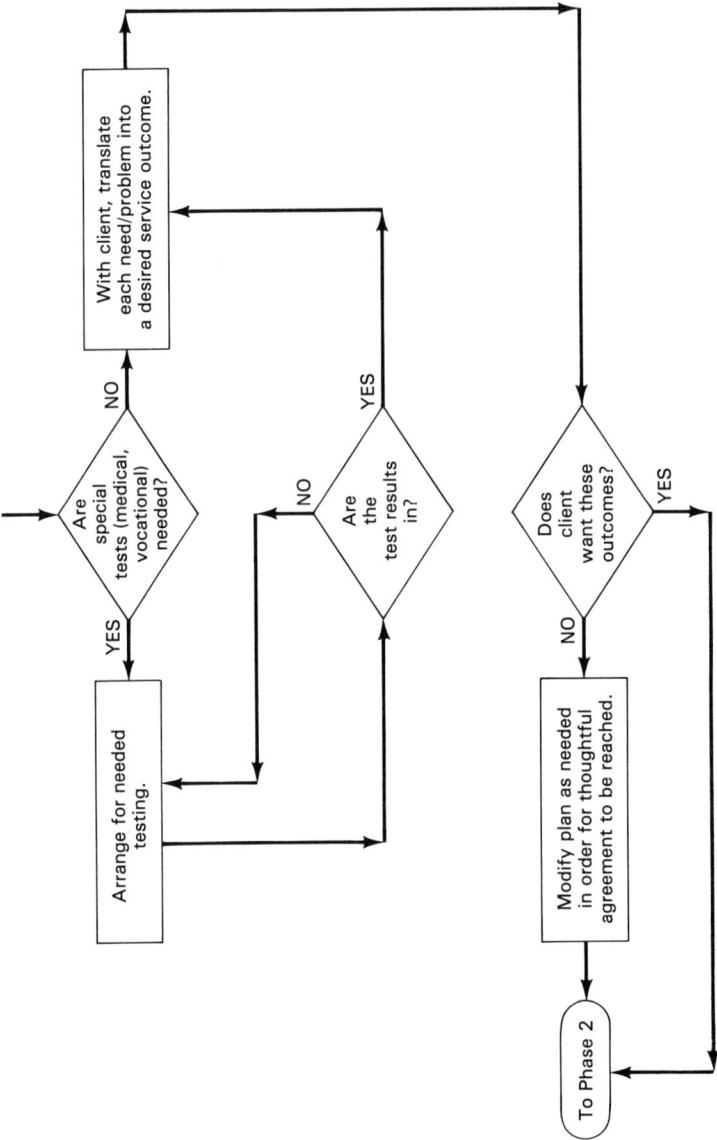

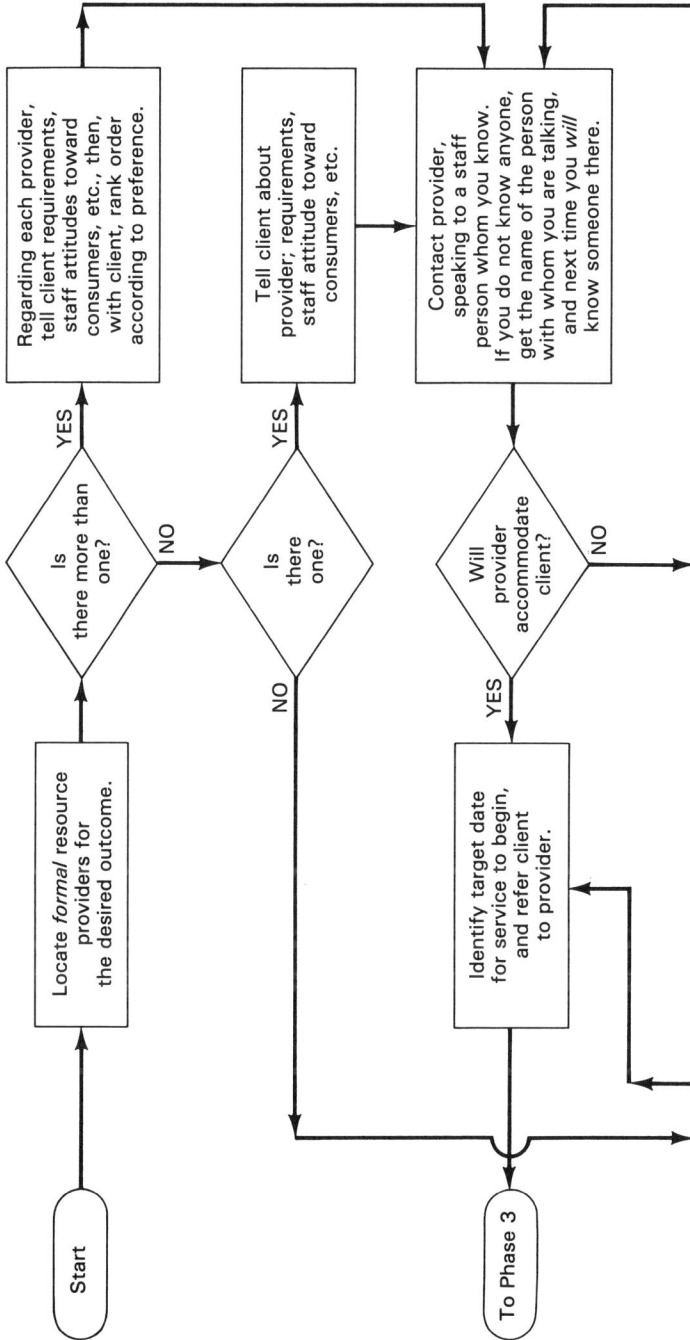

FIGURE 9.3. Process Guide to Case Management in Planning Phase: Phase 2

Regarding each provider, tell client requirements, staff attitudes toward consumers, etc., then, with client, rank order according to preference.

Tell client about provider; requirements, staff attitude toward consumers, etc.

Contact provider, speaking to a staff person whom you know. If you do not know anyone, get the name of the person with whom you are talking, and next time you *will* know someone there.

Is there more than one?

Is there one?

Will provider accommodate client?

Locate *formal* resource providers for the desired outcome.

Identify target date for service to begin, and refer client to provider.

YES

NO

YES

NO

YES

NO

Start

To Phase 3

173

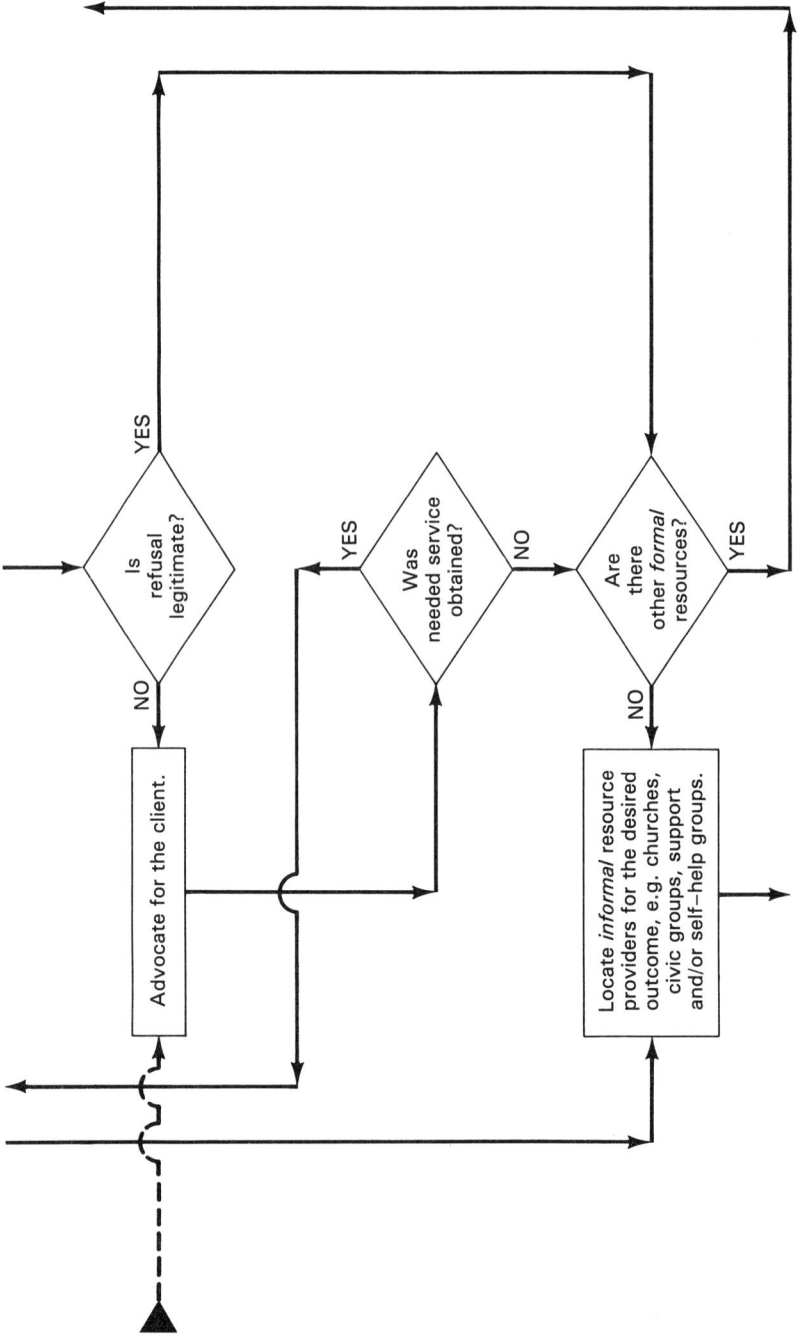

Is refusal legitimate?

YES

NO

Advocate for the client.

Was needed service obtained?

YES

NO

Are there other *formal* resources?

YES

NO

Locate *informal* resource providers for the desired outcome, e.g. churches, civic groups, support and/or self-help groups.

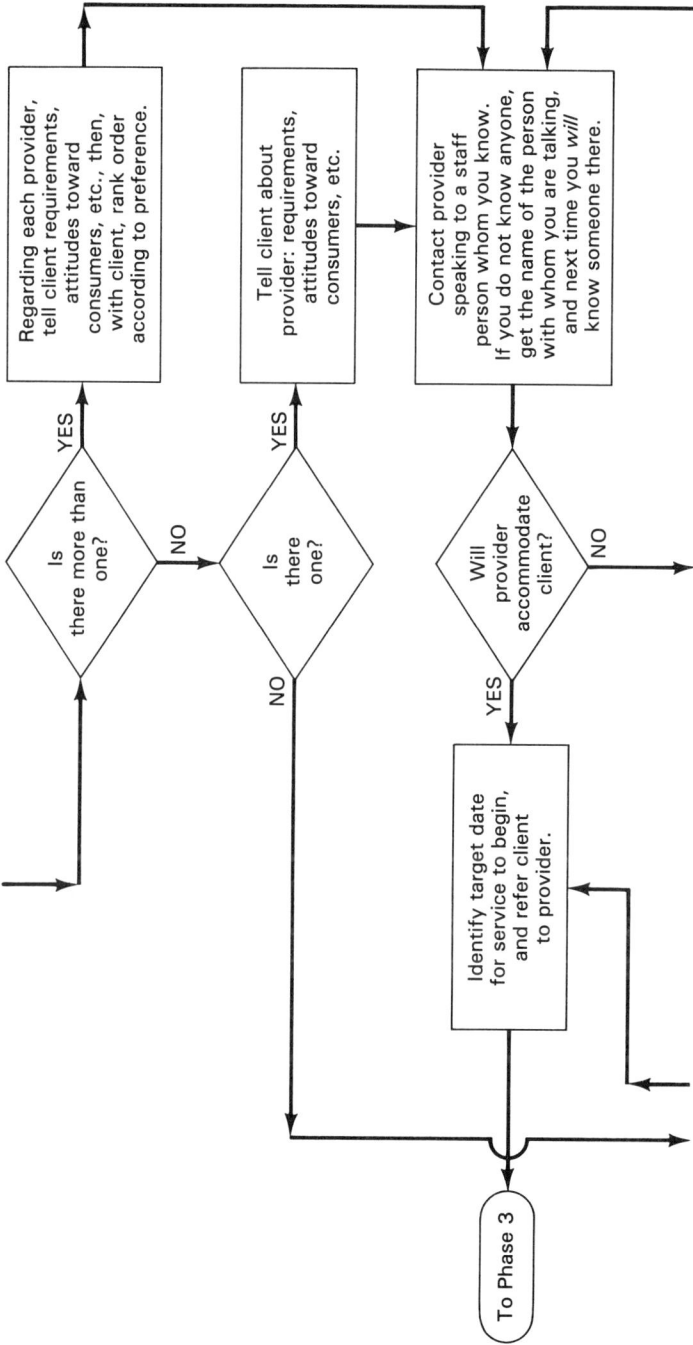

Regarding each provider, tell client requirements, attitudes toward consumers, etc., then, with client, rank order according to preference.

Tell client about provider: requirements, attitudes toward consumers, etc.

Contact provider speaking to a staff person whom you know. If you do not know anyone, get the name of the person with whom you are talking, and next time you *will* know someone there.

Is there more than one?

YES

NO

Is there one?

YES

NO

Will provider accommodate client?

YES

NO

Identify target date for service to begin, and refer client to provider.

To Phase 3

175

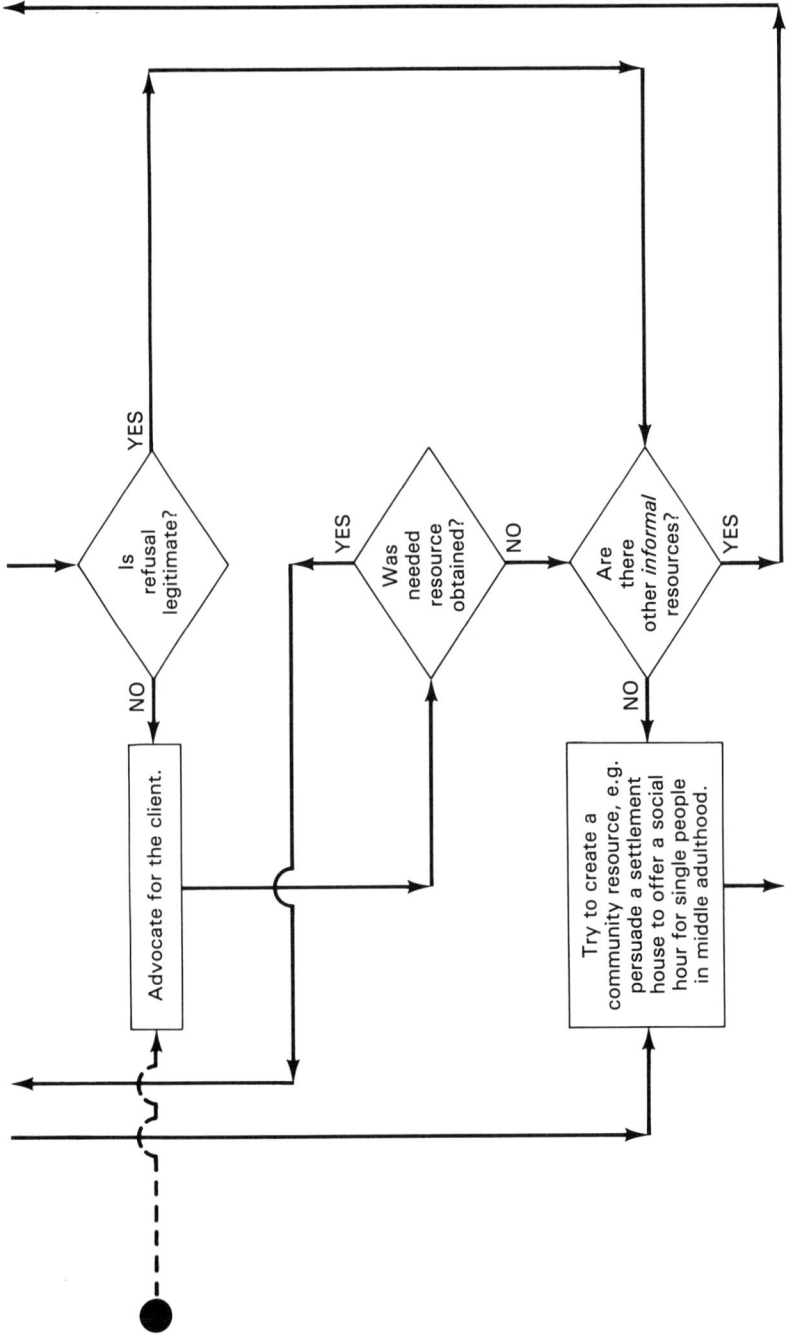

YES

Is refusal legitimate?

NO

Advocate for the client.

Was needed resource obtained?

YES

NO

Are there other *informal* resources?

YES

NO

Try to create a community resource, e.g. persuade a settlement house to offer a social hour for single people in middle adulthood.

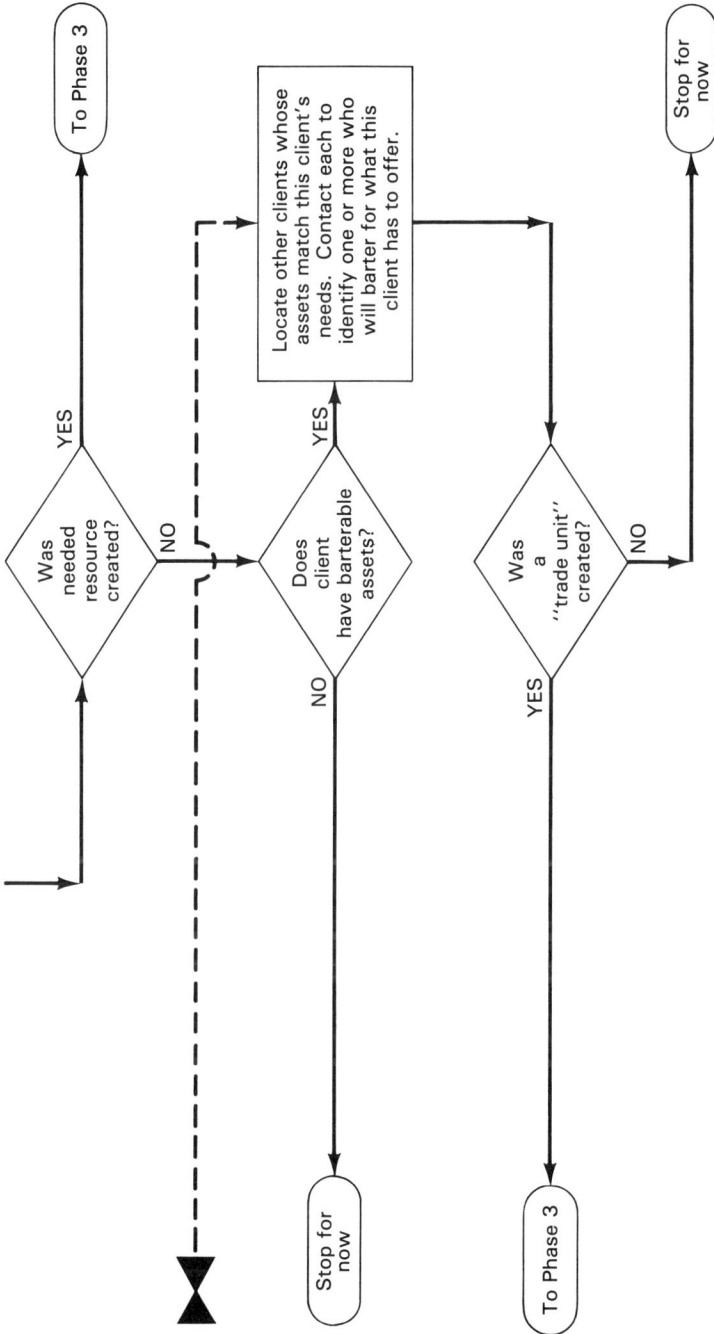

Was needed resource created?

YES → To Phase 3

NO

Does client have barterable assets?

YES → Locate other clients whose assets match this client's needs. Contact each to identify one or more who will barter for what this client has to offer.

NO → Stop for now

Was a "trade unit" created?

YES → To Phase 3

NO → Stop for now

FIGURE 9.4. Process Guide to Case Management in the Linking Phase: Phase 3

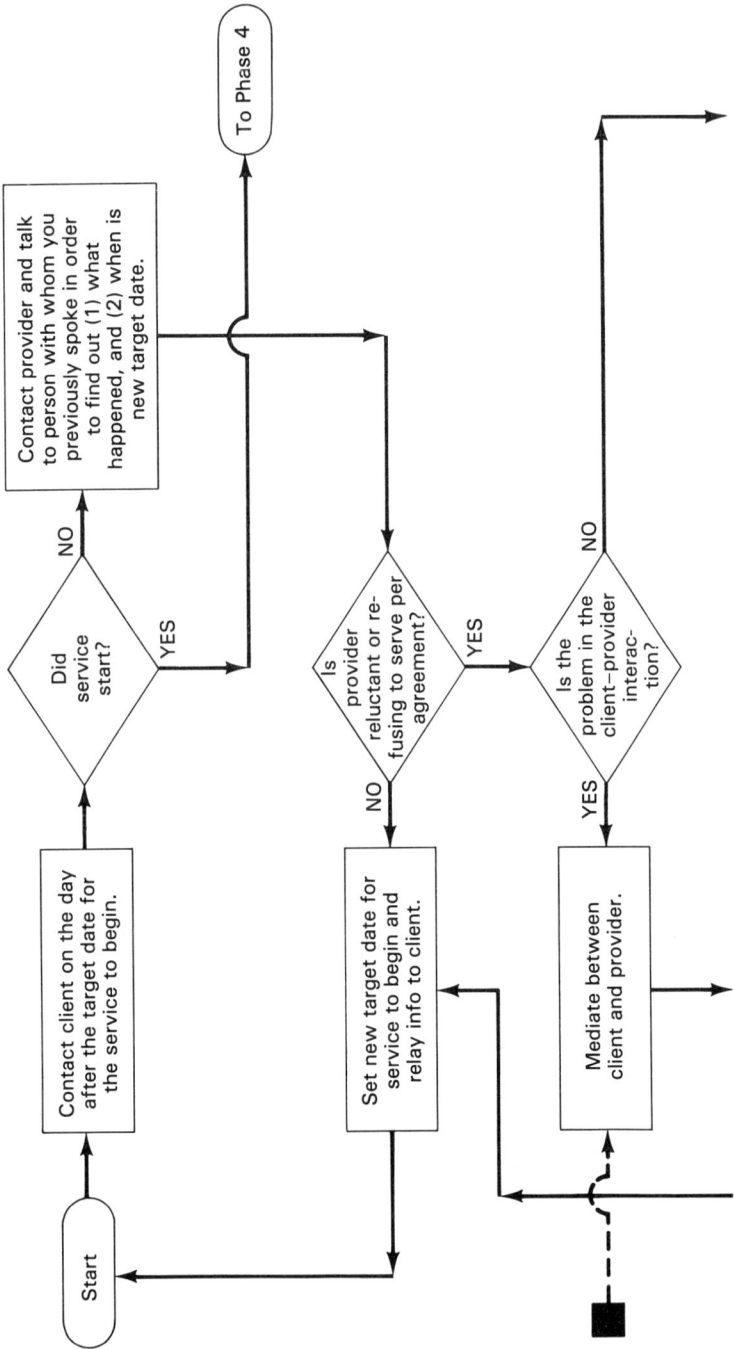

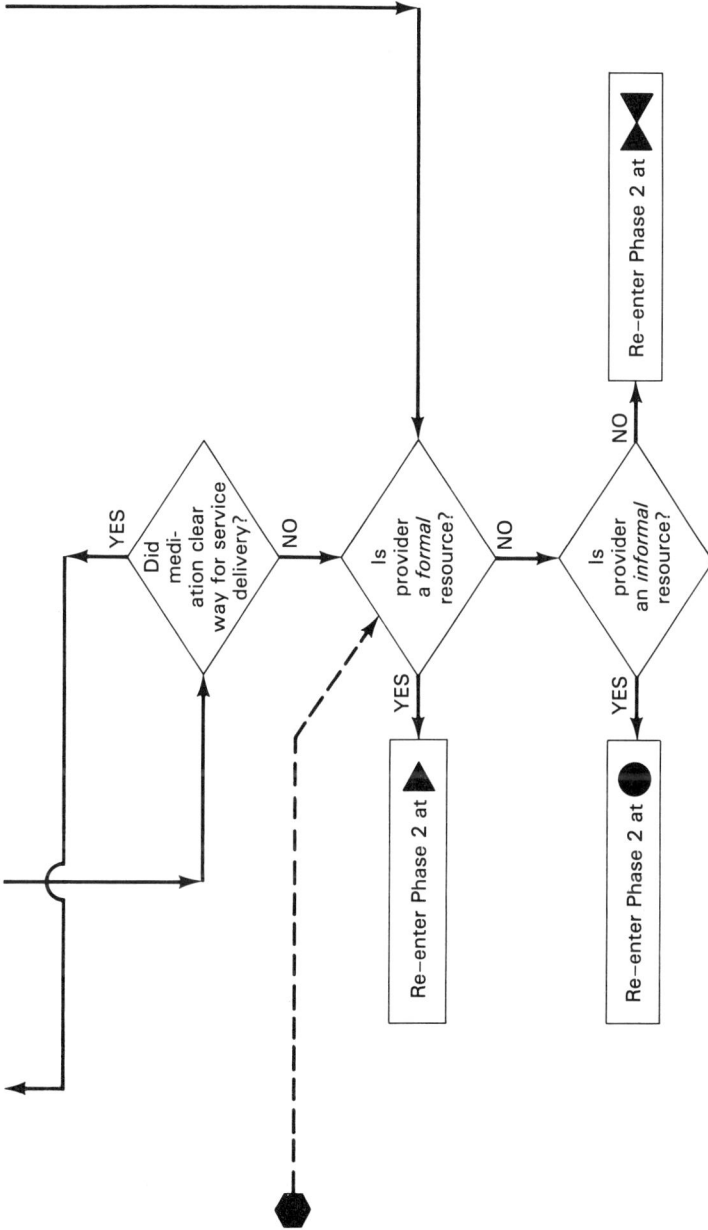

Did medi-ation clear way for service delivery?

YES

NO

Is provider a *formal* resource?

YES

Re-enter Phase 2 at ▲

NO

Is provider an *informal* resource?

YES

Re-enter Phase 2 at ●

NO

Re-enter Phase 2 at ⧗

179

FIGURE 9.5. Process Guide to Case Management in the Monitoring Phase: Phase 4

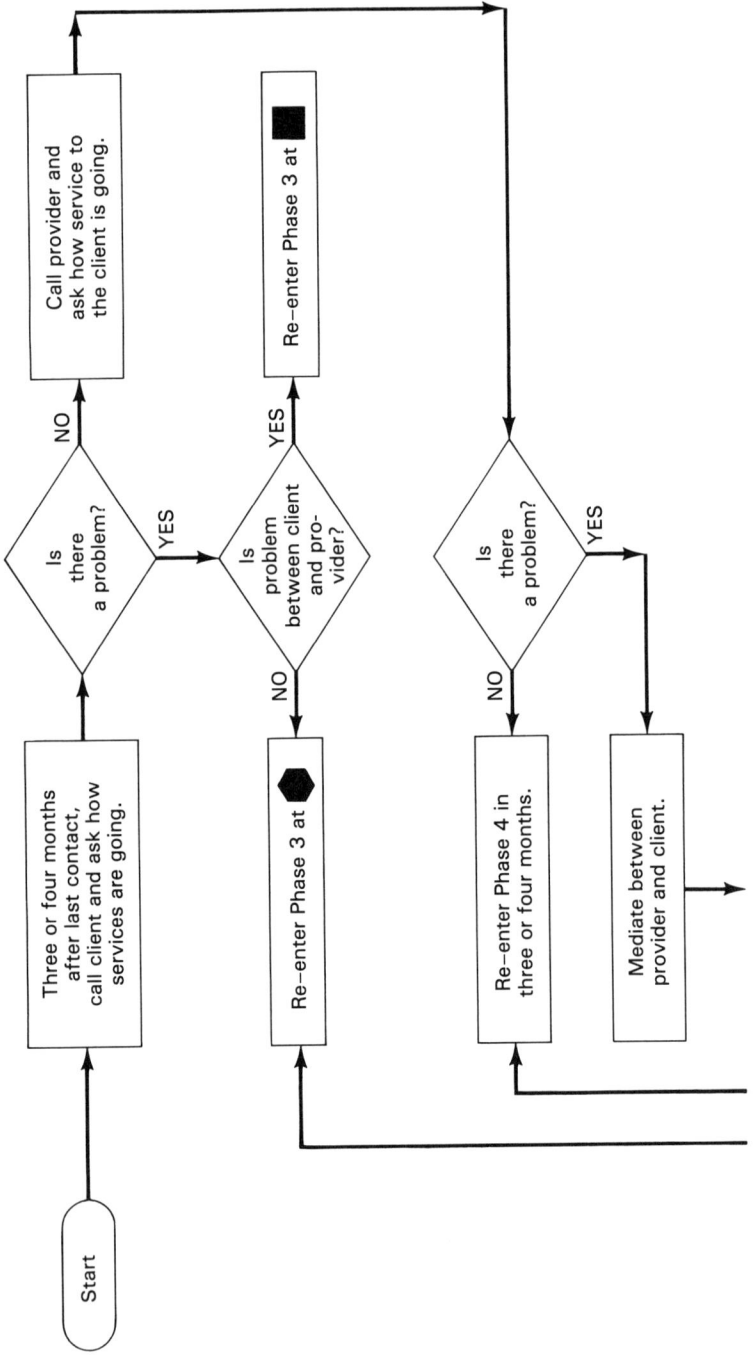

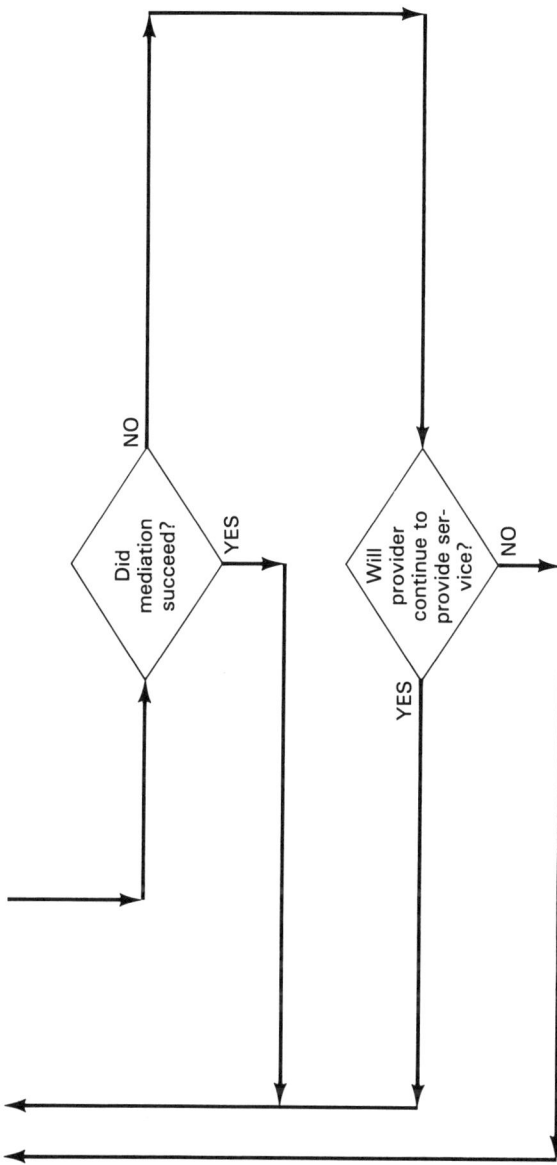

181

10. The Group in Structural Social Work Practice

Second-Order Work: Group Work

The group is at the heart of structural social work practice. And *the awareness of groups,* as critically important in the lives of individuals, is obvious to all social workers who practice from a structural frame of reference. Recall the directive at the outset of the work, a component of the principle of following the demands of the client task: "look beyond the client to see if others are in the same plight." This directive immediately urges workers to consider more than a one-by-one approach to problem situations, to work with individuals in their human contexts along with others similarly affected. Workers also may work with groups in any of the four quadrants, and they will assume the roles of conferee, broker, mediator, or advocate according to the requirements of their groups' situation. They are also urged to work with different numbers of people, not merely individuals.

Then, there is the principle of maximizing supports in the client's environment (often being other persons and groups) which emphasizes, "do not occupy the central position in the helping process"—change and create structures so that you can work yourself out of the (helping) job. Taking these imperatives seriously requires the practitioner to put great faith in the basic helpfulness of groups and others in the client's life.

Thus, it becomes exceedingly important to appreciate groups and their workings, to understand the skills practitioners must know and use to connect with these workings so as to maximize and do no violence to the inherent processes and dynamics of the clients' groups. For the professional helping relationship is a temporary one. It is the clients, their groups and families, that will persist; and they can be helped to help each other.

In this chapter we shall focus on groups with clients. But groups are also critical in work on behalf of clients and others—staff meetings, committees, task groups, case conferences, and so forth. These will be considered in chapter 11 as Metawork.

We shall discuss certain key components of groups to give a general idea of the workings of any group. We shall also illustrate work with groups to present a clear picture of how workers approach and deal with groups. A major emphasis in this chapter will be on distinguishing support groups, self-help groups, and treatment groups from psychotherapy groups. While therapy groups are frequently led by social workers, they are intrapsychic in emphasis ordinarily; such groups are aside from the main thrust of the structural approach. Interpersonally focused groups (which we shall designate as treatment groups), support groups, self-help groups, and social action or advocacy groups are prime examples of *social* work with groups and are congenial with the concepts discussed in the previous chapters of this book.

We see the use of groups, much as we see case management (chapter 9), as *second-order* work. That is, given the Structural Approach, this framework will define and limit, as we shall see, how the practitioner uses groups with clients. The practice orientation discussed up to this point will operate and underlie all that the worker will do when working with a group.

The Basic Group

Individuals cannot exist for long in total isolation, for they ordinarily long for the companionship of others. It is practically impossible to escape the ties that bind persons to persons. And it is no accident that the concept *network,* the workings of a net or string of personal relationships that enmesh people with their others or may be awakened to "catch" a drifting person, has a currency almost jargon these days. Network captures the flavor of the usual interconnectedness of individuals. The natural state of individuals is to be linked with others in the main, not isolated and alone, and not merely in a dyad—be it mother/child, husband/wife, or any other twosome.

"Alone" should be distinguished from "lonely." Some people can be alone happily. They can use, even relish, their solitude and not be lonely. Others can be lonely in the midst of a busy workplace, or marriage, or set of social obligations. While physical aloneness need not breed loneliness, it can encourage it by its separating quality. The very popularity of home entertainment systems, video tape recorders, and telephone "chatlines" where strangers pay up to 99 cents a minute for group conversations,[1] suggests how some are trying to fend off loneliness when alone.

The vocabulary that is used to talk about loneliness tends to make it into a personal, private experience particular to each person. It is described psychologically rather than socially with such expressions as lack of intimacy, inability to relate, a poor communicator, introverted, and narcissistic.[2] When one uses such discriptors for loneliness, the "solutions" would also need to be private ones. But we see loneliness as more related to the circumstances of everyday life—to the changing conditions of the world, to the economy, to the state of technology, to demographic shifts, and in short, to a *structural* perspective—a perspective that looks first to public, societal conditions that may create miseries for many.

NATURAL AND CONSTRUCTED GROUPS

One can think about groups in two ways. There are the natural groups through which people carry out their activities of daily life, such as the family, and there are the social groups at school, church, or workplace. Then there are the constructed, small groups which people choose to join or to which they are assigned. The constructed group may be for an educational, diversional, inspirational, spiritual, consciousness raising, corrective, empowering, advocacy, recreational, socializing, or therapeutic purpose. Regardless of the purpose, in order to do social work through such constructed groups, the practitioner needs to be able to "think group," i.e., understand the structure and dynamics of groups and the special ways of working with more than one person at the same time.

In considering the small group in North American culture, we cite two main natural groups—the family and the social group. We see five types of constructed groups—the theme group (seminar or class); the psychotherapy group; the treatment, support, and self-help groups; the task or committee group; and the empowerment or advocacy (social action) group. Table 10.1 identifies these categories of small, constructed groups, differentiated according to the focus (purpose) of the work and the major activity of the worker.

The family is a basic group, primarily of biological origin, through which the young are cared for and socialized, i.e., introduced to the physical, psychological, socio-cultural, and spiritual worlds. The social group is an informal arrangement where friends get together to enjoy themselves, pursue common interests, and plan activities of interest. Ordinarily these two group-types function on their own without professional attention. Families seek help only when their natural living processes become too difficult to manage on their own. The social group becomes a candidate for professional concern even more rarely, if at all. Sometimes social workers may encounter social groups when the group members, as volunteers, plan a project to help others.

Table 10.1 identifies and differentiates five types of constructed groups. In all types of groups the communication, in addition to talking, may be through activity, action, or experiential approaches— nonverbal expressiveness being as important as talking. In fact, the "doings" of groups, "immersion in activities in which rules, order of performance, roles, and expected behavior are known to the participants may be seen as the natural home of speech. What is negotiated and variable is turns at talking."[3] The doing-approaches are especially

TABLE 10.1. Five Types of Constructed Groups

Type of Group	Focus	Main Worker Activity
Psychotherapy	Intrapsychic	Interpreting/counseling
Support/self-help/treatment	Interactional	Mediating; consulting; counseling
Theme	Educational	Teaching
Task/committee	Instrumental	Facilitating
Empowerment/advocacy	Instrumental	Facilitating; consulting

necessary in work with children, teens, and older adults, where many can be involved at the same time unlike in the talking situations. And work pursued through the nitty-gritty, through the ordinary activities of everyday living with group participants on their own terms and turf is especially valuable with the hard-to-reach, with populations that make the community uncomfortable, and where mistrust and inaccessibility prevail.[4] We shall return to certain other distinctions among group-types after first considering some aspects which are pertinent to all group work.

GROUP AND INDIVIDUAL SERVICE APPROACHES

It is as natural to approach individuals through their groups as to see them one-by-one despite the traditional emphasis in social work on a case-by-case approach. In fact, work with individuals can be understood as a temporary removal of the person from one's groups in order to intensify, augment, remediate and/or speed up developmental, enhancement, or restorative processes. Consistent with this perspective, we can think of the person who applies for social services as one who has temporarily and probably reluctantly removed herself (or has been removed) from her groups, in order to get some need met that her natural groups are not providing.

Although social agencies are set up to provide resources or services mainly through an individual-by-individual pattern, this should be seen as the agency's convenience and tradition or perhaps the workers' comfort, not necessarily the client's preference. Therefore, two implications for service delivery seem important: 1) the constructed group is a reconstructed modality that replicates a context already familiar to the client, and may be a temporary, congenial service mechanism, and 2) the individual interview may be appreciated as a special instance of temporary separation from one's natural others. In fact, one can appropriately construe the interview as one form of a temporarily constructed, instrumental group, i.e., a dyad or two-person task group.

For many, the constructed (or better, the re-constructed) group can become a microcosm of the person-in-situation which is the peculiar heritage of concern for the social work profession. It is the social situation which is the basic social unit of human functioning and experience, a situation comprised of people and physical objects in time/space.[5] And it is the group that mediates between persons and their situations or environments.

To View Groups

There is a simple, analytical way of looking at the group regardless of its particulars. This involves a foursome mentality,[6] or four-sided, pyramidal view, as follows:

ME (the worker) looking at

US (the group, with me in it), in

CONTEXT (time/space; the here-and-now and the history) with a

PURPOSE (treatment, theme, support/self-help, task, empowerment).

All of these components comprise a continuous transactional field of force that in combination makes up the group situation.

The *me* looking at *us* suggests that the worker always be mindful that she is seeing things through her own biases, cultural background, professional screen, and other limitations that focus her judgment of what is *really* going on; and that she realize that her presence as part of the group also changes the group situation. The group itself, moreover, is a continuously moving, changing entity. The *context* directs attention not only to what is happening in the moment, and to where the group is in its current process (e.g., at the beginning, or midway, or near ending if a time frame has been stipulated). But context encompasses also previous experiences of the group-as-a-whole and each individual's experiences with groups (if possible) as pertinent to what happens in the here-and-now. Finally, why the group is here, or its *purpose,* and whether it is a natural or constructed group, a voluntary or required experience, a closed or open group, will have a major impact on all that happens.

We think that much social work intervention in response to diverse human need can be accomplished best through a group rather than an individual approach simply because the client(s) may be familiar with and more comfortable there. Whether it be offering a service to clients or dealing with colleagues in team or committee meetings, much of the business of social work happens (or could happen) in groups. Unfortunately, workers often avoid the group, perhaps out of fear, as if intimidated by the unknown mystique of *groupness*.[7] Yet, groups will become more "worker-friendly" as their doings are understood, and as workers practice putting themselves into group situations.

FEAR IN WORKING WITH GROUPS

Here are some of the common notions that may create a fear of working with groups. They are presented as an internal dialogue:

1. "There is such a lack of technical knowledge, i.e., the vocabulary and concepts."

There *is* some additional information unique to group work that must be acquired but it is *not* inaccessible.

2. "Part of my control is given up."

Yes, this is a scary reality. It will only be appreciated as the plus it can be when you experience the exhilaration that comes with the group's launching ahead on its own.

3. "Others can help, maybe more than me."

There are, in fact, many helping relationships going on. This may be an assault to your ego, but it won't kill you.

4. "What do I do with the forces set in motion?"

This is a subtlety related to the control issue. Experience may help you live more comfortably with this situation. It is, after all, important for client empowerment—a cardinal value of social work.

5. "There are so many of them and only one of me."

Yes, living with this takes faith in the other(s), faith that they will use well their opportunities on their own behalf.

6. "What is my role ultimately? To make waves? To keep the lid on?"

A complex point. The answer here is related to the context of the work with the group, i.e., the agency and the service contract developed with the group.

7. "Being in a group makes me think of my teenage days."

I was always uncomfortable then in such situations, never particularly popular. But I can know this was back then, not now. I am different now in so many ways and, besides this, I have a special role with them.

8. "There is a lack of privacy for this work."

In other words, I am doing my social work publicly where many see and hear me rather than in the comfort of my office. There it is only myself and the client. This difference can be intimidating, but any public forum can lead to stage fright at first.

Any of these ideas may discourage a worker from venturing into group work. But they should be considered and dealt with: through additional know-how, through risking the new even if uncomfortable at first, and through practice in this different area. Hopefully, some of the content in this chapter will serve to launch any reluctant person toward working through groups, and make the work easier.

BASIC GUIDELINES

Three general axioms for working with groups are:

1. To work in a group context, one must be comfortable there or willing to be uncomfortable for a while.

2. Regardless of one's theoretical orientation to practice, the use of certain group-related skills is in order so as to be able to use

group knowledge in the service of others and be in control of one's group-actions.

3. Whether one notices it or not, there is always a group process going on. Much between-participant communication happens all the time (even nonreaction is reaction). The challenge becomes: how should the worker connect with the transactions already in motion?

Core Structure and Process Elements

It will help one understand the workings of groups to realize that all groups have certain structural elements. These include size, norms (openly or subtly enforced rules of conduct), roles, attraction links among various participants, interaction behavior (who talks to whom; who talks after whom, etc.), motives and goals, decision-making patterns, and so forth. These structural elements exist regardless of the length of the group experience or whether the group-type is a natural or constructed one.

All groups also have certain common, core processes stemming from their groupness. These will vary according to how tight or loosely the practitioner keeps control of the experience. A particular group's experience is partly dependent upon who the individual participants are, partly upon the influence, frame of reference, and skill of the worker, and always it is affected by the overall objectives for the group experience and the form of its main content (talk, interaction, party, etc.). But regardless of the individuals' or practioner's qualities, the activities or purpose, certain predictable group effects will interact with individual needs. The worker will need to understand, expect, respect, value, and go along with these core processes.[8]

Any small group which meets for even a few sessions will reveal at least these core processes:

- development of cohesion: related to a sense of being accepted and accepting others, to concern for others.

- conformance with group norms: related to establishing and be-having in certain valued ways, e.g., expressing feeling, listening; and refraining from other behavior by such means as not domi-nating, not being too personal.

- expression of emotion: related to risking positive and negative feelings within the group situation as they occur, rather than talking about them—within limits.

- use of the group to work on problematic ways of relating: related to trying out alternative behaviors on the others in the group, that is, on participants and worker.

- experience of power and influence: related to shifting clique and subgroup loyalties, alignments with others, interpersonal attrac-tions and dislikes, and testing one's own power and attractive-ness.

- experience of role taking and different group functional and dysfunctional acts: related to trying out various ways of behav-ing, e.g., clarifying, initiating, confronting.

- development of increased intimacy: related to closeness with others over time, to the probability of comfort with familiarity.

- pursuit of group purpose: related to accomplishment of the avowed outcome, to increased experience with reflection and thinking about the experience retrospectively.

The challenge to the worker is to recognize that these processes persist with or without one's intervention, and to find ways to connect with these powerful group forces rather than oppose them in any way.

COMMUNICATION PATTERNS

Along with these eight core processes, there is some pattern of com-munication in every group. This becomes established as a way of being together, often determined through the informal leadership and power structure of the group, or through who talks the most or the loudest. The communication/interaction patterns are influenced by the theoretical preference and values of the practitioner and by the group purpose, size, and other structural elements. It is useful for the practitioner to know of the several interactional patterns that are possible for a given group. These may fluctuate in different sessions or even within any one session.

THE MAYPOLE: the practitioner talks to individuals one-by-one. Individuals direct responses to the worker. There is little between-member communication. The worker dominates and controls.

THE ROUND ROBIN: each participant speaks in turn (usually clockwise) in relation to a given focus set by the practitioner, e.g., how did you spend your holiday? The worker is still in control, often nonverbally signaling the progression via eye contact and head nod, "Next!"

THE HOT SEAT: the worker engages in an extended back and forth discussion with one participant while the others are a watchful audience. It may be John's turn this week, Joan's next week. The worker establishes this pattern, which is then followed each week.

THE AGENDA-CONTROLLED: in task groups and more formal associations, the minutes, old business, new business, and so forth form the sequence of "business." Other Robert's Rules structure who, how, and to whom participants may speak.

THE FREE FORM: participants take responsibility to speak with any other person according to what is being said and who is contributing or silent. In this pattern, a large degree of responsibility for the flow and form of the discussion rests with the participants who learn to observe matters of turn-taking, consideration, risking, and so forth.

GROUP PROCESS OVER TIME

All groups have some overall pattern of development over the duration of each particular session and over the life of the group. The one-session dynamics will reveal themselves to the careful observer. Does the group start and end on time? Or dribble in? Or want to stay overtime? Is there a slow start? Do "important" matters come out at the very end? Schwartz spoke of this as "doorknob therapy:"

> Within the life of any particular group we have found that the last few minutes of every meeting yield us the most significant material; that is, people will raise their most deeply-felt concerns as a "by-the-way," almost with a hand on the doornob. We find, further, that these themes do not lend themselves to easy reintroduction at the beginning of the

next meeting. The intention to "start with that at our next meeting" is more often subverted, and the theme reenters only at the next doorknob period. The point is that beginnings and endings are hard for people to manage; they often call out deep feelings in both worker and members; and much skill is needed to help people help each other through these times.[9]

Group process in a more overarching sense (i.e., over the life of the group itself) differs according to whether the group is an open or closed one. The open-ended group is like an elevator with persons getting on and off when they reach their special destination, the exact composition differing from time to time. There is no beginning or end. People enter and leave, but the elevator remains and keeps moving. In contrast, a closed group has a stipulated beginning and end. As soon as an end is determined (e.g., five sessions, one semester), the group will be moving in a *linear* developmental framework, the most familiar and prevalent mode in Western, urban thinking with its notions of progress and growth. There are, in addition, two other group development models possibly encountered—*helical* or *cyclical* (a more Eastern spirit). We will identify these three models briefly.

LINEAR: there is a definite beginning, a middle, and an end. In fact, as soon as the group begins, the move is toward the end, through fairly predictable stages or phases. The focus on the group elements of the process if *future* oriented, with goal attainment, development, and achievement ordering the worker's and groups' thinking. There are more than 100 different formulations of group process in a linear mode.[10] Any one of these will help the worker realize that what happens in a given session might be related to where the group is in the overall process, and not just to the personality dynamics of the participants or to the worker's skillfulness or lacks in a given session. Linear models are useful for understanding dynamics in task groups and committees, short term treatment, skill training, consciousness raising, advocacy, family life education, etc.

HELICAL: this model is taken from the helix concept, a spiral with an ever-deepening focus. Here the focus is on the *past* and the process emphasizes regression, spiraling and ever deepening the focus on a few pertinent issues peculiar to the participants in the group. Once a theme surfaces, it develops in a predictable pattern from superficial to deeper levels of significance. The group is viewed as a microcosm with such metaphors as family, tribe, nurturing breast expressive of its ambiance. The focus in these groups is on the contextual elements of the process. This model fits psychotherapy groups, especially analytic oriented ones.

CYCLICAL: in these groups, the process is in constant motion returning to a starting point as part of a circular cycle. The focus is on the individual elements of process; and the emphasis is *present* oriented. There is tension between basic polarities (such as intellect and feeling, interaction and silence), followed by resistance to change and increased polarity. Then the group develops an awareness of change, and begins to struggle to resolve the polarity. Next, attempts at synthesis are made, and the product of the synthesis becomes a new pole. The group again increases the polarity and resists change and the cycle continues. This seems to describe gestalt groups and personal growth groups.[11]

It will be useful to the practitioner to consider whether the basic thrust of the group is future oriented, past valued, or in-the-moment focused, and act with this main time frame in mind. It will also help to view the overall process of the group as moving ahead toward more of "something," as digging deeper/coming up for air/and digging down again, or as an ongoing circling, much as night and day or the seasons of the year, with no beginning or ending. These notions will help one understand and bear with the group's process with more tolerance and appreciation.

By having some knowledge of the group-related structures, core processes, communication patterns, time foci, development-over-time formats, and main theme or purpose requirements, the practitioner has a choice as to what kind of group may be offered to meet particular clients' needs over how long a period of time. As table 10.1 revealed, workers may be involved diversely with various group-types and may assume different stances in terms of whether they are doing therapy, or assertion training, or developing a widow-to-widow group. The widow-to-widow group would be the most likely one for the structural social worker to have. In the therapy instance, this worker would probably make a referral elsewhere or create and facilitate a support group. For assertion training, the worker would probably arrange for some other person knowledgeable in the area to teach this content.

Worker Roles

Using the structural perspective, the worker with groups always starts in the conferee role in order to discuss how the group will work with the prospective members and obtain their agreement. That is, the particulars (ground rules) are jointly worked out and agreed to by all concerned, and a working contract is arranged. This will clarify dates, hours, and objectives of the group worker and of the participants. Beyond this generic planning, workers' stances will be variable. They may act as expert (therapist or teacher) or clinician (facilitator, mediator, or resource/consultant) according to their preferred practice theories and the group's purpose. The workers' basic orientation may range from controlling/dominant to permissive/participative. The group's purpose and the sponsoring agency's mandate or mission also will affect how the group and practitioner work together.

For example, some groups are developed for participants to learn new behaviors or to give up undesired ones. The worker in such a group would be viewed as the expert and act as assessor/teacher. These workers would determine where the individual group participants were at the outset, teach different behaviors, and determine whether or not the new behavior was learned. If, for example, the group was for learning assertive behavior, the worker-as-expert might model, role play, coach the participants in the "right" behavior for particular situations, assign homework practice and observation, and prescribe other outside activities. In this instance, the worker is controlling so as to move participants to predetermined outcomes deemed desirable. The following illustration shows the worker-as-expert, controlling the process in a stress management group:

> I asked them to divide into pairs much as we did last week. "The coaches from last week will now be the trainees. The trainees should sit in the chairs and try to relax. The coaches should stand to one side. Fine! Coaches should watch to see that the trainees follow the instructions. I will tell you how to do the tensing and relaxing."

With a support group, on the other hand, the worker's expertise would be devoted to maximizing the group members' potential for helping each other. The worker would adopt a mediating stance and help the group members learn to take over their own leadership and direction. The focus would be on mutuality, on interpersonal transactions, not on demands for behavioral or intrapsychic change. Worker interpretations would be process notations which benefit the group as a whole. Workers would voice the potential for mutual help and gradually work out of any special role, calling attention to the sense of empowerment that accompanies the group's successes in helping each other. Workers in support groups model the use of empathy and support, and emphasize the group's achievements of their goals.

In the next example we see the social worker with a group of older adults in a community center clarify the contract as they deal with the purpose of the group:

> The group has a hard time getting started at its fourth session. At the previous meeting some members had questioned my training and qualifications, and some were now embarrassed. . . . Doris told the group about how the psychology courses she had taken were organized and run. Jean joined her. They said the teacher presented a topic every week, like love or jealousy, and then the class would discuss it.
>
> Lee agreed that it was a more structured thing and was better than what goes on in this group. She said the discussions were "about things in general" and it was more interesting. Everyone who spoke directed their words to the group but glanced often at me. After several minutes I said that it sounded like the group was angry at me. Jean asked, "Why should we be angry at you?" I asked why she was. She said I wasn't running things right. Lee told me that I should plan topics and teach them something about psychology. I said that was not my job, that I was not there to teach psychology. Jean said it would be better if I did.
>
> I said I understood that it would be easier for the group if that were my job with them, but that I was here to help them do what they said they came together to do—to discuss the problems they were facing, try to give help to each other and get help from each other, learn something about how they talk to people and how people respond to them. Jean said that opens up a lot of sores. I nodded and said that I knew how painful talking about yourself and looking at your own behavior could be. I said that I sometimes get

very upset about things I do and that there are times when my feelings frighten me and I feel very much alone. Frances asked me if I really got that way, too. I nodded yes. She turned to the group and said, "Let's get down to what we came for."

In each of these two group-types the worker brings to bear certain expertise. But the distinctions are quite different. With the behavior-change group, the worker's special knowledge/skill resides in methods of teaching, reinforcement, and so forth. With the support group, the expertise is in matters of groupness. This difference must be made known to the group members who may want to turn the group session into a psychotherapy or behavior-change event. Some group participants may have more experience with group therapy, or notions of a therapist-worker from watching Bob Newhart or other characters on television. Even when the avowed purpose of the group is self-help or mutual support, this focus must be reinforced by the worker any time the discussion veers into the intrapsychic or therapy realm so as to keep the group on track. The group can be *therapeutic* without being *Therapy* with the capital *T* if the worker values and knows how to use group enhancing skills; and holds to an interpersonal or group level focus.

The following excerpt also shows the worker setting a tone and focus for a support/self-help group experience in a first meeting. She is meeting with six AMACs, adults (sexually) molested as children, in a Parents United program. Part of the requirement for participation in this program is that each group participant also be in therapy aside from the group. At their initial meeting, the women were polled to see if they did have a therapist. The mutual aid aspect of the group meetings was emphasized and distinguished from group psychotherapy at the outset:

> You will be helpers to each other in this support/self-help group, and the help will come as you talk with each other about your pain within the safety of these meetings. You are the experts in your situation, not me. But I can help you talk with each other. My help comes through knowing about groups and how they work.

Strictly speaking, this was a support group and not a self-help group even though they knew the word "self-help" better. The self-help

aspect came in their weekly business meetings attended with participants from other groups in the Parents United program, in money
raising events, public speaking engagements, etc.

In a later meeting of this group, we see the worker using focusing
skills to continue to clarify the mutual aid emphasis of the group as
distinguished from an intrapsychic one.

> S is divorced and lives with her two children. She is finishing her
> senior year in college. She talked about a recent surprise visit from
> her father with great excitement. He lives in Texas with his second
> wife and S hasn't seen him since he left home when she was little.
> Her mother had always bad-mouthed him. Now, right after he left,
> came the ESP: a telephone call from her mother. This resurfaced
> the old problems S has always had with her mother. She asked the
> group for any suggestions as to what she could do. The group
> seemed startled; they didn't know her struggle with her mother
> enough to say much. I asked softly if this was something she might
> talk with her therapist about since there was a lot of history to all
> this. S said she would be seeing her therapist tomorrow and planned
> to do so. I said the group could not help her deal with "*her* old
> problems with mother," but they may have mother-handling expe-
> riences of their own. Several sympathized with S and recounted
> their comparable incidents.

LEVELS OF INTERVENTION

Practitioners have a choice as to the focus and level of their interventions which will depend upon their overall theoretical orientation and
the purpose of the group. For instance, let us take Joe speaking to
Bernie in a group session:

Joe says, "Whenever anyone in this group has a good idea, others
always shoot it down."

The worker can say, "You seem angry from that remark, Joe. What
is going on with you?"—(Intrapersonal level). Or, "You're looking at
Bernie. Is there something between you two?"—(Interpersonal level).
Or, "Who else can connect with what Joe is feeling?"—(Group level).

Here is an example of a worker beginning a session with her focus
on the group-as-a-whole:

I opened the meeting and said I had been thinking of them during the week; how they had worked together as a group; how they helped each other. I acknowledged that some here today were not here for a week or two, and were back now. I welcomed those persons back and said they were joining into a good group. There were smiles as I glanced around the circle at all.

Change Processes of Groups

When workers begin to work with groups, they do not have to give up the theories held for work with individuals, or become a totally different kind of practitioner. The group knowledge is added to whatever explanatory theories the worker uses. It merges with the other theories. The process is one of addition, not substitution. Since we see group work as second-order work within the structural approach, we have emphasized the support group. But beyond the particular orientation and strategies of the practitioner, there are basic change processes and factors characteristic of all group-types.

Let us consider the change processes in psychotherapy groups, and then those in self-help groups. Some of the processes will be similar; others are unique to each group-type.

Yalom's identification of "therapeutic factors" in psychotherapy groups has been influential for many clinicians. He cites eleven therapeutic factors:

- instillation of hope

- universality

- imparting of information

- altruism

- corrective recapitulation of the primary family group

- development of socializing techniques

- imitative behavior

- interpersonal learning

- group cohesiveness

- catharsis

- existential factors

Some of these refer to actual mechanisms of change and others are more considered as conditions for change.[12]

The change processes in self-help groups are somewhat akin to those of the therapy group,[13] but are also different.

- cohesiveness

- perceived similarity or in-the-same-boat mentality

- different from "them"

- family-like—a primary group

- the stimulation of emotionality

- a context for social comparison

- gaining information

- feedback on behavior inside and outside the group

- altruism—being helped through helping others

- getting advice from others

- sensing the universalities of one's situation

- modeling

- influence of special ideology

- inspiration and hope

Such change factors as cohesiveness, stimulation of emotion (or catharsis), gaining (or imparting) information, modeling (or imitative behavior), altruism, universality, and hope are common to both group-types, to therapy and self-help groups.

Perhaps the greatest difference between the self-help and therapy groups (aside from the person of the practitioner) stems from the role of ideology in self-help groups. The ideological orientation prescribes certain behavior and proscribes other behavior. The ritual, special language, history, and other factors unique to the special group experience increase cohesiveness and bind participants to each other and to the program and its objectives. Ideology plays a central organizing role in the self-help group much as the therapist does in a psychotherapy group.

The self-help groups' major change mechanism is the interdependence of the fate of their members. This in-the-same-boat mentality may come to prevail in therapy groups since the participants are "in the boat" of being together in *this* group and have expressed intimacies, often generalizable to the others in the group. But for the self-help group the very raison d'être is the common secret or situation.

The members of the self-help groups publicly "confess" their qualifications for membership, an important criterion for joining the group. They speak a common language, often with in-group special jargon, and operate horizontally rather than hierarchically. Emphasis is on a peer or team or collegial structure. Additional special features include: locus of control in the participants, emphasis on positive reinforcement of effective behavior rather than intrapsychic personality change, emphasis on strengths and health, imitation of others' successful coping behavior, and alteration of perspectives.[14]

The social work treatment group, an alternative to psychotherapy groups, is an orientation to group work adopted by many social agencies as a component of the treatment plan. Some clinical social workers prefer the treatment orientation to that of therapy, especially when the work focuses on family or related others whose aim is to support the client, e.g., with foster families. It is often more palatable for others to see themselves as partners in a treatment group than as persons who need therapy. The focus in the treatment group (much like that in the mutual aid/support group) is interpersonal, helping participants to communicate with and help each other. It is also in our view, actively directed to link the participants with other forces in their living situations, i.e., with the reality circumstances of their worlds—economics, jobs, and the nitty-gritty of each day.

SELF-HELP AND SUPPORT GROUPS: FOCUS ON THE GROUP

Self-help and support groups are often lumped together and referred to interchangeably as if they were one and the same thing. Both group-types share certain common elements: similarity of members' problems; emphasis on strong cohesiveness that builds trust, self-esteem and confidence. Yet there is a difference in the source of the leader's expertise. With the self-help group the leader has experienced the same problem or stress; with the support group the leader's special knowledge/skill is in having know-how about the workings of groups. Self-help groups are often anti-intellectual (even anti-professional), deliberately intent on turning away from dependency on professionals. Having "been there" and working through the problem is seen as the basis for emotional understanding. Support group leaders, on the other hand, are professionals, clinicians who encourage cognitive learning to supplement the experiential awareness and do not share a total identity with the group members. They are not "in the clients' boat"; their help comes from other sources.

Self-help groups exist for every conceivable problem or situation. They may deal with conduct reorganization or behavioral control (AA, Weight Watchers), with a shared status or stressful predicament (Parents without Partners, Survivors of Suicide), with consciousness raising or survival issues for the stigmatized or oppressed (gay and lesbian groups, Black Panthers), and with enhanced effectiveness and personal growth (Integrity group, Parents United). The group becomes a family, a context for social comparison processes.[15] An atmosphere of acceptance, belongingness, and risk taking is created and, especially with stigmatized persons, a we-ness mentality is stimulated, and difference from "those others" is ultilized.

The support group is well known in the history of social work with groups. Arising from the settlement house movement, the roots of social group work nourished "normal" persons in transition (from the farm to the city, from foreign lands to America). These "support" groups were also devoted to issues beyond the participants—to issues of social reform, for example, to the eight-hour work day, or to interracial dining in restaurants. The groups were to help the individuals and to pursue socially desirable goals.[16]

The major focus for social group work, at least through the 1950s, was its experience and achievement in dealing with the common human needs of all persons, pursued mainly through problem-solving and special interest (activity) groups. The "territory" for social group work was the utilization of the group experience for developmental, preventive, and enhancement purposes. This kind of group work focus was on shared responsibility in decision making and outcomes, on learning the "rules" of living, and on experimenting with the roles for future social relationships from one's experience with others in a group.

The support group, conceptualized by William Schwartz as a *mutual aid group*,[17] has probably become a generic, basic orientation for social workers who are knowledgeable about groups. Those with little schooling in the evolution of group approaches within social work and with little exposure to groupness skills have, in the main, followed the conceptual and practice lead of psychologists and psychiatrists, and focus upon the individual in the group context. This emphasis has been helped along in the mental health field by an insurance policy which reimburses for particular individuals, not for group work.

A group-type with a long tradition in social work since the time of Jane Addams, Lillian Wald, and other settlement house pioneers, is the outreach group that pitches to the hard-to-reach, the disenfranchised, the oppressed and powerless, and those diverse others who struggle to survive the assaults of urban pressures. Although the popularity of such group work may ebb and flow according to the national political climate, the resulting funding possibilities for support, and the social work profession's internal "political" climate, a commitment to this uniquely *social* work remains. A conceptual orientation congenial to serving such populations has been presented throughout the previous chapters of this book.

Current work in this tradition is exemplified in the writings of Lee, who describes

> the horrors of the front line ... working with oppressed, homeless women in a public shelter ... strengthening or restoring human connection through the use of the primary group. ... Two layers of work with oppressed people [are] 1) restoring human relatedness and strengthening transactions between people, and 2) strategies for political action (to help people) realize their potentials and change oppressive systems.[18]

Support groups may turn into advocacy groups (totally or partially) as they turn their attention to social action.

THERAPY AND THEME GROUPS: FOCUS ON INDIVIDUALS

Group psychotherapy differs from support groups or from social work with groups in several ways. In these groups, the worker is seen mainly as an expert in individual or personality dynamics. The leadership is somewhat permissive (although central and dominant), and spontaneity is encouraged. Usually, there is no pre-planned agenda. Session content depends on what the participants bring to the group. There is an emphasis on experiencing feelings. In order to achieve this, an atmosphere of mutual trust is promoted, always dominated by the overt or subtle influence of the therapist.

The psychotherapists may differ in their approach to the group aspect of the work in diverse ways. There are varieties of attentiveness to group aspects. Lang's review of the place of the group in various accounts of group therapy is instructive:

> Use ranges from approaches which disregard totally the use of groups in any sense (Berne, Perls, Slavson); to those approaches which value a developed, cohesive group only as a context supportive of therapeutic procedures, or as a means of generating interactional processes which will form the substantive content for analysis in the therapy (Foulkes, Yalom); to those approaches which characterize and interpret interactions of the participants solely as indicators of collective group themes (Bion, Ezriel, Whittaker, and Lieberman); to those which undertake a group-psychoanalysis (Wolf). In almost all of the group therapies the unit of attention is the individual and his treatment.[19]

Yalom's discussion of therapy captures the essence of an individually focused group therapy. It differs from a concern with the group: "group therapy is a highly individual process. Each patient will enter, participate in, use, and experience the group in a uniquely personal manner. The end of therapy is no less individual."[20] Even in a group setting, individual goals are held by each participant and/or for each by the therapist. The participants begin as strangers to each other and for the most part remain strangers although they learn more about themselves over time and hear the others also learning about themselves. In fact, therapists often caution participants against socializing with each other outside the group since this would contaminate the therapy process. Or, if outside contacts between members are seen as inevitable, then the members should be told it is their responsibility to discuss the key aspects of the encounter with the group.

In theme groups where the focus is upon learning a specific content, (e.g., social skills, managing stress), the main focus is also on the individual. The group becomes only the context for the learning. Usually, these are time-limited learning situations with predetermined, explicit goals shared with the participants at the outset. Plans or strategies are developed to help the participants move toward the identified individual goals via a cognitive/experiential format that emphasizes feedback and self/other assessment. The worker may be viewed as trainer, teacher, or consultant and plays a central, expert, controlling role.[21]

While group psychotherapy, as described by Yalom, and special interest, theme groups ordinarily focus on the individual in the context of the group, social work through groups and the support or treatment groups focus on the group as well as the individuals comprising it, and emphasize interpersonal interdependence and helpfulness. This is a way of dealing with the person *and* the environment. And this connection of persons with others and with their outside environments is a hallmark of social work, especially important in the structural approach.

SOCIAL WORK TREATMENT AND SOCIAL WORK WITH GROUPS

We see four criteria that distinguish *social work with groups*.[22] All four are related to the groupness aspect of the group. Many social workers work with groups, do treatment or psychotherapy, or skill training through group work. But unless their work meets these four criteria, we see them as doing group work but not necessarily social work with groups. Not everything a social worker does is social work! When the social worker drives a car or shuts a window, it is some activity but it is not social work. Likewise, the social worker may be doing individual therapy in a group and holding an intrapsychic focus, but misses the social work of the work. The conditions we see as characterizing social work through groups follow.

The practitioner begins by helping the group members gain a sense of each other and their groupness. They need to answer the questions:

who is here with me? what can groups do? what are the possibilities for this group? The group members and the worker are involved in transactions from the outset as they deal with these questions.

First, the worker must focus on helping the members become a system of mutual aid by deliberately encouraging between-member communication. Next, the worker must actively understand, value and respect the group process itself as the central change dynamic it is. Then, the worker must hold a basic attitudinal orientation of working herself out of a job. From the very first group meeting, the worker helps the group increase its autonomy so that it can continue as a support group after she either withdraws completely or changes her role to that of consultant or sponsor. This would apply except with a group of children or severely limited adults. Then the worker helps the group become as autonomous as possible. Fourth, and finally, the worker must help the group members to re-experience their groupness at the point of termination. This could happen in several ways— verbal and/or nonverbal, e.g., joint reminiscing, compiling a scrap book, a final event.

EMPOWERMENT AND ADVOCACY GROUPS

These groups deal with undervalued, stigmatized, alienated, and angry populations—people whom mainstream culture often tries to ignore. Examples may include the "warehoused" elderly, mental patients, delinquents, homosexuals, the homeless, persons with AIDS, the disabled, and so forth. Also included in empowerment groups are those who see themselves as disadvantaged (politically, economically, socially): women, racial, ethnic, religious minorities, or the many others who suffer the pangs of disaffection with their realities.

Two main routes toward empowerment pursued through group work are consciousness raising groups and advocacy groups. Often the first step is in the consciousness raising realm where participants may gain a new sense of their potentials and strengths. Usually these groups have a professional person as facilitator (a special instance of a support group),[23] but occasionally they are true self groups that develop among friends or work associates in order to increase their sense of self-worth or enhance morale (avoid burn out).[24]

Ordinarily, the advocacy groups develop through some professional leadership ordinarily to deal with oppressive aspects of "the system." In the case of the homeless women referred to earlier, Lee not only helped the women to help each other in their group and discussed how they might make the shelter a better place to live. She also helped them get out of the shelter to get back on their feet again outside. She met with the top city administrators, and helped the group share knowledge of their situation through media and alliances with other established groups.[25]

Working toward empowerment through advocacy entails special strategies and tactics in the political realm, a range of power pressures by the members and worker. Social workers with groups are becoming more knowledgeable in this arena.[26]

Group-Focused Skills

As we have learned, a major distinction among different types of therapies and social work with groups is the degree of attention to the group itself as the central helping medium, with the worker devoted to helping this happen. We think this could occur more often if workers had greater awareness of group processes and dynamics, and more opportunity to learn and practice group-focused skills. Several group-focused skills are described and illustrated in *Skills for Direct Practice in Social Work*.[27] These include:

Thinking group

Scanning

Fostering cohesiveness

Verbalizing unspoken norms

Encouraging development of traditions and rituals

Selecting communication patterns purposefully

Voicing group achievements

Preserving group history and continuity

Turning issues back to the group

Reaching for consensus

Reaching for difference

Reaching for a feeling link

Reaching for an information link

Amplifying subtle messages

Softening overpowering messages

Redirecting messages

Inviting full participation

These group-focused skills are used in addition to the various other skills that have been described as important for working with one person at a time.[28]

In the following excerpt, the worker's focus is clearly on the group. This is a meeting with ex-mental patients living in a halfway house. These women have lived there for more than ten months and have had three meetings as a group with the worker.

> Sara broke the silence and said, "When you're good at things, people don't like you." The other five women turned toward Sara, apparently in response to her emotion rather than the message itself. I asked if everyone understood what Sara was saying. There were several no's. I wondered if the group could ask her more about it, and Liz asked Sara what she meant. Sara said that when you are good at things, other people say you think you're better than they are and they don't like you. Her affect was still very strong. I commented that Sara seemed to have very strong feelings about this. She said she does, because it makes her stop doing anything too well because that's the only thing she can think to do. She said everyone wants to shoot you down, and it just plain isn't worth it. I wondered if anyone else had ever felt that way, and Liz said she did sometimes. . . . Amy said she does too. I said it must feel very uncomfortable. There were a few nods.

We see the social worker here assuming a mediating role, turning comments back to the group and to the individual (Sara) rather than answering herself. She did *not*, for example, say, "Sara, could you explain what you mean further?" She asked the group if they understood and if they would ask for more clarity. We also can see how this stance involves the group and takes away from an assumed role of expert in content for the worker. It is a subtle but important shift in emphasis.

It may strike one as strange, that probably the most useful and necessary skill for the worker with groups to have and use is *silence*. Actually, this should not be surprising since common sense tells us that only one person can speak at a time with any degree of impact. The more the worker speaks, the less "air time" there is for the group members. It is hard for learners of group work to master deliberate, timely silence, but they can when they are supported in its importance. Total silence (passivity) works out the same as total domination by the practitioner. Both are control more than support. The "trick" is to be differentially, sensitively silent when this encourages the group members to take over the issue at hand.

In this next excerpt we see such encouragement of the group helpfulness:

> I looked at James (who had revealed his problems last week) and asked how he was doing. He said he wants to disappear after all that he talked about last week. I was silent. The group members said that is just how they felt when this happened to them. Jerry, Sue, and Terry all talked about experiencing this kind of feeling. There was lots of agreement about talking and then feeling awful. James seemed to relax more and told of saying something to a girl he knows while in the hall, even though it was hard. He got approval for the risk he took; what if she had not responded to him! He was quiet. They said this was still movement on his part.

It takes relatively little time to help the individually focused practitioner develop a consciousness that begins to see the group itself instead of only the individuals who happen to be in the group, and then uses group focused interventions. In one recent instance, a student social worker in field work at a general hospital taught a psychiatric nurse twelve special group-focused skills in one two-and-a-half-hour session. The nurse was the leader of an outpatient bulimia group. In a pre- and post-observation, the trainer found that the nurse increased her group-focused skills by significant amounts. There was a gain in frequency in all but two skills. For example, within one twenty-minute segment of the meeting, the worker used "we" and "our" in dealing with the group. Before the training she was observed for a comparable time and never used these words.

In-Group and Extra-Group Life

The potential helpfulness of member-to-member contact outside the group is discouraged in psychotherapy groups. Citing Yalom again, "The therapy group teaches one how to develop intimate, long-term relationships, but it does not provide these relationships."[29] A rule of confidentiality concerning all that is said in the group is crucial for all group work so that the inside-group talk can be freely expressed within a safe atmosphere for sharing personal thoughts and feelings. This safety factor has much to do with the discouraging of member "friendships" outside the psychotherapy group. On the other hand, this very sharing (in the group and outside) has much to do with the strong bond of the self-help groups. One member of a rape victims' group brought out her sadness when a person she knew from this group refused to recognize her on the outside as they saw each other in a restaurant. The discussion of this "affront" lasted for about twenty minutes and was heated and critical for the group's evaluation of their faith in the group.

The various self-help, support groups, and social work with groups (in terms of our definition) are at the other end of the continuum so far as deliberate use of the members' connectedness goes. These emphasize the exchange of telephone numbers and mid-week communications among group members. For example, in the ideology of such groups as adults-molested-as-children or various substance abusers, emphasis is placed on the frequent member-to-member phone calls as equal to or even more important than the weekly group meetings. In support groups, it is not unusual also for the practitioner to telephone members between sessions. The worker has entered into the life situation of the group members and demonstrates this in actuality from time to time. Parties, trips, "graduations," and other special events are shared by the worker and group participants.

Conclusion

We have highlighted certain features of group work in this chapter with the intention of demystifying groups and encouraging increased attention to the potentialities such services can offer. The most basic issue in work with groups (as with most' experience in everyday living) is a matter of power. It can be summed up in this way: can you, do you dare to share your power as group leader and helper with the group members? Deciding to meet this challenge can bring exciting consequences that are amply rewarding. It can be a thrilling adventure to be part of others' increasing power and strength.

.

PART FIVE

Surroundings

11. The Metawork

Beyond dogma of the past, and habit, are possibilities for enhancement of the basic work of agencies—once all levels in the present hierarchy are scrutinized from the perspective of effective service rather than role-related self-interest. As one means for moving toward such a review, we propose the concept of metawork to stand for all the work about the work, and argue that whether or not this metawork actually enhances the work of the service delivery is open to question. Toward the end of stimulating increased interest in self-evaluation of service (rather than waiting for others to do this to the service systems), we present some data derived from time/cost studies, some brief consideration of the red tape that ties up the bureaucracies, and passing attention to the politically determined external influences that may have diverted the administrators of social agencies from deploying primary attention and resources to the quality of work life of the staff. Our aim in highlighting these internal and external complexities which the social welfare organizations will continue to have to contend with is to leave the reader with the challenge that effective services will be offered more readily when the obligation for continuous change rests equally upon the organization and its staff.

If we were to look around us at the social workers we know and make a private list of those whom we regard as especially effective, as movers of others, as imaginative innovators, chances are that those on our list would reveal a particular competence in managing the work to be done. They are most likely able to process quickly the diverse stimuli that demand differentiated responses, to sort out and cut through a morass of detail, and to set priorities. Issues involved in viewing one's work and allocating time differentially, which are matters of skill in priority setting, are major determinants of who will be effective and who will simply be actors in other people's scripts.

This component of priority setting and managing the work exists within all social work jobs, and in fact within all work. Social workers have some measure of control over how they spend their energies and how they organize their work. And yet, precious little attention is given to helping workers and students learn to do this. Such know-how is mainly picked up through trial and error if at all. Yet, it is interesting to note that some of the most popular workshops "sold" these days (in and out of social agencies) are those on time management and stress management.

Often, how one organizes the work is left to chance or determined by personal preferences or comfort with parts of the work, rather than by the imperatives of the tasks of service delivery or client need. This aspect of the work, the "discretionary component," refers to areas where workers are expected and/or required to use their own judgment in planning and executing the tasks, or in other words to exert authority in decision making rather than follow prescribed directions.[1] A job whose tasks require only following prescribed routines can hardly be thought of as "professional."

As we look back upon the past, a serious charge can be raised. Social workers have been busy people, but have they consistently exposed their work to such questions as: "Is all this really necessary?" "Are all of these activities really important?" We think not. Some of these activities might well be abandoned altogether. Habit, faith, dogma, and tradition have often ordered the thinking about the "good" service, the "proper" intake procedure, and the necessary recording, more than has a continuous critique of the actual merit of these tasks.

The Work and the Metawork

Considering the many activities that bid for worker time and energy, it seems important to separate the work of the direct practice tasks from what we term "metawork." The metawork concept will distinguish certain activities, those that facilitate the actual work, from the work itself. In this sense, metawork is *work about the work*. It is work that supports the direct worker/client engagement but is aside from it.

In chapters 3 through 11 we described many varied activities which are concerned with the client in need and are pursued as the worker's response to the client according to the service contract they develop together. These activities may be with clients, with others in behalf of clients, and with clients in behalf of themselves and others (Quadrant A, D, or B activities). From the worker's perspective, all activities to meet the demands of the client task can be thought of as the service delivery work: some is direct work, some is metawork.

When the rationale for being involved in a particular activity is that it is a response to the clients' understanding of what is happening in their behalf, then this is the work involved in service delivery. This is the service delivery work whether it occurs directly with the clients, whether in person or on the telephone, or whether it happens in person or by telephone with people other than the client. All other work that may be once-removed from direct engagement with clients (or unknown to the client) is the metawork—the activities that may enhance the work but are aside from the work itself.

Adopting this perspective, such activities as recording, attending staff meetings, team meetings, treatment conferences, or attending conferences, institutes, or workshops are either agency work or professional development work. These activities, plus participating in supervision as supervisor or worker, receiving or offering training or staff development, are metawork.

In this category also must be placed dealing with all the red tape, the elaborate accounting and billing systems, and the formal, written communication systems that have grown out of the organization's need to be accountable for the work. Once a distinction is drawn between work with clients and all the "supportive" work directed to facilitating this work, it may be easier to look at this huge superstructure of metawork to determine its actual versus its illusory enhancement of the basic work. The plight of workers in bureaucratized systems who cannot find time to serve their enormous number of clients at least partially springs from the disproportionate amount of metawork to work, ritualized by the agency through history and tradition.

To a certain extent, computerization of the organization's information systems has made for a more efficient workplace and a speedier capability for dealing with the huge amount of data needed to operate.

And yet the requirements for information have increased exponentially, offsetting much of the gain in speed that computers bring.

If we consider all the in-person conferences and meetings, plus all the paper communication as time spent in the name of service *to* clients but not *with* clients, then certain questions must be posed: what proportion of human energy and time within the total operation is directly concerned with clients, as opposed to that spent in behalf of the agency's administrative needs? What proportion of the energy and time is consumed by the accountability systems? Following these questions, we must consider whether things should stay this way.

Time/Cost Studies

A benchmark study of these issues was conducted by the Family Service of Philadelphia during 1951–52.[2] This was the first major systematic study of its kind that applied to social services the cost accounting principles drawn from the world of commerce and business management. The total staff (administrative, supervisory, casework, and clerical) recorded use of time to the nearest five-minute interval in terms of its ultimate purpose over 252 randomly selected working days not known in advance by the individuals. Eight cost centers were derived from about two hundred activities that staff might perform. Of these, four were considered the basic activities or "production costs" (casework, group education, professional education or student training, and community activities and planning). The remaining four were viewed as collateral or "share-of-service" costs; that is, those efforts aimed at maintaining the proper quantity and quality level in the basic activities—staff education and development, research, public relations, and general administration.

Further, each of the eight cost centers had a detailed breakdown of activities comprising the category. For example, casework specified subcategories as follows: in-person interviews in the office and outside the office; telephone interviews; collateral in-person interviews in the office and outside the office; collateral telephone interviews; supervision; case consultations; case conferences; case recording; and case assignment routines.

As table 11.1 shows, $63.66 of each $100 agency expenditure (or

65 percent of all staff time) went to the four basic activities, (production costs), while $36.34 (35 percent) went to the collateral activities, (share of service costs). Within the 65 percent devoted to the basics (casework, group education, professional education, community activities and planning), casework accounted for 56 percent while the other three basic services received 2.9 percent, 2.1 percent, and 3.3 percent respectively. Eighty-six percent of the time spent on the basic activities went to casework, a finding "gratifying" to the executive. A further breakdown of casework by organizational role revealed that it consumed approximately 82 percent of the caseworkers' time, 50 percent of the supervisors' time, 39 percent of clerical time, and 4 percent of administrative time. But what proportion of casework's 86 percent was spent with clients? As the table reveals, only about 27 percent of the casework services (the production part of "interviewing costs") was actually devoted to the direct delivery. We shall consider the other 73 percent metawork.

Discussing these findings, Ormsby called for new administrative standards and norms regarding the ratio of total resources to the basic activities and the collateral activities as well as the proportion of in-person interviews to processing procedures (dictation, evaluation, conferencing, consultation, preparation for specific activities) so as to get away from programs "built up piecemeal and without design other than traditional patterns."[3] Following this elaborate time study, agency attention was aimed at diverting more resources to client interviewing and less to meetings, supervisory conferences, and the detail work required in compiling "much seldom-used data."[4] As a result of the impact of seeing that combined recording and supervisory costs ex-

TABLE 11.1. Distribution of $100 Among Casework Services

	Total Cost	Production Cost	Share of Service Cost
Interviewing costs	$42.49	$26.80	$15.69
Case recording	32.15	20.27	11.88
Supervisory conferences	13.17	8.30	4.87
Case consultations	5.77	3.64	2.13
Miscellaneous	6.42	4.29	2.13
Total	$100.00	$63.30	$36.70

ceeded interviewing costs, case summaries were reduced from the usual six or eight pages to two, with oral presentations during supervisory conferences, rather than following the requirement for detailed process recordings. Encouraging as these efforts seem to be, Ormsby also commented:

> It is obviously impossible to expect a caseworker to have, on the average, more than three client and collateral in-person interviews per working day, plus necessary telephone interviews, *unless ways can be found to reduce drastically demands on the worker to record, carry out community and public relations assignments, attend staff meetings, and so forth.*[5] (emphasis added)

Now, years later, social agencies have not yet found the means to reduce the demands on the worker as suggested by Ormsby. In fact, we are hard put to find more than a handful of agency-initiated time-cost studies in the literature. Family Service Association of America (FSAA), now known as Family Service America (FSA), encouraged other member agencies to apply time-analysis studies to measure agency operations quantitatively[6] and in 1971 reported to its membership a summary of studies conducted by fifty agencies.[7] Although analysis of these data from agencies of various sizes and program emphases did not account for the differences in time expenditures by either agency size or program, the amount of staff time devoted to program-related activities was found to be 86 percent, just as in the Hill-Ormsby study. Of this amount, 39 percent was spent directly with or on behalf of clients, three quarters of which time, or 29 percent, was in interviews with families (a median amount 2 percent higher than in the original study). Recording averaged 14 percent, supervision 11 percent, and preparation, staff development, and other activities 21 percent.

Despite frequent blasts in the news media that aim to expose mismanagement and waste, there has been little discussion of similar attempts by agencies to tackle the metawork issue. The situation today remains much as it was before the Hill-Ormsby study, except that agency executives cannot feel quite so comfortable with 86 percent of basic activity devoted to casework and 3.3 percent for community activities *(sic!)* and planning.

In 1972, with fewer systematic controls than the FSAA study, a study of the time allocation of six direct service workers was undertaken in a children's agency. Here it was found that 19 percent was devoted to interviews with clients while 81 percent went to activities needed to support this work (dictation, phone calls, record reading, interview preparation, conferences, meetings, court hearings, and travel). Further, it was found that diagnostic evaluations consumed a minimum of eleven and a half to thirteen hours per child and might take twenty-one and a half hours; maternity intakes could range from three hours and ten minutes to five and a half hours; and foster home applications required from two hours and fifty minutes to three and a quarter hours. We must remember that only one fifth of all these hours was spent with the clients.[8] Briar and Miller discuss this aspect of metawork:

> Clients generally do not come to caseworkers simply to be diagnosed—they want and legitimately expect to be helped. . . . Diagnostic efforts are justifiable only insofar as they contribute to the effectiveness of the intervention. . . . If the practitioner has only one treatment approach in his repertoire, then diagnosis is not only unnecessary but meaningless. . . . In many social agencies, it is not uncommon for staff conferences convened to discuss cases to devote fifty-eight minutes to "diagnosis" and two minutes to intervention planning with little apparent connection between the two discussions.[9]

The time/cost investment in meetings has continued to be an area of concern and investigation, especially as resources have been curtailed in the last decade. Meetings are expensive. According to Tropman's studies more than half of staff time (and of highest paid staff) is consumed by meetings, not counting the preparation time involved![10] Attention to the tasks of group problem solving, decision making, and effective committee meetings has gained increased consideration in the literature, perhaps as one approach toward decreasing the expense of organizational meetings.[11]

Recording

A key aspect of the metawork is the recording system. The process record, a timeworn standard operating procedure, in the past was the greatest consumer of worker time. Despite the difficulty of obtaining information on the ratio of clerical time to professional time necessary for completed dictation, and the obvious differences among agencies due to matters of size, auspices, and objectives,[12] one estimate drawn from a large, public system indicated that each minute of worker dictation demanded from 3.38 to 5.2 minutes of clerical time for its transcription.[13]

We discuss the process record, not because it is much of a component of the metawork today, but because it is of enormous importance in considering the development of professionalism in social work. The detailed written (process) record of the worker's engagement with the client was a major means for on-the-job teaching, learning, and surveillance. Perhaps the time investment, inclusive of dictating, transcribing, and reviewing (reading and discussing by the workers and their supervisors), would have been justifiable if we were convinced that such procedures made for a better service. But this issue has never been documented. Probably valuation of this laborious, voluminous written work stemmed more from the time-honored system of supervision than from the demands of the service.

These written records aimed to demonstrate workers' sensitivity to diagnostic cues. They were focused upon the client and the client's problem. The accounts mainly revealed the client's reactions and feelings plus the workers' judgments of their meaning. They did not equally record the workers' reactions and feelings as one major element that affected everything the client did. Usually, the workers' part of the transaction was taken as a given. For example, workers did not record moments when they felt intimidated or bored or uncertain, nor do they ordinarily admit in the written review that the anger noted on the part of the client might have been aroused by their ineptitude.

The worker's detailed record of the client's response to the effort to help often contained as much biased and possibly perjorative information as it did facts. And while the facts and bare history provided continuity when workers left, agencies might have had fewer "hopeless" clients if workers were freed from the biased accounts of their predecessors, and could form their own impressions out of the freshness of a new contact.

Supervisors reviewed these accounts and used them to help workers see their blind spots, biases, or other insensitive behavior by making their own inferences from what was and what was *not* recorded.

This process could become the game of "I see something you don't see," an important mechanism for assuring some supervisors that they really knew more than the workers and held a vital place in the agency hierarchy.[14]

Another question must be raised about the case record that focused on a description of client behavior. Did clients know that a written record of their cases would be kept which would reside in the agency files for all time? Did they know that their attitudes, feelings, and so forth might be recorded there, possibly subject to court order if evidence about them was desired at some future time, possibly open to public scrutiny? The social work profession has not yet achieved community sanction for privileged communication, as have psychiatry, law, and the ministry, and cannot completely assure confidentiality to the client. Surely, we believe, clients' understanding here and agreement to such documents should have been a sine qua non for work in their behalf. And written documents should be kept with the hazards of public exposure in mind.

We question this time-intensive process record for its susceptibility to subjectivity, and its potentially dangerous misuse in the legal arena. It was the instrument by which the supervisor could know what each worker did with the clients, since the actual transaction was usually conducted in office privacy. Thus, the record was the tool for the supervisor and was used for attending to the quality of services. But it was not lawyer-proof!

Some critics believed that workers were kept too long from performing as autonomous professionals, responsible for the quality of their own work. Workers, also, were often not allowed to deal with other professionals without checking or clearing first with their supervisors. These considerations are of less consequence now, since the ACSW certification of NASW and the states' licensure requirements are standardized approaches to (assumedly) determine competence. Other opportunities for examining and upgrading one's practice skills in the workplace now may include such experiences as peer self-help groups, case conferences, training sessions, and videotaped and critiqued samples of practice.

Realistically, the written process record is an impossibility in present day agency work except as it may be used as an educational tool with students. Even here, more popular means of "seeing" what workers do with others is obtained through watching behind one-way mirrors, co-leading groups, reviewing selected segments of audiotaped or videotaped sessions, or even supervisors "sitting in" (being there in person while the learner does a session with a client). Obviously these techniques are time-savers for supervisors, which is what justifies them in the hectic work-a-day agency whirl. They are not sounder educationally.

Laborious as the process record might have been, still it contained within it the seeds of professional development for workers. Now, it is "out" and workers are still consumed, perhaps even more so, with metawork, with paperwork. There are tremendous controls in every field of practice: the UCRs (Uniform Case Record) and DRGs (Diagnostic Related Guidelines), the DSM III and other insurance reports, and the many other technical restrictions to deal with so as to make for more accountable, efficient work. Alarm is expressed concerning the growing technical culture surrounding social services and professional practice, and the imposition of external bureaucratic controls on professional practice in the public and the voluntary agencies as well. There is uneasiness with the encroaching controls of guidelines that must be followed, exemplified by such key words as "specific task," "discontinuous processes," "scientific management," and "management by objectives."[15]

The shift throughout social work's history from "craft" to "assembly line" practice (in large public-sector agencies) has been described in frightful detail. For example, the organization is seen as a factory; the work is viewed as trivialized (reorganized into small specific tasks where workers have little control over or knowledge of outcomes); the *output* is valued more than the *outcome*. Here, the quality emphasis is getting the statistics in on time and moving cases through the process within a limited time frame Quality is quantity! Workers are deskilled, client problems are fragmented, and discretionary decision making by workers is eliminated.[16]

The process record has been a valued part of the profession's tradition, but it is now eclipsed in the work of the metawork as we have suggested. It is the vestigial appendix of the organization's information system. Yet, it remains a qualitative means for professional learning with its demand for reflection, conceptualization, and examination of one's blind spots and values. It has not entirely disappeared from student professional education as an instrument for learning and growth. We believe some modified form of process recording, perhaps following one case of the worker's preference, and reviewed with the supervisor or with peers at a stipulated "professional-time" each week might add quality to the workplace and "heart" to the workers.

Other Approaches to Record Keeping

Records serve several purposes: accountability, reimbursement documentation, continuity, on-the-job training among others. These purposes should be clearly separated from each other to insure the integrity and utility of each. The accountability aspect is statistical and has to do with numbers of contacts, numbers of inquiries, kinds of problems, hours spent, monies spent and so forth. These accounts are also necessary for reimbursement purposes. Continuity is provided by a record of service, which should also be factual and summarized. Each agency has certain purposes for which these records of service are used, and these should be known by the workers before they produce written records.

Probably the purpose (and thus the format) will differ according to who uses the records and to what ends. For instance, when social workers are in interdisciplinary settings and their notations are placed centrally along with those of physicians, attendants, or other staff, the nature of the information will differ from the recording made within the social service department or a social agency. In chapter 12, preconditions for responsible practice are introduced. One of these preconditions is "to communicate in exoteric language," to understand the medicalese and other technical languages and yet speak and write simply.

In the instance that follows, we find the social worker taking the initiative to insert exoteric language in a multidisciplinary setting:

> I work in a residential school for multi-handicapped children. I often find myself overwhelmed by the professional jargon our medical and therapy staff introduces to our parents at conferences. Many have never before been informed as to their child's condition, and they do not understand the complex vocabulary nor ask for expla-

nations. The other specialists, when I raised this issue, expected
that the social worker would translate the information for the parents at some later time.

I took a different approach. I identified each of the terms used by
the therapy departments most often and requested they define the
terms. I made a minidictionary comprised of terms like spaticity,
hypertonic, athetosis, *pes planus,* and much more, that could be
given to parents at meetings. Our staff group continued to work on
this communication problem. Each department compiled a list of
self-help books. We decided to make an attractive reading room.

While this began in the interactional level of communication, the new
awareness crept into the written work also. This staff became committed to making their exchanges and writings understandable.

Another use (misuse?) of records is for dealing with the legal
system, a situation in which social workers are now vulnerable professionals. Issues related to reporting suspected child abuse, neglect,
and other child welfare matters—all of which can be generalized to
other areas—are detailed, as are worker liability protection, guidelines for interviewing, and cautions for worker written and oral behavior.[17]

Generally, records are a collection of information that is needed to
document or convey detail to another source concerned with the
agency's program and services. The kind of information detailed in
case records, forms, and all written accounting should always be
viewed from the perspective of what its use will be. For example, the
elaborateness of social histories containing voluminous questions on
the client's background should be reivewed from the perspective of
how all this information will help in offering services, and each non-
essential question should be viewed with alarm.

Many social workers have discovered that an ecomap,[18] a graphic
diagram developed in discussion with the client, is not only a parsimonious record of information about the many impinging forces on a
client, but an excellent means of involving clients in presenting key
information in a simple way. The DSM III (Diagnostic and Statistical
Manual) coding system developed by the American Psychiatric Association and the PIE (Person in Environment) developed by the California Chapter of NASW are both attempts to control descriptive lan-

guage through specifying definitions and reducing assessment to numerical codes that are parsimonious.

Agencies do not expect new workers to attack the record-keeping system as a first order of involvement. However, as workers become familiar with the setting, it is not beyond the realm of possibility that some of their energies will be directed at this aspect of the work as one way to push the organization to engage in continuous self-appraisal.

As a general heuristic, the practitioners' focus in their record of service should be on *their* activities with the client. For example, their written account might include date of contact, tasks performed, telephone calls and contacts made with various sources in behalf of the client, outcomes of these contacts, and next appointment or other steps arranged. Furthermore, the record should *not* be about the client's behavior or responses to the worker.

This type of service record would provide continuity, enable new workers to pick up with clients and know what had happened in the past, and avoid many of the problems of biases, value judgments, and misuse. Clearly, this approach to recording with its emphasis upon the specific things done with or on behalf of the client rather than upon detailing client responses to worker statements or the worker/client relationship dynamics, is a key element of a structural approach to practice. The emphasis here is upon the task to be accomplished and the steps taken toward the goal. The relationship develops out of work on the task.

Other kinds of written records might be undertaken for the avowed purposed of worker on-the-job training. These might form the basis for teaching and staff development in individual or group supervisory conferences, team meetings, training sessions, and so forth. For these purposes as much detail as possible is desirable, especially in those portions of a contact with a client that workers see as problematic and with which they wish help. The detailed written account of the worker and client in action, screened through the grid of the worker's judgment of the essential elements after the event, can be a vital teaching/learning instrument. It is, of course, screened, being workers' versions of what happened; limited by what they noticed and remembered, their willingness and facility in using words to describe the total transaction, and the capability of words for expressing experience.

This record might be composed of two parts, narrative and analysis. In the narrative portion, the minutiae of the transaction are detailed in process, in "client said-I said" fashion. The workers' preparation for reviewing their work should include underlining and noting in the margin what skills they used, what principles they were following, and so forth. In the analysis portion, workers would discuss why they did what they did, what underlying theory or theories they were operating from, and what questions they have.

Another form of on-the-job records for worker development are the notes kept by the workers for their own use, perhaps as reminders of themes to pursue, issues to raise in the future, shifts in the patterns of interaction. As workers form the habit of keeping their own logs aimed toward particulars upon which they wish to focus their energies and attention, they will come to feel a special kind of responsibility for their own progress on the job.

The use of one-way screens where others can view and evaluate the work is another approach that might stimulate worker learning and improved performance. For on-the-spot feedback and suggestions, a telephone can connect the worker and the viewer behind the one-way screen so that suggestions or cautions can be telephoned in while the transaction is in progress. Clearly, the only way to obtain a complete account of a transaction is through videotaping so all that is said or not said can be captured. And even this mechanism is limited by the focus of the camera at any particular moment; hence its account is not fully complete. Audiotapes can provide documentation of the verbal part of the transaction, possibly useful for later study and review.

It may seem that electronic equipment is too expensive for agencies to mount. New technology, computerization of the record keeping system, and other electronics have been installed in the business side of the organizations; many agencies have found the means to invest in the person-side of the system. New modalities and formats for on-the-job training inevitably will replace older patterns and forms, especially since moves are on to reorganize and retrench personnel. We have received good reports on the agency workers' use of a computer-based teaching system, *I-View Skills: Interviewing Skills for the Human Services*,[19] which workers follow at their own pace in their own time.

A primary implication, not fully elaborated here, is that a new culture surrounding agency work must be established. This would include new norms for transforming the privateness and loneliness of a practice shared only with the supervisor (or with no one, in some agencies) into a public matter open for group attention and peer-directed learning.

Supervision

We think workers cannot accord self-determination to clients when they, themselves, suffer from a gross lack of professional self-determination within the bureaucratic hierarchy. Unlike the client, workers cannot stop going to conferences when they believe that these are not helpful to them (without placing their evaluation or very job in jeopardy). Nor do they possess ready-made action groups to advocate for *their* professional entitlement against the power structure of the agency. We have suggested some collective action in chapter 3, with Principle 6, the Self Principle which assumes that it is a professional imperative to act so as to help "the system" correct itself in particular areas.

Here is how one worker reflected on the situation:

> Many social workers deal with caseloads far too large to manage successfully. I have worked in situations where colleague expertise was valued, and also where workers operated individually. I found that when I had colleagues who voiced opinions and lent assistance, my feeling of being overwhelmed was lessened. We, as social workers, expect a good deal from our clients. Can we not make the same expectations of ourselves and our fellow workers? Just as the structural approach assumes clients are adequate, so we, as workers, might first assume that the workers are adequate; often it is the service delivery system which must be targeted for change.

Even in precarious economic times, when unions are attacked and all workers fear for their futures, strategic change-focused behavior by workers may be seen as insurance, as prevention which ultimately saves services' quality as well as quantity. We see this as work against burnout, as work on behalf of the service system.

The influence of supervisor upon worker is potent and flows from several bases of power: legitimate (the agency sanctions this role); expert (though sometimes questioned, the supervisor knows more); informational (the supervisor has particular information to which the worker does not have access); reward and coercive (the evaluation, promotion, often the increment, and thus the image, of the worker rest in the supervisor's hands). There also may be a referent power base operating—that is, power derived from likeness of race, ethnicity, gender, age, and so forth.[20]

Goffman viewed the social behavior of persons as careful performances that create a "front" or an impression. Individuals define the situations they encounter in such a way that they guide and control the impressions that others obtain of them; by using various techniques, they aim to present a favorable self-image.[21] As one obvious case in point, consider the airline flight attendants with their "well managed smiles,"[22] laboriously cultivated so as to please the tired business men passengers, a requisite for successful employment. Their smile is cultivated in special training sessions; performances are periodically evaluated.

With respect to their supervisor, social workers, from their low power status, expend considerable energy on their "impression management" out of self-interest. Their differences with the supervisor might be labeled overreactive or unconscious resistance or denial.[23] To approach the problems that stem from such normative judgments by supervisors, agencies must begin somehow to convey the message to the workers that they have the skills necessary to accomplish their work, and set about deploying the energies of the higher echelon staff to devise ways for systematically stretching horizons and stimulating all the service staff to exploration of the practice.

The complexity of the supervisory role in social work, a role that combined administrative and educative functions in one person, has been discussed extensively in the literature,[24] starting with Austin's highlighting of this dilemma and urging that these two functions be separated.[25] But as Hanlan pointed out, there have been no formal, permanent, structural revisions within agencies to support attempts to redefine the supervisor's role.[26]

As the social work profession was professionalizing itself, the teaching of workers by supervisors in the agencies was the major avenue through which the knowledge and skills needed for practice were conveyed. Classical accounts that emphasized the teaching and learning components as dominant in supervision include those of Robinson, Reynolds, Towle, and Williamson.[27] Consider, for example, Bertha Reynold's ideas:

> We are not so greatly concerned with how much he can repeat from books the preserved experience of others. . . . Books may interpret, but cannot supercede living experience. . . . (as Sir William Osler, a great teacher of medicine told his students), medicine is learned at the bedside and not in the classroom. . . .
>
> There is need of flexible and richly associating minds capable of both analysis and synthesis; of sensitivity to people, ability to feel with them and yet to see them in perspective; of ability to express feeling and yet keep in balance with all the forces in the situation. When we think of such an educational goal, we are perhaps worried because we feel as if we had to *make* a professional personality. We have only to let it grow.
>
> How much time does a professional self need to grow?[28]

Reynolds did not offer a specific answer to this question. It was an "all depends" matter, depending on how much the learner practiced and also on how skilled at teaching the supervisor was. She thought some students might graduate and never gain the stage of awareness of the use of one's professional self in working with others. As Reynolds put it so eloquently, "the temple of learning is not to be entered carelessly or with muddy shoes."[29] On-the-job teaching and learning through supervision was an unending arrangement during the profession's developing years; the more "professional" the agency, the more the practitioner could expect to have close supervision—an arrangement purporting to be for the practitioner's learning interests but also to assure some uniformity and accountability in the agency's interests.

Kadushin's survey of supervisors and supervisees (1974) yielded a view of the creeping change taking place in the valuation of educative supervision. Supervisors wanted to teach more than supervisees wished to be taught! Twenty-six percent of the supervisors saw themselves as teachers, but only 3 percent of the supervisees saw themselves as students. Supervisees described their relationship as that of colleague-collaborator (60 percent), while only 30 percent of the supervisors described it in that way. The supervisors' view of their teaching role was further underscored by their reported satisfactions in supervising:

first came helping supervisees grow and develop in professional competence, third came sharing knowledge and skills. Kadushin commented that his findings reflected the interference of work pressures with instructional goals.[30]

Gradually, the role of the supervisor has shifted markedly in terms of the teaching function. Partly, this is a consequence of new time constraints and priorities in the workplace, new technical and mechanical tools which capture, store, and retrieve data differently, and "jazzy" training opportunities outside the workplace. And as if these factors were not enough to do traditional supervision in, those practitioners who have known such supervision firsthand through their own learning experiences are dying out. In fact, they are an endangered species!

Interestingly, in the early 1980s, a time study of supervisory activity in private social agencies found *teaching* occupied only 13 percent of the supervisor's time while *administering* averaged 35 percent. These supervisors, when questioned on their preferred use of time, said they desired *teaching* an average of 21 percent and *administering* 13 percent.[31] Subsequent informal reports in class discussions indicate that the time allotted to the teaching function by supervisors approaches zero these days!

The disappearance of the teaching function is accompanied by the demise of *supervision,* itself: not the title "supervisor," but the varied tasks that were the supervisor's forte so far as professional enhancement was concerned—imparting practice orientations, considering ethical and value issues, helping workers toward a conscious use of self. "Supervisor" is out and "manager" is in! This goes for agency work and professional education classes as well. The workplace becomes more like a business. The valued knowledge to impart is more in the realm of technical aspects: how to use the computer, how to measure client progress, and so forth.

Returning to a consideration of traditional supervision, it was not merely unending and time-consuming. Its almost exclusive reliance upon the mechanism of close one-to-one supervision as the major means for keeping agency practice in tune with service requirements has been increasingly questioned in the literature in regard to its influence upon conformity rather than innovation, its power over the professional destinies of the staff, and its anti-egalitarian emphasis.

It was seen by increasing numbers of practitioners as inhibiting to the avowed professional norm of individual autonomy. It was authoritarian in consequences. Chernesky claimed that it was incongruent with feminist principles and values, a "patriarchal model of power expressed as a hierarchy, with those higher up on the pyramid controlling and dominating their subordinates."[32] It is intriguing to speculate on this "patriarchal arrangement" for a profession whose gender distribution, as indicated by NASW membership, was only 27 percent male in 1986.[33]

Middleman and Rhodes questioned the emphasis in the literature on only two or three supervisory functions (administrative, educative, and supportive),[34] and proposed a more complex arrangement to account for what supervisors actually did: nine functions that express three organizational imperatives, as shown in table 11.2. Without elaborating these organizational imperatives and nine supervisory functions, it is apparent that the supervisor's assignment in today's organization is complex.

We have reviewed recording and its uses for purposes of accountability, continuity, reimbursement, and on-the-job training because of a concern that the time invested in writing and processing records through conferences with supervisors exceeds that spent directly with clients. This suspicion has only increased in recent times, with addi-

TABLE 11.2. Supervisory Organizational Imperatives

Organizational Imperative	Supervisory Function
Stability (and survival)	Integrating Functions Humanizing Managing tension Catalyzing (idea generating)
Adaptability (to internal/ external forces)	Linkage Functions Administering Advocating (for workers) Changing
Effectiveness (quality of services and how delivered)	Product/Process Functions Teaching Evaluating Career socializing

tional pressures regarding accountability and numerically justifying
services for reimbursement—for agency survival!

Supervisors, Managers, Trainers, and Team Leaders

We have suggested the need for differentiation among the purposes
of records and proposed some new formats which might be utilized to
distinguish the record of service that is kept assumedly in the client's
(and agency's) behalf from the documents whose primary raison d'être
is teaching the workers. Naturally, any restructuring of the record
keeping system calls into question the type of supervision that such
recording supports. We cited the need for change in the traditional
supervisory arrangements of agencies, a conclusion also reported in
Schwartz and Sample's research which found traditional supervisory
arrangements did not contribute to the most effective performance of
practitioners.[35] We have identified also some of the forces that have
conspired to transform supervisors into managers. It seems imperative
that agencies critically review present hierarchical supervisory arrangements and restructure roles so that becoming a supervisor is not
the only route upward in the organization.

The role of trainer seems especially important as an alternative to
an emphasis on supervision. When the educational function is separated from the administrative function of supervision, then attention
can be devoted more efficiently both to quality control and to the
needs of staff for innovation and learning. Manpower studies suggest
the efficacy of team approaches that include members of diverse
professional and educational backgrounds for delivering better services than have certain approaches in the past.[36]

Trainers should be specialists in using group approaches with staff
and able to teach staff to work in teams. Implied here is a group-based
training approach within agencies, one featuring lots of workshops.
At the staff level the use of the team for idea exchange and decision-
making, as has been demonstrated in other commercial organizations,[37] provides opportunities for creating new norms within the
service delivery systems that stress peer judgment and mutual responsibility in practice.

One organizational restructuring approach which aimed to turn the "semi-autonomous unit supervisors" in a large public agency into "collegial team leaders" is described in Wijnberg and Laury. It is an example of such group-based training, a team approach to turn:

> [the] isolated, disconnected and often despairing practitioners into integrated groups of workers with a shared vision, mutual concerns and caring attitudes . . . [to] share knowledge and skills, provide one another with mutual support in coping with stressful tasks, and increase the visibility of the case resources and neighborhoods.[38]

The retraining of the supervisors consumed several years and emphasized the learning of leadership behavior and small group process. The effort was described by the authors as a response to a "fundamental change in the profession of social work":

> The transfer of practice from community agencies to bureaucratic organizations; the shift from intrapsychic to problem solving orientations; the changes from long term invisible strategies to short term visible phenomena; from perceptions of the client as "ill" to perceptions of the client as "coper."[39]

To a great extent in current organization practice, supervision for quality work and practitioner learning has been transformed—away from the one-to-one model of the past, to the team meeting and treatment conference as the mechanisms for quality control and professional development.

The Team

The team, a group of professionals, case aides, specialists, and sometimes volunteers, collaborates to achieve a specified service goal, perhaps for general programmatic direction or for a particular client. They discuss in advance the activities to be accomplished to achieve the goal, and then various assignments toward this end are made by the team leader. Ordinarily, the team has a regular meeting time in the agency's schedule and has a fairly stable composition with the occasional addition of those with special expertise in response to a particular problem or client situation. The flavor of the team influence can be seen in these reflections by a hospice social worker:

Our interdisciplinary team is comprised of five nurses, two social workers, a chaplain, an expressive art therapist, and any volunteers who are assigned to the families we are working with. We meet twice a week—once to review all our current cases, update our plan of care, and plan the week's work, and again to hear presentations of new cases. Our supervisor is there to answer any questions we may have about agency policy as it affects our work with a particular family, and to take notes for the ongoing written plan of care. No one person is considered the leader of the team. All the team members working with a given family are equal members of the team, including the volunteers.

The team meetings demand careful listening and thinking because we depend upon one another to help us clarify thinking and to broaden our perspectives in the problem-solving process. They also serve as a stress management tool within the agency. In the team meeting we can "let our hair down" about problems and frustrations, and know that the other persons there are colleagues who understand what we are about out of their own experiences, and what difficulties we may face. I would hate to think of having to do my work alone, without my team's expertise and support.

A literature about teams and their workings has developed since the 1960s, concurrent with mental health services' movement into the community and social work's involvement with professionals in health systems.[40] The growth of new mental health disciplines and interdisciplinary practice with the elderly, chronically ill, and disabled have also necessitated a team approach.

The team notion accompanies the growing interest in holistic ideas about the individual and environment and is a move away from fragmentation of persons, especially possible in our Age of the Specialist. It is a way to bring many points of view and expertise to bear in consideration of a particular situation. Teams involve strategic collaboration, conferring, consulting, and coordination toward the goal of comprehensiveness of care. As implied in the hospice worker's remarks, one doesn't have to go it alone; others are in that same boat with you.

Multidisciplinary teams should be distinguished from interdisciplinary ones. The multidisciplinary team is hierarchical with leadership and control vested in the physician (who has medical expertise and legal responsibility) in the health area, in the principal in a school setting, in the superintendent in corrections, and so forth. The various disciplines are represented, but have clearly defined and separate roles. The interdisciplinary team integrates, not merely coordinates. It involves interdependent talents of different persons, each contributing particular knowledge and skills, and some blending or overlapping of roles based on the client's needs rather than traditional definitions of professional roles. The chair of these team meetings is apt to fluctuate from session to session according to the issues at hand.

Work as a team member requires practitioners to possess and project a clear self-image of what they are about, i.e., have a clear professional identity. They must be willing and able to learn what others (providers and clients) can do and cannot do in different situations. They must be able to accept and include others as appropriate to the situation. They must be able to analyze the system in which the interrelationship between one's self and others occurs, and be willing and able to use communication, confrontation, and group skills to work with others in solving problems.

Empirical studies of the workings of treatment conferences and psychiatric teams found their major drawback was time consumption, which workers saw as detracting from direct service to clients. Other disadvantages (in psychiatric settings) included status conflicts and competition for power and control, fragmentation, and pressure to conform. Otherwise, the benefits of the treatment teams included: improved services, increased staff accountability for client progress, up-to-date information on each client situation, increased collective awareness of treatment programming and differences in client behavioral responses, and heightened staff morale.[41]

One area of interest in the small group literature over the years and, more recently, in social work literature is whether groups make better decisions than individuals working alone. In general, groups have *not* been found superior, but participants have been more likely to implement the decisions if they had a hand in their making. However, from extensive study of meetings, Tropman claimed that decisions are almost always the result of some group process, and their quality is likely higher if groups make them.[42] Other research suggests that group members may be stimulated to be more explicit about reasons for their choices if the process of decision making is public.[43] The complexities involved in studying this issue confound any conclusive results,[44] even when participants possess equal access to needed information. Clearly, with interdisciplinary teams, their very purpose is the pooling of diverse knowledge and expertise. This greater cumulative perspective and potential for increased staff morale (if the teams are conducted supportively) would seem to justify their value.

Conclusion

In considering the issue of work and metawork, we have inevitably been drawn into areas previously excluded from the core curriculum of the student in direct service emphases. Such areas as organizational theory, superior/subordinate role relationships, and their variable patterns have been largely reserved for those choosing to specialize in administration, management, and policy/planning. Preparation of the direct service practitioner concentrated on the complexities of the worker-client relationship.

Our central thesis is that service deliverers must know as much about their interrelatedness to others within the system, to the ways organizations move and shift or stick and stay, as they need to know about their own roles with clients. For, in large part, their work with clients is as much affected by the forces of the organization within which they operate as by their own efforts with a given client. The organizational environment is not neutral!

As long as the organizational arrangements are viewed as givens, and workers direct their professional understanding only toward the client, then they ignore potent areas of potential change. The social agencies will continue to operate with the bureaucratic hierarchical structure predominant, and the pressure which brings low morale, frustration, conformity, and undistinguished individual performance will persist. Burnout is the ultimate "solution." We turn to these organizational matters in chapter 12.

12. The Organizational Context

Six priorities confront social work practitioners today and loom important for practice—one is a matter of values, five are in knowledge/ action areas. In fact, they may be thought of as preconditions for responsible practice:

1. *To work from a social conscience and consciousness.* Social work has been looked to in the past as *the* profession with a major responsibility for supporting stability in social structures and roles. But social workers have stopped being unquestioning gatekeepers of a status quo that causes or increases social distress for oppressed populations. And they have been advocates for new, diverse, and untraditional social roles. Although there is ideological diversity within the profession (as with any profession), social workers must be animated by belief in the dignity of persons and a history of engagement with unpopular causes and ugly situations, whether or not this is an easy task.

2. *To look with planned emptiness.* Emptiness is not necessarily a negative thing. In the past, ideas lived longer than people. Once established, thinking changed only slowly and over generations. Now, technology and science have speeded up change and reversed matters: people live longer than ideas! They must change their ideas in order to keep up in the world. Planned emptiness involves maintaining a blank, a free area in one's mind that is reserved to receive the unknown, the new and perhaps alien idea or experience. In short, it is an undogmatic stance.

3. *To communicate in exoteric language.* Esoteric language is well known as a mark of power and prestige in some professions, signifying years of education, elite status, and distance from the "person on the street." It is difficult to understand, abstruse, foreign to the public

(Latin lingo takes care of this!), and is confined to a small circle or school of thought. "Exoteric," a word that has disappeared from everyday vocabularies through disuse, means a public and popular vocabulary that is easily understood. This is how social workers must talk with their clients. And yet, they must understand also the esoteric languages of other disciplines and professions. They need two vocabularies—to speak understandably, and to understand complexity.

4. *To maintain pivotal readiness.* This implies having a posture of alert, poised-for-action responsiveness that is free to move in a variety of directions: an anticipatory stance. Such a view emphasizes and enjoys preparing for contingencies, expects the unfamiliar, and meets it with a sense of tentativeness and tolerance for ambiguity. The emphasis is on being ready to *do* something, even with an awareness that one may count on encountering situations which will have no obvious positive results, nor see these as cause for self-blame or self-doubt.

5. *To give away one's special know-how to others.* This involves empowering others—individuals, groups, families, communities—by giving knowledge and skills away to the extent possible so that others will become more expert and powerful, will have "tools" and personal resources to improve their life situations. Social workers will not "go out of business" if others are helped to do-it-themselves. There will always be enough distress around to keep everyone busy! George A. Miller, while president of the American Psychological Association, advocated "giving psychology to the people who need it (to the "unwashed")—and that includes everyone," making everyone into a psychologist.[1] We see no less of a goal for social workers.

6. *To demonstrate the social value of collective service arrangements.* Social work is essentially a bureaucratized profession. There is ample evidence that the context of service seriously affects the impact and effectiveness of what social services look like and can mean to clients. The best direct practice skills in the world can be eclipsed by aversive organizational arrangements. Organizations, mainly bureaucracies in form, have fixed jurisdictions, rules established by others, hierarchical command systems, job entry, promotion, and tenure awarded via uniform performance of tasks, examinations, certification, degrees, or longevity, and the work broken down into small units. However, the way things are need not remain fixed. Bureaucracies

are shifting systems and should be amenable to workers' tactical inputs and ways around blockages.

This chapter is devoted to matters concerned with these collective service arrangements—the "home" for most social workers. And yet, the sponsorship base for social work is shifting yearly, the exact extent of which is difficult to know. It has been estimated that the number of social workers entering private practice has doubled every five years since 1925.[2] According to Barker, most educated guesses put the count in the mid-1980s at between 10,000 and 30,000 for part-time workers and 4,000 to 10,000 for full-time practitioners.[3] And internally focused, psychologically-heavy, practice theories of individual aberration seem to appeal to increasing numbers of practitioners (and educators). Figures obtained from the National Association of Social Workers reveal two-thirds of the social workers doing psychotherapy either full time or part time in 1986.[4]

Most practitioners are attracted away from organizations not simply by money, but by hopes for more autonomy and freedom from a crushing bureaucracy. Social workers flee, just as many in the teaching and nursing professions do, to escape the constraints of "mass production" services. This seems especially interesting in light of a trend in the legal and medical professions away from solo practice toward working within a multi-specialty group practice, in larger firms or organizations, or in the public sector where the merit system has always fostered very specific specialized job descriptions and boundaries. For example,

> The urban hospital, law firm or denominational headquarters is as different from the practice of the small-town doctor, lawyer, or minister as the factory is from the family farm. Even such newer fields as electronic data processing, once regarded as highly professionalized, are now taking on the characteristics of factory work.[5]

Social workers are well acquainted with a "factory work" ambiance. But perhaps the "small is beautiful" organizational format may eventually come to predominate for the delivery of social services—a loosely linked arrangement, centralized in certain aspects but individually operated. This has certainly proved remarkably effective for the Convenience Food Stores.

The role strain many practitioners face is often heightened by their professional education to the point where they may withdraw from organizations and abandon social work as a career, organization-hop in hopes of finding some "ideal" agency where professional (read "treatment") skills can be actualized, conform to an organizational identity, and abandon all but the most routine components of their role, or assume other survival tactics. The dissonance between the "is" and the "what ought to be" can only be understood as some huge puzzle where agencies try to fulfill their missions with dwindling resources, where retrenchment of funds and services and personnel is routine, and where the measure of quality is cost effectiveness.

Consider one worker's view of her workplace, an account written for her supervision course in a MSW program:

> My current position is a AFDC caseworker for the state. The job itself is a tension giver, but in our office it goes deeper than just the job itself. Our supervisor is a very degrading, egotistical, self-centered individual. He does not delegate work in a manner in which workers can ease into gracefully. It is more like being slapped in the face with a concrete slab. For example, at staff meetings suggestions are given for ways to improve office production. All of these are handled in one of two ways: shoot it down, or it's no solution. On occasion, he has called workers, "Ass holes," "Bitches," and so on.

Let us hope that this is an extreme and unusual picture.

Wasserman's study of newly graduated social workers in public child welfare agencies found one-half suffered varying degrees of physical fatigue and emotional upset. The predominant source of the difficulty was supervision. They had little sense of being members of a professional collectivity with whom they could consult on the basis of common experiences, concerns, and needs.[6] The name for this game is *burnout,* a popular concept these days!

A "burnout" is someone who works harder and harder while accomplishing less and less; one who may take work home or work late, but seems to have lost the enthusiasm and optimism about the possibility of applying ideas that professional preparation may have ignited. It is easy to succumb to being a burnout as organizations become more complex, red tape becomes more circuitous, rules, regulations, and service arrangements are changed with almost predictable regularity, and the person-to-person part of the job (that was its original attraction) becomes more remote and obscured by myriad details.

We found that students are relieved to learn of the Self Principle, discussed in chapters 3 and 9. They get permission, as it were, while studying and formulating their approach to practice, to see the legitimacy of doing things to take care of themselves. In a sense, they are forewarned (in case they are new to social agency contexts) or reaffirmed in the realm of considering strategic agency work to be "professional," critical work. A key imperative for self-survival is working to humanize the work place. This happens more readily when workers have some conceptual understanding of how things work, a matter to which we now turn.

In a sense, social workers must have double vision: they must partly focus on those coming for service, partly on the arrangements within which they must work, so that their energies directed to the latter help the agency remain accountable and responsive to client need. For just as clients are central in defining the pressures they face, so are the workers the ones who know best how their agency environment supports or hinders their work. They must bring to bear as much knowledge, understanding, and skillful handling of self and others within the organization as they know they must bring to the worker-client relationship. Rather than being guided only by emotion, belief, or hunch, social workers need to use planful and purposeful behavior in their role within the system to help the organization renew itself from the inside. They are interested parties who can contribute to the evolution of new structures, patterns, and processes if they understand and take this part of the professional assignment seriously.

Thus, while our primary concern is with the actual delivery of service, we intend to emphasize by some, albeit cursory, attention to the organizational arrangements in which the service is offered that the worker's knowledge and legitimate deployment of time and energy to conceptualizing this aspect of the work affects the effectiveness in the delivery of services. More complete discussion of organizations as context and the implication of these forces upon social services can be found in the literature.[7]

When a problem is sufficiently widespread that it threatens the

SURROUNDINGS

general welfare of the community, it is recognized as a social problem, and at least part of it is marked for public action. That action may be aimed at alleviating or managing the problem, or diminishing the potency of its deleterious effects. Because public action requires resources that may have been or potentially will be committed to other aspects of community life, because different vested interest groups in the community designate different aspects of community life as priorities in the allocation of resources, and because what is problemmatic for some segments of the community is advantageous to other segments of the community, there is conflict over both goals and means. These conflicts are resolved through a process of trade-offs among the competing groups; hence, the social task that emerges and the amount and type of resources committed for its accomplishment represent a compromise,[8] as opposed to a determination reached by parties exclusively concerned with resolution of the problem.

The compromise-task is then assigned to an agency charged with accomplishing it with the limited resources allocated. It should be noted that this political compromise is frequently responsible for the off-target activity of many social agencies which bear the brunt of public criticism for not accomplishing what they were never mandated to accomplish. In the decade of the 1980s, a conservative federal administration has divested itself of responsibility for as much of the social programs as possible, diverting increasingly scaled-down resources to the states to disburse.

Within the restrictions of the political definition of the task to be accomplished and the amount and kind of resources allocated for this purpose, the agency which is established must organize itself to deliver and account for services delivered. To a great extent, the point of organization is to limit the number of behavioral alternatives available to individual members of the system so that performance is more predictable. To this end, roles with expectations supported by a system of rewards and punishments are elaborated, and rules for the interaction of role incumbents are set down. These rules specify both particular actions to be performed and the conditions under which their performance is to occur, and are codified in a formal set of policies and procedures. In general, role differentiation in an organization is based on the the unequal distribution of power rather than on functional specialization, although the latter is not entirely absent.

That is, less powerful role incumbents report to, and are directed by, more powerful role incumbents, such as supervisors, who, in turn, report to, and are directed by, incumbents of roles at still higher levels in the hierarchy. In contrast to this is the divisionalized corporation with specialized units for promotion, design, research and development, training, and so on.

In terms of functional specialization, however, in multidisciplinary settings the person with the background nearest to the manifest purpose of the organization wields the most power. It is this person's expertise that the service seekers seek. Thus, in hospitals the physicians have greatest power, in schools the principal, in correctional facilities the superintendent, and so on.

We have mentioned the drift, especially in the large public agencies, to a factory-like workplace. The situation has been described as one where fiscal retrenchment is routine and cost effectiveness is the measure of performance.[9] Middleman and Rhodes have described social work's organizational context and ways bureaucracies may be organized as, for example, by:

profession or discipline (social workers, psychologists)
work process and function (counseling unit, personnel)
time (intake, treatment, discharge, follow-up)
client (age groupings, problem types)
output (typed reports, filled prescriptions, meals)
place (catchment area, district)[10]

This has been called a horizontal view of the bureaucracy, a cross section. Or alternatively, we can take a vertical, a hierarchical, view which would then yield a scene of 1) workers—those who do the basic work with the clients; 2) supervisors—middle-level staff who link workers and administrators; 3) staff specialists—consultants such as researchers, planners, accountants, and attorneys, whose work is related to design and control of the work; and 4) support staff—those who provide indirect services or handle information-processing chores; 5) administrators—those at the top who make the strategic, long-range decisions.

Each of these staff units may work together harmoniously, or when the task expectations outstrip the ability of the collective components to respond adequately, may be pitted unit against unit in the resulting tensions. It becomes all too easy to apply a victim-blaming mentality to organization-based tensions, tensions in which the incumbents are cast with little individual discretion. Understanding the organization qua organization will not automatically solve such problems, but will provide certain overview insights which might lead to the application of strategic action, possibly in concert with other role occupants.

Forces Confounding Agency Operations

It is perhaps the most theoretically interesting and pragmatically de-moralizing organizational phenomenon that maintenance of the roles and rules initially devised to facilitate accomplishment of the service goal ultimately becomes a goal of equal, if not greater, importance than that service goal. That is, means become ends in themselves, frequently obscuring, if not usurping, the primacy of the original mission. And beyond the formal role relationships based on power differentials, an informal organization based on interpersonal attrac-tion develops, the maintenance of which diverts still more energy from accomplishment of the service goal. To the external impediments to the service delivery posed by political decisions regarding definition of the social task and allocation of resources, are added the internal obstructions posed by institutionalized efforts to maintain the estab-lished patterns of formal and informal role relationships.

Further confounding service delivery is competition between vested interest groups at the agency level. Professionals from different disci-plines with diverse primary orientations, bureaucratic functionaries, clients, and those who say they speak for clients all have special subgoals for which they seek organization acceptance in the form of resource allocation. In view of this, Heraud suggests that organization theory predicated on such assumptions as common goals, shared values, and unity of purpose (an integration model) is not useful for understanding social agencies and should be replaced by a theory that presupposes no central value system, multiple, vague goals, and goal conflict that arises from forces outside the organization as much as from those within it (conflict model).[11]

Adding to goal conflict, as well as means conflict, in the social agency setting is the issue regarding the viability of method-based

orientations for the delivery of social work services. And a challenge
to method is a challenge to the historical justification of professional
social work activity and the huge body of policies and procedures,
agency rules, and professional norms that evolved to support such
practice—the fabric of agency life.

Fabricant calls the 1980s a "watershed period" in social agency life,
characterized by shifts in practice, new demands made on social work
by an increasingly turbulent environment, and new forms of practice,
all of which are symptoms of major transformations in social services
and the meaning of practice.[12] Practitioners' control over the nature
and quality of their work is especially in jeopardy. And at the administrative level, Neugeboren laments "declining enrollments in macro
social work education and an invasion by the MPAs, MBAs and MPHs
into the leadership of the social welfare agencies,"[13] where they have
assumed positions of authority and power, and social work influence
over this sector has been eroded.

It is one thing to distinguish work from metawork, and another to
recognize the unresolved issues surrounding both concepts deriving
from disagreement over goals and means. Further, with so much
power and vested interest deployed to the metawork, including sta-
tuses and identities tied to the current role expectancies, the problems
inhering in restructuring roles are complex. For roles are filled by
people, and new role expectancies demand different skills.

Still another conflict characteristic of social agencies is that between professional autonomy and administrative control. Much as in
the fields of health, education, and business, the strain within the
social service system is between those forces supporting standard
agency policy and practice and the new, the "heretical," the different
way of thinking and acting. On one side is the administrator's push
for quality control, for assurance that all clients can expect to receive
a somewhat similar kind of attention and response at a given agency,
no matter who their social worker is, while on the other side is the
push for autonomy from the individual social workers.

All too often, much as idealistic young schoolteachers gradually
sink into the morass of the public education system as they are systematically shown by the system's rewards and sanctions that their
beliefs and goals are naive and misguided, so are the newly arrived
social workers often gradually ground down to fit the status quo under

the guise of being taught by their more experienced peers and supervisors the realities of life. The workers bent on their own image management, find chances for advancement greater if they meet the expectations of those who evaluate their work. They prefer being liked to being disliked, and may not have the energy and confidence to follow their own internal gyroscope and make waves within the organization. Thus, it is not surprising that many prefer to accommodate themselves to the agency rather than engage in the struggle needed to change it. The trade-off is autonomy and diversity in the interest of uniformity, clarity, and accountability.

According to Bennis, most organizational theorists have concentrated upon the internal structure and dynamics of systems rather than on their relationship to the external environment and their capacity to adapt to and shape it.[14] Using the concepts of reciprocity and adaptability, those dealing with internal forces and those dealing with the organization environment, Bennis thinks the future strains for bureaucracies reside in the organizations' lack of flexibility and adaptability to its externalities. In his view, the future demands organizations that are highly adaptive, rapidly changing, temporary systems attuned to the rapidly changing environment. They should be organized around problems to be solved by people differentiated not according to rank or role, but according to skill and training. These differentiated units should be coordinated by "linking-pin" personnel able to mediate between the various project groups.[15]

A Review of the Organization

If one adopts a structural perspective not only toward clients and their predicaments but toward the organization offering the services, then it follows that agency effectiveness, staff morale, productivity, and possibilities for program development stem, for better or for worse, from the forces impinging upon the workers. They are not created by them. The intricate network of patterned transactions between client, worker, and service delivery system are one focus for attention. Another is the linkage of the organization and its exchange processes with other diverse social institutions and organizations, its external environment.

The focus for development cannot be exclusively upon the staff, no matter how well-intentioned and enlightened the administrator's view; rather, it is the organization that must continuously be developing. In one sense, focus upon staff development, which may appear progressive on the surface, is a gross example of institutionalized victim blaming; it is as if the organization's problems would be solved if only staff were better prepared to do their jobs. To presume that the problems are a function of individual attributes or interpersonal interactions is to approach a complex of forces at the wrong level of analysis.[16] For systems have properties independent of the individual actors; roles and norms may be begun by people, but once established, they exist independently of them and exert a powerful force on the people. No matter how caring individuals may be when they come to work at the Department of Public Assistance, once they are involved in its workings, the rules force them to be otherwise. If the locus of the organization's problems is considered to reside in the staff, then the spotlight is there rather than on the total organization and all the complexities of the internal and external networks that make the organization function.

No amount of staff development can singlehandedly deal with structural problems. Lectures on racism aimed to change staff attitudes will not affect the work if policies and procedures are racist. Nor will community mental health centers work toward their mandated goal of prevention and serve people in the community so long as the center is paid on a per capita basis for only those who walk into the building for treatment. Nor will children's agencies ever devote much real energy to maintaining children in their own homes, and deliver the material and other resources needed to support this program, so long as child welfare agencies are reimbursed per capita for numbers in foster care or group homes. Nor will hospital social workers be able to deal with those gross social problems accompanying illness for massive segments of the population, so long as hospital policy directs major resources to the crises surrounding in-hospital treatment, so long as the physicians decide which patients need the social services, so long as the social workers are diverted to attend only to discharge planning, so long as the insurance policy determines how long and how much attention the patient's physical condition needs.

The profound effects of the external forces, those vagaries of the political climate which become translated into uncertain resources that are always up for question, can make quixotic affairs of even the best conceived plans of social workers. The compromise between what is desirable and what is feasible can make any discussion seem fantastic. Withal, these issues are discussed as if it were possible to follow the desirable. The presumption, then, is that social work as a profession will clarify its priorities. Following this clarification, the profession will need to have a voice in defining its role rather than having this decided by others.

Assuming, then, that social work sees and wants to deliver more than the coping and rehabilitative functions, wants involvement also in preventive and developmental social welfare concerns, and assuming that greater clarity about levels of tasks and skills is being taught to larger segments of the population concerned with human services, then in order to implement new directions those in the social agencies must be ready to bear the anguish of restructuring the delivery system's potential to deliver. Internal reorganization will be unpleasant for those who bear the strain of the shifts. And the internal stresses and strains will obviously be exacerbated by the uncertainties and insecurities that derive from external threats. Likewise, service will suffer while organizations are changing, for there will be less energy for production of services. Maslow questions Theory Y management principles [17] on similar grounds:

> You cannot trust people with a key to the pantry when most people are starving or when there is not enough food to go around . . . if there were one hundred people and there was food for ten, and ninety of these hundred had to die, then I would make sure that I would not be one of those ninety and I'm quite sure that my morals and ethics and so on would change very radically to fit the jungle situation. [18]

The point here is that just as humane attitudes—everyone can be trusted, has the impulse to achieve, does not need the security of role to justify dominance—are dependent upon certain other circumstances, so social agencies can be innovative only when we assume they have succeeded at Maslow's "safety-need" level. [19]

But social agencies stand midway between a watchful, critical public that begrudges and finances reluctantly and minimally the basic social requirements of the poor. On the other side are those who suffer who are hidden from public view as much as possible, and those in need whose alienation, anger, and despair increase daily with their "social" services and the conditions surrounding their delivery. All too often, staff energy is diverted from service provision by the breathless rush to keep up with the needs of the clients, with the changes in requirements and policy regulations, and with the gaps created by the shifting personnel who move through the bureaucracies and on to less troublesome workplaces. One comprehensive study of a public assistance organization reported the probabilities of new direct-service staff staying even one year on the job as only 45 percent.[20]

Thus dependent upon the vagaries of public opinion and legislative enactment of resources, the social welfare organization can hardly be counted upon to provide services from a context of stability. Both the services and the spirit of the staff that delivers them are subject to inconsistent, piecemeal, and shifting resources accorded from year to year by the influentials in the economic/political realm. Social agencies have not "made it" at Maslow's basic safety-need level, and the ethics that order interorganizational life can hardly be humane and benevolent. Rather, interorganizational life is perilous and mirrors the insecurities and uncertainties of the day-to-day lives of the clients.

It is beyond the scope of this book to dwell at length on the organizational arrangements. Our major aim is to suggest that the future of the welfare system demands organizations that dispense social services possess stability, an aura of legitimacy, and value to the larger society (as has the armed forces system) so that the administrators can concentrate upon deploying necessary talent and resources to making the workplace an exciting environment—one with career opportunities and personal enrichment for those who work there. When this happens, it will be possible to devote monies to research and development (a necessary, valued component in commercial enterprises), to refinement and improvement of social welfare's products (services), and to allocation of resources proportionate to the need of any organization for upgrading and attending to the quality of staff performance. Such an orientation to services will depend upon structural arrangements that undergird the values of continuing staff development and training and new linkages with the universities and institutions that can provide specialized educational opportunities for theoretical, methodological, and technical study and advancement.

Conclusion

Proceeding from the assumption that organizational arrangements affect the quality of services as much as, if not more than, an individual practitioner's skill, we have described some of the internal and external forces that impinge upon the social agency and its central resource—its staff. Priority-setting as a skill distinguishes social workers who are in control of their work load from those whose work load is in control of them. And we have found that strategic deployment of energies at the organizational level can be learned at the same time as one learns how to be, and act, with clients. We believe this element has been neglected in the education of students, in favor of concentration upon learning direct practice approaches. One consequence of an intensive focus upon the worker-client relationship and the exclusion of comparable attention to theoretical and practical knowledge about organizational dynamics, has been a view of the agency as a given— perhaps a necessary evil with which the worker must identify, or subvert covertly, or ignore as much as possible ("I will be different from the other workers you knew"). Surely, the consequence has not been a practitioner who sees the organization as potentially fluid and capable of shifts and alternative patterns in its structural organization, not merely in its potential for adding on new practice interventions. Because of our conviction that the circumstances of service provision can make a vital difference if the agency can provide a resource of consequence to clients, we have described some of the organizational arrangements that we believe are variables, that are subject to change provided the practitioner sees them as changeable and devotes energy to devising means for affecting organizational arrangements. Central to employing change efforts toward the organization in which one works is knowledge about the intricacies of the problems and a belief in the possibility of organizational change. A structural approach to practice demands that its basic stance, one of adjusting the environment to the person rather than the person to the environment, also applies to the agency as environment for the worker. This is a difficult, not an impossible, assignment.

We have focused upon certain key elements that are potentially changeable, not once-for-all-time givens. In this category are the timeworn, cumbersome recording practices of agencies and the hierarchically based system of close one-to-one supervision that was congenial to a practice theory that emphasized an individualistic orientation to the client who would grow and change through a relationship with the practitioner. We suggest that workers cannot, at one and the same time, accord the client a central position in determining the tasks they will work on together and experience less than this consideration themselves from their superiors in the organization. It seems to have been far easier for the higher-ups to embrace a client-oriented partnership with those who come for services than to apply a similar orientation to staff decision-making and planning around service emphases, priorities, policies, procedures, and so forth. For there is support for client power in the literature of social work. But there seems to be little support within institutionalized professions such as social work, where the professionals work together under the sponsorship of an organization, for a worker-oriented partnership with the administration. It seems to us to be imperative, therefore, for practitioners to take seriously what we have described as the Self Principle: apply the other five principles to yourself.

13. Conclusion: It Matters

In reviewing what we described in this volume's first edition, we find that the concepts and practice principles have stood the test of time. We have extended and illumined further our ideas in this realm, having the benefit of more opportunities to test their fit with diverse practice situations. We find that others have seen the Quadrant Schema as a valued orientation, suited to help social workers understand their place within the vast network of formal and informal resource systems. Those who work within the Structural Model will use the six guiding principles, and see where their activities related to clients and others are positioned conceptually. They will appreciate and use, with purpose and affect, the diverse roles guiding action in work with individuals, related others, and groups. And they will see the connection (or its lack) between what they do in face-to-face client work, and all the "supportive" work that others of the system(s) do.

But what a fifteen years this has been for the "systems" for services, for the environmental press, and thus for the living situations of clients, of practitioners, and of the general public alike! Volumes could be (and have been) written to capture a description of the world of the 1970s as compared with that of the late 1980s. We leave this task to others.

The social work profession has lived through its ebbs and flows in relation to public opinion, and through its own internal shifts of priorities and imperatives as the dialectics of the times and tasks have fluctuated. And so have other disciplines and professions struggled, for they cannot be separated from the economic/political zeitgeist in which they thrive or try to survive. The social work profession has developed in these years. It has refined, revised, shifted, reviewed, and moved on again.

254

Toulmin sketches such a picture for his discipline—philosophy—
as it related to and kept apart from the history of science and related
disciplines, for sociologism and psychologism, and from the political
zeitgeist. The themes are familiar to us. Between the 1950s and mid-
1970s, he cites many shifts: concern with internal structure and
foundations, formal rigor, and technique, then the breaking down of
fences separating the established academic disciplines and the embrace of the interdisciplinary. The move was:

- from the general, abstract, timeless, and universal to the emphasis on application to specific instances and cases, dynamics of
  particular cultural changes, concreteness, and human actuali-
  ties.

- from means or efficiency, (how to-do-its, and consensual politics) to ends and justice, (what to do and for whom, and confron-
  tational politics).

- from narrowly formal conceptions and analyses to broader functional ones with different intellectual procedures to deal with the
  demands of changing problems.

Toulmin's image for these patterns was that of a folkdance, with its
alternating periods of marching and weaving:

> For a time, the different academic professions march forward sepa-
> rately but in parallel, each in its own special way; then, for a time, they
> join hands and work together on the general problems arising in the
> areas where their techniques overlap; only to break away once more
> into separate lines, and march along in fresh directions until they are
> ready to join hands again.[1]

Have we not known periods of marching and weaving? Of shifts in
ideological or theoretical orientations? Of organizational sponsor-
ships? Of collaboration with this or that profession or discipline? Of
acceptance or disfavor by the general public? Have we not "disappeared" into some collective entity termed "therapist" in the mental
health or family realms, or shifted toward other social workers at a
NASW symposium? Only recently have we begun to acknowledge in
the literature, without self-consciousness or apology, that there may

never be one, clear public image of "social worker" since the circumstances, imperatives, and tasks are diverse.

Will social work become more élite, specialized, and "private"? Or more "public," more involved in the political and social policy realms where the "big" decisions about public well-being are strategized? It is interesting to consider that European social workers look to U.S. social work for the latest techniques and innovations in individual and family practice, while we look wistfully at their governmental traditions of national health insurance and support (albeit with high taxation) for the expected living-needs of the citizens. Perhaps the very diversity of the social work profession in the United States will trend toward corporate, private, emergent institutions and will seek to decouple itself from welfare. This may happen especially if formulas, standardization of provisions and tasks, and computerization assume more of the decision-making tasks (a frightening, not impossible, scenario). Or practitioners may work with less immersion in the routine *because* computers make certain determinations which free the workers to assume leadership tasks demanding human attentiveness and quality judgments which they know how to make. Computers may trivialize workers' duties, take the discretionary judgment away, and substitute their unknown decision rules and theoretical biases already programmed into their "brains." Or they may offer more free time and space for inspired actions and creativity in the ambiguous realms.

In the *Handbook of Social Intervention*, contributors with social work credentials had almost no visibility, a surprising fact in terms of the focus of the volume. Social work was acknowledged as an historical entity that "has been where most of the action was in human services and public policy."[2] The many forms of political action were cited as social workers' historic contributions—for example, advocacy for the oppressed and powerless, presentation of evidence as technical experts, and influencers of social policy.

These moves, the historian claimed, aimed more at reform of social arrangements and institutions than at fundamental systems change. They stayed within institutional and ideological bounds, and used consensus more than conflict approaches.[3] But who wants to bite the hand that feeds you (and family)? To march to a different drum, and risk being drummed out of the parade? To be a whistle-blower and whistle your tune alone? These social workers were people just like us—not martyrs! And they were involved (and are still involved) in issues that many others have abandoned.

It is "interesting" that most lawyers have fled from their brief enchantment with poverty law, with defending poor and oppressed persons: they seem happier with corporate law. And some idealistic, environmental scientists have moved away from the frustrations of the Environmental Protection Agency's commandments (which prevent them from doing what they know technically should be done). Or they may capitulate and find their safe place in the agency out of their own personal survival needs.[4] And, of course, some social workers avoid the huge bureaucracies which now predominate in determining and dispensing resources to the poor, the children, the frail, the stigmatized.

In any profession there will be some who choose to join the lot of the oppressed and powerless. Perhaps they have known powerlessness themselves. The social work profession has always had the lead mandate in this arena and continues to need practitioners with such an orientation. Consider this account of one worker's activities undertaken in behalf of homeless women in a New York City shelter:

> investigation of the city's shelter system; visits and assessments of various shelters; data collection on the extent of the problem(s); direct work with the homeless residents (arranging transfers for some to better circumstances, excursions "away" for groups of others, being/talking with them); drafting a reform proposal and presenting it to city officials; recording and publicizing the experiences; enlisting other individuals and groups in this cause; developing supportive help networks.[5]

We see this work as ranging through all of the Quadrants. In this instance, however, the social worker was free to "call it as she saw it." She was a highly qualified *volunteer,* not *of* the system. She was not directly biting the hand that fed her, and yet this work took courage, intelligence, and skills.

Social work has been described as a "foreign body" within mainstream marketplace capitalism.[6] It values human dignity and need over profit (either agency or individual economic gain). In its embrace of such ideas as full employment, guaranteed income, adequate medical coverage for all, decent housing, and so forth, social work has gone against the grain of the dominant cultural values. Social work's values are not popular ones (concern for minorities, for AIDs victims). Foreign bodies (children, students, the unemployed, those on annuities, welfare recipients, women working in the home, criminals) *cost* society rather than *gain* for society. There is a tension between human rights and profit, irritating in the short run but necessary.

A foreign body is an irritant. A grain of sand in the eye must be extruded. Yet this same grain of sand in an oyster can be cultivated to become a pearl, a valuable thing of beauty in the long run. It is such a stance that has characterized social work and its value base, norms, ethical imperatives, and traditions. It is a mentality concerned with social costs, human loss, and the long run.

The title of this concluding chapter is "It Matters." Where does this come in? If we try to peer ahead toward a murky, cloudy "future", it looks frightening. It is scary, regardless of how much or how long persons may have saved for "the rainy day," or how vulnerable others have grown to feel they are.

- *It matters,* especially for the social work profession, that it continue to attend to oppressed people. No other profession has held this societal mandate. By "oppressed" we do not mean merely "the poor," financially. We mean gay and lesbian persons, AIDs sufferers (their partners, and their families), raped and molested persons, battered women and children, and the many other strugglers who have the pressures of life-circumstances stacked against them. Oppressed persons and social workers are well known to each other.

- *It matters* to this profession that the average real income has increased in this country, not because average working-class families are better off, but because the highest-income families have had such a tremendous increase in their incomes. It matters to us that the Congressional Budget Office announced, "the poorest one-tenth of Americans soon will pay 20 percent more of their earnings in federal taxes and the richest one-tenth will pay almost 20 percent less."[7]

- *It matters* that projections for this nation's four and five-year-old children conclude that 1 in 4 will be poor, 1 in 6 will have no health insurance, 1 in 5 will live in a family where neither parent has a job, and 1 in 7 will be at risk of becoming a teen parent. "In rich America (sic!), poverty kills 10,000 children every year, or one every 53 minutes."[8]

- *It matters* that practitioners working from a structural perspective master the process dynamics of short-term relationships, including what is needed in "working yourself out of a job." We have learned an important lesson out of the experiences connected with deinstitutionalization, with people hastily discharged from mental hospitals to become unattended wanderers in the community. Practice orientations seem to grow shorter (as monies grow sparser). Hopefully, this will not diminish the vitality of the worker/client transaction.

- *It matters* that we are involved with persons different from ourselves and we have the obligation to reach out to each other person with compassion, with humanness. The differences may be obvious (age, gender, race, family situation) or subtle (ethnic, marital status, neighborhood), yet each difference is profound and capable of obscuring a meaningful working connection. The awareness of and use of process in working with others may be the component that makes the worker/client relationship "work."

- *It matters* that all practitioners take seriously an obligation to work for social change. This mandate should not be left for only the macro-focused social workers to pursue. It should be a central part of each practitioner's professional responsibility. It represents an encouraging mind-set, both for oneself and for the "face" one shows to others.

- *It matters*, finally, that there never be an end to the *"it matters list,"* that you add your own "it matters" to ours, and check yourself from time to time to see if you are attending to them. You will undoubtedly add and subtract (or march and weave!) as you refine your practice. Meanwhile, these shall serve to give you a start.

Notes

INTRODUCTION

1. See, for example, Joseph Anderson, *Social Work Methods and Processes* (Belmont, Calif.: Wadsworth, 1981); Wynetta Devore and Elfriede G. Schlesinger, *Ethnic-Sensitive Social Work Practice* (St. Louis: Mosby, 1981); and Elfrieda G. Schlesinger, *Health Care Social Work* (St. Louis: Mosby, 1985).

2. Carel B. Germain, "Technological Advances," in Aaron Rosenblatt and Diana Waldfogel, eds., *Handbook of Clinical Social Work* (San Francisco: Jossey-Bass, 1983), p. 50.

3. June Axinn and Mark J. Stern, "Women and the Postindustrial Welfare State," *Social Work* (July–August 1987), 32(4):282–286.

4. George Gebner, "Television's Populist Brew," *ETC.: A Review of General Semantics* (Spring 1987), 44(1):3–7.

5. Neil Postman, "Amusing Ourselves to Death," *ETC.* (Spring 1985), 42(1):13–18.

6. *New York Times*, April 20, 1984, p. A3.

7. Donald Schön, *The Reflective Practitioner* (New York: Basic Books, 1983), pp. 17–18.

8. R. Buckminster Fuller, "The Wellspring of Reality," *Synergetics* (New York: Macmillan, 1975), pp. xxv, xxvii.

9. Herbert J. Gans, "The New Egalitarianism," *Saturday Review* May 6, 1972, pp. 43–46.

10. Harvey Brenner, "Estimating Social Costs of National Economic Policy: Implications for Mental and Physical Health and Criminal Aggression," in *Achieving the Goals of the Employment Act of 1946* (Washington, D.C.: GPO, 1976), p. vii, as quoted in Thomas Keefe, "The Economic Context of Empathy," *Social Work* (November–December 1978), 22(6):460–465.

11. See John L. Palmer and Isabel V. Sawhill, eds., *The Reagan Record: An Urban Institute Study* (Cambridge, Mass.: Ballinger 1984) for a fuller discussion.

12. Burton Gummer, "The Social Administrator as Politician," in Felice D. Perlmutter, ed., *Human Services at Risk* (Lexington, Mass.: Lexington Books, 1984), p. 31.

13. *New York Times,* April 30, 1985, p. C1.

14. Gummer, pp. 23–36.

15. Robert Barker, "Sliding Fee Scales: A Return to the Means Test?" *Journal of Independent Social Work* (Spring 1987), 1(3):3.

16. The implications of this perspective in terms of planning and offering social services are elaborated by Charles F. Grosser, "Changing Theory and Changing Practice," *Social Casework* (1967), 48(1):16–21.

17. Charlotte Towle, "Social Work: Cause and Function," *Social Casework* (1961), 42(8):385–397.

18. Max Siporin, "Situational Assessment and Intervention," *Social Casework* (February 1972), 53(2):91–109.

19. Carel Germain, ed., *People and Environments* (New York: Columbia University Press, 1979); Carel Germain and Alex Gitterman, *The Life Model of Social Work Practice* (New York: Columbia University Press, 1980); Carel Germain, *Social Work in Health Care: An Ecological View* (New York: Macmillan-Free Press, 1984).

20. See, as one example, Murray Levine and Adeline Levine, *A Social History of the Helping Services* (New York: Appleton-Century-Crofts, 1970), p. 8.

21. For an earlier discussion, see Nathan E. Cohen, *Social Work in the American Tradition* (New York: Holt, Rinehart, and Winston, 1958).

22. Lawrence A. Cremin, *The Transformation of the School* (New York: Knopf, 1961), pp. 345–353.

23. Levine and Levine, *Social History.*

24. Mary Richmond, *What Is Social Case Work?* (New York: Russell Sage Foundation, 1922), pp. 224–225.

25. Barbara Wooton, *Social Science and Social Pathology* (London: Allen and Unwin, 1959), p. 286.

26. Charlotte Towle, "New Developments in Social Casework in the United States," *British Journal of Psychiatric Social Work* (1955), 1(2).

27. Charlotte Towle, "Social Casework in Modern Society," *Social Service Review* (1946), 20(2):175.

28. Bertha C. Reynolds, "Social Casework: What Is It? What Is Its Place in the World Today?", *The Family* (1935), 16:238.

29. Joe M. Schriver, "Harry Lurie's Critique: Person and Environment in Early Casework Practice," *Social Service Review* (September 1987), 61(3):523–524, 529.

30. Jerome C. Wakefield, "Psychotherapy, Distributive Justice, and Social Work," *Social Service Review* (June 1988), 62(2), pp. 187–210.

31. Grosser, "Changing Theory," elaborates this viewpoint and distinguishes it from a pathology viewpoint; for a comparable discussion in the area of prevention and mental health, see George W. Albee, "A Competency Model Must Replace the Defect Model," in Justin M. Joffee, George W. Albee, and Linda D. Kelly, eds. *Readings in Primary Prevention of Psychopathology* (Hanover, N.H.: University Press of New England, 1984), pp. 228–245.

1. A FRAME OF REFERENCE FOR SOCIAL WORK PRACTICE

1. Allen Pincus and Anne Minahan, *Social Work Practice: Model and Method* (Itasca, Ill.: Peacock, 1973).
2. Carel B. Germain and Alex Gitterman, *The Life Model of Social Work Practice* (New York: Columbia University Press, 1980).
3. The type of research suggested here is descriptive only; hence the findings will function like a road map, illustrating where things are in relation to each other. The driver will decide, based on criteria external to the map, where to go and which route to take. It should be noted too, that even an evaluative study that reveals route X to be more effective (shorter, safer) than route Y, does not, in and of itself, say, "Use X!" although presumably the study was conducted for the purpose of making such a decision. The point is that research measures; it does not command.

2. THE PHILOSOPHICAL BASE FOR STRUCTURAL SOCIAL WORK PRACTICE

1. For further discussion of this issue, see William Ryan, *Blaming the Victim* (New York: Pantheon Books, 1971).
2. Eliot Studt, *A Conceptual Approach to Teaching Materials* (New York: Council on Social Work Education, 1965).
3. For a classic example of this, see Francis P. Purcell and Harry Specht, "The House on Sixth Street," *Social Work* (1965), 10(4):69–76.

3. BASIC PRINCIPLES OF THE STRUCTURAL APPROACH

1. Robert K. Myers, "Some Effects of Seating Arrangements in Counseling," Ph.D. dissertation, University of Florida, Gainsville, 1969.
2. Edward T. Hall, "A System for the Notation of Proxemic Behavior," *American Anthropologist* (1963), 45:1003–1026.
3. Martin Rein, "The Social Service Crisis: The Dilemma—Success for the Agency or Service for the Needy?" *Trans-Action* (1964) 1(5):3–8.
4. Peter M. Blau, *The Dynamics of Bureaucracy* (Chicago: University of Chicago Press, 1955).

5. THE CONFEREE

1. Theodore Kemper, "On the Nature and Purpose of Ascription," *American Sociological Review* (1974), 39(6):415–431; Barbara Bovee Polk, "Male Power and the Womens Movement, *Journal of the Applied Behavioral Sciences* 10(3):415–431; Rhett Jones, "Proving Blacks Inferior: 1870–1930," *Black World* (February 1971) pp. 4–17.

6. THE BROKER

1. Lillian D. Wald, *The House on Henry Street* (New York: Holt, Rinehart, and Winston, 1915); Murray Levine and Adeline Levine, *A Social History of Helping Services* (New York: Appleton-Century-Crofts, 1970), ch. 5–6.
2. Scott Briar and Henry Miller, *Problems and Issues in Social Casework* (New York: Columbia University Press, 1971), pp. 3–31; Brian J. Heraud, *Sociology and Social Work* (Oxford; Pergamon Press, 1970), pp. 5–6.
3. Briar and Miller, *Problems and Issues,* pp. 237–240, provide an interesting example of a social worker in a mobile trailer serving the diverse needs of San Francisco's skid row population, and outline the complex requirements of this role.
4. William Ryan, *Blaming the Victim* (New York: Pantheon Books, 1971).

7. THE MEDIATOR

1. William Schwartz, "The Social Worker in the Group," in *New Perspectives on Services to Groups* (New York: National Associaiton of Social Workers, 1961), pp. 7–29; William Schwartz and Serapio Zalba, eds., *The Practice of Group Work* (New York: Columbia University Press, 1971).
2. Peter Kropotkin, *Mutual Aid: A Factor of Evolution* (New York: Knopf, 1925).
3. Schwartz, "The Social Worker," p. 17.
4. This list of expectations partially derives from the work of Schwartz, "The Social Worker."
5. For a fuller description of this, and other ulterior motives that stand as obstacles to satisfactory relatedness to others, see Eric Berne, *Games People Play* (New York: Grove Press, 1964).
6. Gale Goldberg Wood and Ruth R. Middleman, *Interviewing Skills for the Human Services* (Park Forest, Ill.: OUTP ST Software, 1987).

8. THE ADVOCATE

1. Lillian D. Wald, *The House on Henry Street* (New York: Holt, Rinehart, and Winston, 1915).
2. Jane Addams, *Twenty Years at Hull House* (New York: Macmillan, 1910).
3. Jacob Riis, *How the Other Half Lives* (New York: Scribner's, 1917).
4. Nathan E. Cohen, ed., *Social Work and Social Problems* (New York: National Association of Social Workers, 1964); Scott Briar, "The Social Worker's Responsibility for the Civil Rights of Clients," *New Perspectives* (1967), 1(1):89–92; George A. Brager, "Advocacy and Political Behavior," *Social Work* (1968), 13(2):5–15; Ad Hoc Committee on Advocacy, "The Social Worker as Advocate: Champion of Social Victims," *Social Work* (1969), 14(2):16–22;

Willard C. Richan and Marvin Rosenberg, *The Advo-Kit* (copyright Richan and Rosenberg, 1971).

5. Willard C. Richan, "The Public Welfare Worker—Advocate or Adversary," paper presented at Northeast Regional Conference of the American Public Welfare Association, 1970.

6. Willard C. Richan, "Presto: You Are a Social Work Advocate," paper presented at Eastern Regional Institute, National Association of Social Workers, 1969, p. 15.

7. Theodore R. Sarbin, "Notes on the Transformation of Social Identity," in Lehigh M. Roberts, Norman S. Greenfield, and Milton H. Millers, eds., *Comprehensive Mental Health: The Challenge of Evaluation* (Madison: University of Wisconsin Press, 1968) pp. 97–115.

8. Robert K. Merton, *Social Theory and Social Structure* (Glencoe, Ill.: Free Press, 1957); Robert Rosenthal, "Self-Fulfilling Prophecy," *Psychology Today* (1968), 2(4):46–51.

9. Richan and Rosenberg, *The Advo-Kit,* p. 1.

10. Erving Goffman, "On Cooling the Mark Out: Some Aspects of Adaptation to Failure," *Psychiatry* (1952), 15:451–463.

11. Carel B. Germain and Alex Gitterman, *The Life Model of Social Work Practice* (New York: Columbia University Press, 1980), pp. 173–174.

9. THE CASE MANAGER

1. Marie Weil, James M. Karls, and associates, *Case Management in Human Service Practice* (San Francisco: Jossey-Bass, 1985).

2. Gerald G. O'Connor, "Case Management: System and Practice," *Social Casework* (February 1988), 69(2):97–106. For other descriptions of case management, see also Dennis A. Bargossi and Leonard P. Pollane, "Case Management in Mental Health," *Health and Social Work* (Summer 1984), 9(3):201–211; Charles A. Rapp and Ronna Chamberlain, "Case Management Services for the Chronically Mentally Ill," *Social Work* 1985, 30(5):417–422; Peter J. Johnson and Allen Rubin, "Case Management in Mental Health: A Social Work Domain?" *Social Work* 1983, 28(1):49–53.

3. O'Connor, p. 103.

4. Frank Baker and Robert S. Weiss, "The Nature of Case Manager Support," *Hospital & Community Psychiatry* (September 1984), 35(9):925–928.

5. Joel S. Kanter, "Case Management of the Young Adult Chronic Patient: A Clinical Perspective," in J. S. Kanter, ed., *Clinical Issues in Treating the Chronic Mentally Ill: New Directions for Mental Health Services* (San Francisco: September 1985), no. 27, pp. 77–92.

6. "MSWs Lead in Private Case Management," *NASW News,* January 1986, p. 16.

7. These five major functions of case managers have been identified by the Joint Commission on Accreditations for Hospitals (JCAH), by the NIMH Community Support Program and Community Support System (CSS), and by

various states in their job descriptions for case management personnel. See also *NASW Standards and Guidelines for Social Work Case Management for the Functionally Impaired*, professional standards no. 12, for a comparable description.

8. Theodore J. Stein, "Macro and Micro Level Issues in Case Management," *Case Management: State of the Art*, Proceedings of the National Case Management Conference, National Conference on Social Welfare, Indianapolis, Ind., 1980 (Washington, D.C.: Administration on Developmental Disabilities, 1981), p. 85.

9. Betty Reid Mandell, "Blurring Definitions of Social Services: Human Services vs. Social Work," *Catalyst* (1983), no. 15, pp. 5–21.

10. Juanita B. Wood and Carroll L. Estes, " 'Medicalization' of Community Services for the Elderly," *Health and Social Work* (Winter 1988), 13(1) pp. 35–41.

11. Ibid.

12. David Austin, "Observations on the Search for an Institutional Base for Social Work," *Social Work* (September–October 1984), 29:5:285–287.

13. Michael Fabricant, "The Industrialization of Social Work Practice," *Social Work* (Spetember–October 1985), 30(5):389–395. See also, Michael Lipsky, *Street Level Bureaucracy* (New York: Russell Sage Foundation, 1980), for a comprehensive study of human service bureaucracies.

14. Jerome H. Zimmerman, "Negotiating the System," *Public Welfare* (Spring), 45(2):23–27.

15. Jeanette M. Jerrell and Judith K. Larsen, "Policy Shifts and Organizational Adaptation: A Review of Current Developments," *Community Mental Health Journal* (Winter 1984), 20(4):282–293.

16. Information sheet for Board of Directors of NASW, 1984.

17. Nancy Ratliff, "Stress and Burnout in the Helping Professions," *Social Casework* (March 1988), 69(3):147–154 provides an excellent review of the literature on stress and burnout among human service professionals.

18. Marybeth Shinn et al., "Coping with Job Stress and Burnout in the Human Services," *Journal of Personality and Social Psychology* (1984), 46(4):864–866.

19. Bruce Bower, "Neuroleptic Backlash," *Science News* (July 20, 1985), 128(3):45–46.

20. Ruth Sidel, *Women and Children Last* (New York: Penguin, 1987); Alice H. Collins and Diane L. Pancoast, *Natural Helping Networks* (Washington, D.C.: National Association of Social Workers, 1976).

21. Stuart R. Schwartz, Howard H. Goldman, and Shoshanna Churgin, "Case Management for the Chronic Mentally Ill: Models and Dimensions," *Hospital & Community Psychiatry* (December 1982), 33(12):1006–1009.

22. Annetta Miller, Carolyn Friday, and Sue Hutchison, "The New Volunteerism," *Newsweek*, February 8, 1988, pp. 42–43.

10. THE GROUP IN STRUCTURAL SOCIAL WORK PRACTICE

1. Julia Lawlor, "The Year of the Phone," *USA Weekend*, March 25–27, 1988.

2. Louise Bernikow, *Alone in America: The Search for Companionship* (New York: Harper and Row, 1986) deals with aloneness in some detail.

3. Ruth R. Middleman, "Interaction and Experience in Groups: Doing as Life-Learning," in Carel B. Germain, ed., *Advances in Clinical Social Work Practice* (Silver Spring, Md.: National Association of Social Workers, 1985), 159–170.

4. Ruth R. Middleman, ed., *Activities and Action in Group Work: Social Work with Groups*, 6(4):4; Richard D. Casey and Leon Canter, "Group Work with Hard-to-Reach Adolescents," in Middleman, *Activities and Action*, 9–22; Ruth R. Middleman, *The Non-Verbal Method in Working with Groups* (New York: Association Press, 1968; Hebron, Conn.: Practitioners' Press, 1982); Margot Breton, "Nurturing Abused and Abusive Mothers: the Hairdressing Group," *Social Work with Groups* (Summer 1979), 2(2):161–174; Anne Brooks, "Group Work on the Bowery," *Social Work with Groups* (Spring 1978), 1(1):53–63.

5. For further elaboration of "situation," see Max Siporin, "Situational Assessment and Intervention," *Social Casework* (February 1972), pp. 91–108.

6. Ruth R. Middleman and Gary B. Rhodes, *Competent Supervision: Making Imaginative Judgments* (Englewood Cliffs, N.J.: Prentice-Hall, 1985) describes this metaphor more fully.

7. "Groupness" is a term invented to incorporate a wide variety of qualities, forces, and elements comprising a group, and was first used or appealed to as a concept in Ruth R. Middleman, "Returning Group Process to Group Work," *Social Work with Groups* (Spring 1978), 1(1):15–26.

8. Martin Lakin and Philip R. Costanzo, "The Leader and the Experiential Group," in Cary L. Cooper, ed., *Theories of Group Process* (New York: Wiley, 1975), pp. 205–235.

9. William Schwartz and Serapio R. Zalba, *The Practice of Group Work* (New York: Columbia University Press, 1971) p. 18.

10. For example, a linear model of group process—developed out of social work with groups by James Garland, Hubert Jones, and Ralph Kolodny—cites the stages of pre-affiliation, power and control, intimacy, differentiation, and separation. Consult Saul Bernstein, ed., *Explorations in Group Work* (Boston University School of Social Work, 1965); a model developed by William Schutz out of experience with the human potential movement and dealing with interpersonal relationships cites the phases of inclusion, control, and affection; and as the group moves toward ending, it again deals with issues associated with the phases of control and inclusion (or rather, *exclusion,* this time).

11. Anthony Banet, "Yin/Yang: A Perspective on Theories of Group Devel-

opment," in William Pfeiffer and John Jones, eds., *The 1976 Handbook for Group Facilitators* (La Jolla, Calif.: University Associates, 1976) 169–184.

12. Irvin D. Yalom, *The Theory and Practice of Group Psychotherapy*, 3rd ed., (New York: Basic Books, 1985) pp. 3–4.

13. Morton A. Lieberman and associates, *Self-Help Groups for Coping with Crisis* (San Francisco: Jossey-Bass, 1979) 194–233; see also Pearl P. Rosenberg, "Support Groups: A Special Therapeutic Entity," *Small Group Behavior* (May 1984) 15(2):173–186.

14. Lieberman, *Self-Help Groups*.

15. Leon Festinger, "A Theory of Social Comparison Processes," *Human Relations* (1954), vol. 7, pp. 117–140.

16. Gertrude Wilson and Gladys Ryland, *Social Group Work Practice* (Cambridge, Mass.: Riverside Press, 1949); Catherine Papell and Beulah Rothman, "Social Group Work Models: Possession and Heritage," *Journal of Education for Social Work* (1966), 2(2):66–77.

17. William Schwartz, "Between Client and System: The Mediating Function," in Robert W. Roberts and Helen Northen, eds., *Theories of Social Work with Groups*, (New York: Columbia University Press, 1976); William Schwartz and Serapio Zalba, *The Practice of Group Work*.

18. Judith A. B. Lee, "Social Work with Oppressed Populations: Jane Addams Won't You Please Come Home?" in Joseph Lassner, Kathleen Powell, and Elaine Finnegan, eds., *Social Work with Groups: Competence and Values*, Proceedings of the 6th Annual Symposium of the Committee for the Advancement of Social Work with Groups (New York: Haworth Press, 1987); Joan Shapiro, "Single Room Occupancy: Group Work with Urban Rejects in a Slum Hotel," in Schwartz and Zalba, *The Practice of Group Work*, pp. 25–44; John A. Brown, "Group Work with Low-Income Black Youths," in Larry E. Davis, ed., *Ethicity in Social Group Work Practice: Social Work with Groups* (Fall 1984), 7(3):197–220.

19. Norma Lang, "A Comparative Examination of Therapeutic Uses of Groups in Social Work and in Adjacent Human Service Professions: Part II—The Literature from 1969–1978," *Social Work with Groups* (Fall 1979), 2(3):197–220.

20. Yalom, *Theory and Practice*, p. 368.

21. Ruth R. Middleman, "The Pursuit of Competence through Involvement in Structured Groups," in Anthony N. Maluccio, ed., *Promoting Competence in Clients* (New York: Free Press, 1981), pp. 185–210.

22. For elaboration, see Ruth R. Middleman and Gale Goldberg, "Social Work Practice with Groups," *Encyclopedia of Social Work*, 18th ed., (Silver Spring, Md.: National Association of Social Workers, 1987), pp. 714–729.

23. Mary Coppola and Robert Rivis, "The Task-Action Group Technique: A Case Study of Empowering the Elderly," in Marvin Parnes, ed., *Innovations in Social Group Work: Feedback from Practice to Theory*, Proceedings of the 5th Annual Group Work Symposium (New York: Haworth Press, 1986), pp. 133–147; Susan Glover Reed and Charles D. Garvin, eds., "Group Work with

Women/Group Work with Men," *Social Work with Groups* (Fall—Winter 1983), 6(3—4):133–146; Naomi Gottlieb, Dianne Burden, Ruth McCormick, and Ginny Nicarthy, "The Distinctive Attributes of Feminist Groups," ibid., pp. 81–93.

24. Jack Kaufman and Richard L. Timmers, "Searching for the Hairy Man," in Reed and Garvin, *Social Work with Groups,* pp. 163–175.

25. Judith A. B. Lee, "No Place to Go: Homeless Women," in Alex Gitterman and Lawrence Shulman, eds., *Mutual Aid Groups and the Life Cycle* (Itaska, Ill.: Peacock, 1986), pp. 245–262.

26. Ruby Pernell, "Empowerment and Social Group Work," in Parnes, *Innovations,* pp. 107–117; Hisashi Hirayama and Kasumi Hirayama, "Empowerment through Group Participation: Process and Goal," in Parnes, *Innovations,* pp. 119–131.

27. Ruth R. Middleman and Gale Goldberg Wood, *Skills for Direct Social Work Practice* (New York: Columbia University Press) forthcoming; Gale Goldberg Wood and Ruth R. Middleman, *I-View Skills: A Computer Assisted Skills Teaching Program* (Park Forest, Ill.: OUTP ST Software, 1986).

28. Middleman and Wood, *Skills.*

29. Yalom, *Theory and Practice,* p. 292.

11. THE METAWORK

1. Sidney A. Fine and Wretha W. Wiley, *An Introduction to Functional Job Analysis* (Kalamazoo, Mich.: The Upjohn Institute, 1971), pp. 2–23.

2. John G. Hill and Ralph Ormsby, "The Philadelphia Time-Cost Study in Family Service," in *The Social Welfare Forum, 1953* (New York: Columbia University Press, 1953), pp. 205–226.

3. Hill and Ormsby, p. 222.

4. Hill and Ormsby, p. 220.

5. Hill and Ormsby, p. 221.

6. "Unit Cost Study," St. Louis, 1958; "Time Cost Study," Lycoming Co., Williamsport, Pa., and Children's Aid Society of Pennsylvania, 1961; "Cost-Time Study for Family Counseling Agencies," New Jersey Council of Family Agencies, 1961; "Time Study of Total Staff," Decatur, Ill., 1962; "A Time and Cost Analysis of the Program of the Family Service Society," Salt Lake City, 1965; "Time Study," Edmonton, Alba., Canada, 1965; "Cost Analysis," Canton, Ohio, 1967; in *Research and Study Proposals of the Family Service Society of America Member Organizations.*

7. Livia Lowy, *Time Utilization in Fifty FSAA Member Agencies* (New York: Family Service Association of America, 1971).

8. Direct-service time is equally encumbered in the public agencies. For example, time study averages for caseworkers' involvement with clients in eight districts of a public assistance agency (August 1968) revealed 17.9 percent spent in the field (inclusive of travel time). The workers averaged 1.7 contacts with clients per day with 45.3 minutes spent per contact.

9. Scott Briar and Henry Miller, *Problems and Issues in Social Casework* (New York: Columbia University Press, 1971), pp. 144–145.

10. John E. Tropman, "Effective Meetings: Some Provisional Rules and Needed Research," *Social Work with Groups* (Summer 1978), 10(2):41–55.

11. John E. Tropman, Elmer J. Tropman, and Harold R. Johnson, *The Essentials of Committee Management* (Chicago: Nelson-Hall, 1969); John E. Tropman, *Effective Meetings: Improving Group Decision Making* (Beverly Hills, Calif.: Sage, 1980); and *Meetings: How to Make Them Work for You* (New York: Van Nostrand, 1984); Harvey Bertcher, "Effective Group Membership," *Social Work with Groups* (Summer 1987), 10(2):57–67; Elaine Finnegan, "The Day the Roof Could Have Fallen In: Some Naturalistic Observations about Board Committees, Professional Behaviors, and the Development of a Working Group," ibid., pp. 69–78; Liane V. Davis and Ronald W. Toseland, "Group versus Individual Decision Making: An Experimental Analysis," ibid., pp. 95–110; Gerald M. Phillips, Douglas J. Pederson, and Julia T. Wood, *A Practical Guide to Participation and Leadership* (Boston: Houghton Mifflin, 1979); Paul H. Ephross and Thomas V. Vassail, *Groups That Work* (New York: Columbia University Press, 1988).

12. According to the FSAA report, Lowy, *Time Utilization,* twenty-seven minutes of clerical time were needed to support one professional working hour. The services of one full-time clerical person were needed for every two equivalent full-time professional and administrative employees.

13. This estimate was made from the clerk-typist job specifications of the Philadelphia County Board of Assistance, DPW 8600 Ratings, July 10, 1963.

14. For further discussion of games workers and supervisors play, see Alfred Kadushin, "Games People Play in Supervision," *Social Work* (1968), 13(3):23–32. Kadushin discusses many games that grow out of the anxieties generated by a situation in which the worker is expected to undergo change. See especially "Treat Me, Don't Beat Me," a game in which workers expose their self rather than their work, and the social-worker part of the supervisor is tempted to respond.

15. Carol H. Meyer, "Occupational Social Work and the Public Services: Gains and Losses," *Social Work,* (September–October 1985), 30(5):387.

16. Michael Fabricant, "The Industrializaiton of Social Work Practice," *Social Work* (September–October 1985), 30(5):289–395; Charles Hoch and George C. Hemmens, "Linking Informal and Formal Help: Conflict Along the Continuum of Care," *Social Service Review,* (Spring 1986), 61(3):442.

17. Douglas J. Besarov, *The Vulnerable Social Worker* (Silver Spring, Md.: National Association of Social Workers, 1985).

18. Ann Hartman, "Diagrammatic Assessment of Family Relationships," *Social Casework* (October 1978), 59(8):465–476.

19. Gale Goldberg Wood and Ruth R. Middleman, *I-View Skills: Interviewing Skills for the Human Services* (Park Forest, Ill.: OUTP ST Software, 1987).

20. For an elaborate discussion of the bases of power and social influence, see Bertram H. Raven and Arie W. Kruglanski, "Conflict and Power," in Paul Swingle, ed., *The Structure of Conflict* (New York: Academic Press, 1970), pp. 69–109.

21. Erving Goffman, *The Presentation of Self in Everyday Life* (Garden City, N.Y.: Doubleday, 1959), p. 253.

22. Arlie Russell Hochschild, *The Managed Heart: Commercialization of Human Feelings* (Berkeley and Los Angeles: University of California Press, 1983), pp. 89–136.

23. Brian J. Heraud cites pertinent organizational research on this point, in *Sociology and Social Work* (Oxford: Pergamon Press, 1970), p. 239.

24. For a summary of this literature, see Ruth R. Middleman and Gary B. Rhodes, *Competent Supervision: Making Imaginative Judgments* (Englewood Cliffs, N.J.: Prentice-Hall, 1985), pp. 1–34; 189–222; Archie Hanlon, "Changing Functions and Structures," pp. 39–50, Alfred J. Kutzik, "Class and Ethnic Factors," pp. 85–114, and Florence W. Kaslow, "Group Supervision," pp. 115–141, in Florence W. Kaslow et al., *Issues in Human Services* (San Francisco: Jossey-Bass, 1972).

25. Lucille Austin, "An Evaluation of Supervision," *Social Casework*, (1956), vol. 37, pp. 375–382. Kadushin formulated a third function, *supportive*, and also added an evaluative function that was operative in both administrative and educative realms. See Alfred Kadushin, *Supervision in Social Work* (New York: Columbia University Press, 1976).

26. Hanlon, "Changing Functions."

27. Virginia P. Robinson, *Supervision in Social Casework* (Chapel Hill, N.C.: University of North Carolina Press, 1936) and *Dynamics of Supervision Under Functional Controls* (Philadelphia: University of Pennsylvania Press, 1949); Bertha C. Reynolds, *Learning and Teaching in the Practice of Social Work* (1942, rpt., New York: Russell and Russell, 1965); Charlotte Towle, *The Learner in Education for the Professions as Seen in Education for Social Work* (Chicago: University of Chicago Press, 1954); Margaret Williamson, *Supervision—New Patterns and Processes* (New York: Association Press, 1961).

28. Reynolds, *Learning and Teaching*, pp. 264–265.

29. Reynolds, ibid.

30. Alfred Kadushin, "Supervisor-Supervisee: A Survey," *Social Work* (May 1974), 19(3):288–297, and *Supervision in Social Work*.

31. Middleman and Rhodes, *Competent Supervision*, pp. 3–4.

32. Roslyn H. Chernesky, "A New Model of Suppervision," in Nan Van Den Bergh and Lynn B. Cooper, eds., *Feminist Visions for Social Work* (Silver Spring, Md.: National Association of Social Workers, 1987), pp. 128–148.

33. June Gary Hopps and Elaine B. Pinderhughes, "Profession of Social Work: Contemporary Characteristics," *Encyclopedia of Social Work,* 18th ed. (Silver Spring, Md.: National Association of Social Work, 1986), p. 357.

34. Middleman and Rhodes, *Competent Supervision.*

35. Edward E. Schwartz and William C. Sample, *The Midway Office* (New York: National Association of Social Workers, 1972).

36. Thomas Briggs, "Social Work Manpower Developments and Dilemmas of the 1970s," Workshops on Training MSW Students to Work with Various Categories of Social Welfare Personnel, Council on Social Work Education, Syracuse University (April 1972).

37. See, for example, Rensis Likert, *The Human Organization: Its Management and Value* (New York: McGraw-Hill, 1967).

38. Marion Wijnberg and Bertha Laury, "Transforming Traditional Supervisors into Team Leaders," *Social Work with Groups* (Summer 1981), 4(1—2):169–180.

39. Wijnberg and Laury, p. 171.

40. P. Kong-Ming New, "An Analysis of the Concept of Teamwork," *Community Mental Health Journal* (August 1968), 4, 326–333; Robert L. Barker and Thomas L. Briggs, *Using Teams to Deliver Social Services* (Syracuse, N.Y.: Syracuse University Press, 1969); Rosalie A. Kane, "The Interprofessional Team as a Small Group," *Social Work in Health Care* (Fall 1975), 1, 19–32; Naomi Brill, *Working Together in the Human Services* (Philadelphia: Lippincott, 1976); Jane Isaacs Lowe, "Understanding Teamwork: Another Look at the Concepts," *Social Work in Health Care* (1981), 7(2):1–11.

41. Ronald W. Toseland, Andre Ivanoff, and Steven R. Rose, "Treatment Conferences: Task Groups in Action," *Social Work with Groups* (Summer 1987), 10(2):79–94; Ronald W. Toseland, Joan Palmer-Ganeles, and Dennis Chapman, "Teamwork in Psychiatric Settings," *Social Work,* (January–February 1986), 31(1):46–52.

42. Tropman, "Effective Meetings."

43. Liane V. Davis and Ronald W. Toseland, "Group Versus Individual Decision Making: An Experimental Analysis," *Social Work with Groups,* (Summer 1987), 10(2):95–119.

44. See Davis and Toseland, "Group Versus Individual Decision Making," for an extensive review of the small-group decision-making literature.

12. THE ORGANIZATIONAL CONTEXT

1. George A. Miller, "Psychology as a Means of Promoting Human Welfare," *American Psychologist* (1969), vol. 24, pp. 1063–1075.

2. Sidney Levenstein, *Private Practice in Social Casework: A Profession's Changing Pattern* (New York: Columbia University Press, 1964).

3. Robert L. Barker, "Private and Proprietary Services," *Encyclopedia of Social Work,* 18th ed. (Silver Spring, Md.: National Association of Social Workers, 1987), pp. 324–329.

4. *New York Times,* November 9, 1987, p. A18.

5. Martin Oppenheimer, "The Unionization of the Professional," *Social Policy* (January–February 1975), pp. 34–40.

6. Harry Wasserman, "Early Careers of Professional Social Workers in a Public Child Welfare Agency," *Social Work* (July 1970), vol. 5, no. 4, pp. 93–106.

7. For example, L. L. Cummings and W. E. Scott, *Readings in Organizational Behavior and Human Performance* (Homewood, Ill.: Irwin and the Dorsey Press, (1969); Amitai Etzioni, *The Semi-Professions and Their Organization* (New York: Free Press, 1969); Rensis Likert, *The Human Organization: Its Management and Values* (New York: McGraw-Hill, 1967); James G. March, ed., *Handbook of Organizations* (New York: Rand McNally, 1970); Brian J. Heraud, *Sociology and Social Work* (Oxford: Pergamon Press, 1970); Ruth R. Middleman and Gary B. Rhodes, *Competent Supervision: Making Imaginative Judgments* (Englewood Cliffs, N.J.: Prentice-Hall, 1985).

8. C. Wright Mills, *The Sociological Imagination* (New York: Oxford University Press, 1959); Elliot Studt, *A Conceptual Approach to Teaching Materials* (New York: Council on Social Work Education, 1965).

9. Charles Hoch and George C. Hemmens, "Linking Informal and Formal Help: Conflict Along the Continuum of Care," *Social Service Review* (Spring 1986), 61(3):442.

10. Middleman and Rhodes, *Competent Supervision*, ch. 6.

11. Heraud, *Sociology and Social Work*.

12. Michael Fabricant, "The Industrialization of Social Work Practice," *Social Work*, (September–October 1985), 30(5):389–395.

13. Bernard Neugeboren, "Introduction to the Special Issue: Legitimacy, Effectiveness, and Survival of Macro Education and Practice," *Administration in Social Work*, (Summer 1987), 11(2):1–4.

14. For a succinct overview of the orientations of several theorists (Barnard-Simon, Levinson, Mayo, Likert, Argyris, Blake, Shephard, McGregor, Levitt, Thompson, and Tuden) and their key differences, see Warren G. Bennis, "Organizational Developments and the Fate of Bureaucracy," in Cummings and Scott, *Readings*, pp. 434–440.

15. Bennis, pp. 444–448. For a discussion of the linking-pin concept, see Rensis Likert, *New Patterns of Management* (New York: McGraw-Hill, 1961).

16. For a full discussion of levels of analysis, see Paul Lazarsfeld and Herbert Mensel, "On the Relation between Individual and Collective Properties," in Amatai Etzioni, ed., *A Sociological Reader* (New York: Holt, Rinehart, and Winston, 1961), pp. 499–516.

17. Douglas McGregor conceptualized two managerial styles: Theory X leaders believe that others avoid responsibility and work and are productive only when coerced by outside forces, while Theory Y leaders assume people are self-directing and if left to their own devices, will seek work and responsibility.

18. Abraham Maslow, *Eupsychian Management* (Homewood, Ill.: Irwin and the Dorsey Press, 1965).

19. Abraham Maslow, *Motivation and Personality*, 2d ed. (New York: Harper and Row, 1970).

20. Edward E. Schwartz and William C. Sample, *The Midway Office* (New York: National Association of Social Workers, 1972).

13. CONCLUSION: IT MATTERS

1. Stephen Toulmin, "From Form to Function: Philosophy and History of Science in the 1950s and Now," *Daedalus* (Summer 1977), pp. 143–162.

2. Edward Seidman, ed., *Handbook of Social Intervention* (Beverly Hills, Calif.: Sage, 1983), p. 19.

3. Clark E. Chambers, "Historical Considerations: Human Services, Natural Networks, and Public Policy," in Seidman, *Handbook of Social Intervention*, pp. 21–32.

4. Deborah Baldwin, "High Anxiety," *Commmon Cause* (July—August 1983), pp. 31–33.

5. "Who's Looking Out for the Homeless" and "From the Chronicles of Judy Lee," *NASW News* (September 1983), pp. 4–5.

6. Buford Farris and James Marsh, "Social Work as a Foreign Body in Late Capitalism," *Journal of Applied Behavioral Science* (1982), 18(1):76–94.

7. *The Courier Journal,* November 11, 1987, p. A6.

8. Marian Wright Edelman, "Lobbyist for Children Sees Work as Ministry," *The Courier Journal,* October 18, 1987, p. B3.

Index